Contents

Collins easy learning

French
Conversation

Salut!

Ça va?

Published by Collins
An imprint of HarperCollins Publishers
Westerhill Road
Bishopbriggs
Glasgow G64 2QT

Second Edition 2015

10 9 8 7 6 5 4 3

© HarperCollins Publishers 2006, 2015

ISBN 978-0-00-811198-4

Collins® is a registered trademark of
HarperCollins Publishers Limited

www.collinsdictionary.com
www.collins.co.uk/languagesupport

Typeset by Davidson Publishing
Solutions, Glasgow

Printed in Great Britain by Clays Ltd, St Ives plc

The contents of this publication are
believed correct at the time of printing.
Nevertheless the Publisher can accept no
responsibility for errors or omissions,
changes in the detail given or for any
expense or loss thereby caused.

HarperCollins does not warrant that any
website mentioned in this title will be
provided uninterrupted, that any
website will be error free, that defects
will be corrected, or that the website or
the server that makes it available are free
of viruses or bugs. For full terms and
conditions please refer to the site terms
provided on the website.

A catalogue record for this book is
available from the British Library.

If you would like to comment on any
aspect of this book, please contact us at
the given address or online.
E-mail: dictionaries@harpercollins.co.uk
 www.facebook.com/collinsdictionary
 @collinsdict

Acknowledgements
We would like to thank those authors
and publishers who kindly gave
permission for copyright material to be
used in the Collins Corpus. We would also
like to thank Times Newspapers Ltd for
providing valuable data.

MANAGING EDITOR
Janice McNeillie

CONTRIBUTOR
Laurence Larroche

FOR THE PUBLISHER
Gerry Breslin
Hannah Dove

MIX
Paper from
responsible sources
FSC™ C007454

Introduction

What is it?

Collins Easy Learning French Conversation is a book for learners of French of all ages. It will increase your confidence in holding a conversation in French, whether you are just starting to learn French, studying at school or at an evening class, or brushing up your language skills. You may be going on holiday or planning to go travelling in a French-speaking country, go there on business, or live there. Whatever your situation, you'll want to be able to communicate effectively and naturally in French.

Why do you need it?

Becoming proficient in a foreign language means being able to use and understand a number of different aspects – vocabulary, grammar, pronunciation, and so on. However, it takes a while to be able to put all these elements together and be sure that what you are saying sounds like natural French. The *Easy Learning French Conversation* has been carefully designed to bring these aspects together and give you language structures which you can use in conversation with confidence, knowing that you will be speaking French as spoken by French speakers.

How is it structured?

Collins Easy Learning French Conversation is made up of 12 units, each illustrating the language used in a particular situation, followed by a summary which brings together the key phrases covered throughout the units. You'll also find the One-stop phrase shop – a unit which contains all the important expressions and turns of phrase that help you to sound more natural in French.

A short grammar and verbs supplement gives you additional language support, ensuring that you have everything at your fingertips. Finally, the English-French glossary covers the most important vocabulary you may need to personalize your conversation.

How does it work?

Language allows us to express ourselves and interact with others. In any given situation, we perform different language tasks, such as asking for information, agreeing and disagreeing, complaining, making suggestions and so forth. To do this, we use linguistic structures (*How...?*, *When...?*, *Could I...?*, *I'd like...* and so on) which can be used in a variety of contexts. Each unit in *Collins Easy Learning French Conversation* gives you all the phrases you might need in a given situation, grouped by structure. English headings help you navigate through the structures to enable you to find what you want quickly and easily. Throughout the units, there are also tips headed Bon à savoir! which highlight important differences in the way English and French work.

A conversation, by definition, is a two-way process. It is as important to understand what is being said to you as it is to be able to respond. At the end of each unit, there is a section headed Listen out for. Each of these sections gives you a variety of the most typical phrases you might hear in a given situation. Becoming familiar with these will allow you to have a successful conversation with a French speaker. For further help with pronunciation, a free download with all the important structures recorded is available on **www.collins.co.uk/easylearningresources**.

Communicating effectively in French isn't just about linguistic competence – it's also about cultural knowledge. For you to feel confident in a French-speaking country, it is useful to know more about French culture and lifestyle. At the end of each unit, the Lifestyle Tips will give you the information you need to gain a deeper insight into the language, the country and its people.

Why choose *Collins Easy Learning French Conversation*?

- **easy to use** all the key language structures you need to give you the confidence to hold a conversation in natural French

- **easy to read** a clear, modern layout which allows you to find what you need quickly and easily

- **easy to understand** the language you may hear from French speakers in a given situation

- **easy to speak** free audio download available on **www.collins.co.uk/easylearningresources**

The *Collins Easy Learning* range

The *Collins Easy Learning French Conversation* is part of the best-selling *Collins Easy Learning* range, which includes the highly acclaimed *Collins Easy Learning French Dictionary*. *Collins Easy Learning French Grammar* and *Collins Easy Learning French Verbs* support you with all your grammatical needs, and the *Collins Easy Learning French Words* allows you to learn and practise your French vocabulary. The *Collins Easy Learning* series is the ideal language reference range to help you learn French.

French pronunciation

There are some sounds in French which need a bit of practice, such as the French **r**, which is much more noticeable than an English *r*, and the very sharp **u** sound to be heard in words like **rue** and **plu**, which is different from the *oo* sound in an English word like *ru̱in*.

Silent letters

As in English, not all the letters in French words are pronounced – especially final consonants. The final consonant is not sounded in the following, for example: **vert** (*green*), **grand** (*tall*), **petit** (*small*), and **ouvert** (*open*). However, if the final consonant is followed by an **e**, for example in the feminine form of the adjective, the consonant i̱s pronounced. The feminine forms **verte**, **grande**, **petite**, and **ouverte** all end with consonant sounds.

French vowels

These are the main ways in which French vowels are pronounced:

a	– *a* as in *fat* (pa̱tte, ca̱sserole)
	aw (ba̱s, ca̱s)
	followed by n: *en* as in *encore* (da̱ns, sa̱ns, pla̱n)
e	– *uh* (le̱, pre̱mier, re̱pas)
	e as in *set* (me̱rci, re̱staurant)
	followed by n: *en* as in *encore* (ve̱nt, e̱ntrer, ce̱nt)
	followed by r: *ay* (parle̱r, dîne̱r)
é	– *ay* (occupé̱, régio̱n)
è	– *ai* as in *air* (pè̱re, règ̱le)
i	– *ee* (i̱l, bi̱llet, vi̱e, samedi̱)
	followed by n: *a* as in *sang* (mati̱n, fi̱n, vi̱n)
o	– *o* as in *spot* (do̱nner, mo̱rt)
	oh (mo̱t, po̱ser)
u	– followed by n: *u* as in *sung* (lu̱ndi, bru̱n)

To make the **u** sound for words like **rue** and **pure**, place your lips as if you were going to whistle and make a sharp *ee* sound at the front of your mouth.

Vowel combinations

ai	– *e* as in *set* (m<u>ai</u>s, l<u>ai</u>t)
	followed by n: *a* as in *sang* (p<u>ai</u>n, cop<u>ai</u>n)
au	– *o* as in *gosh* (g<u>au</u>che)
eu	– *euh* (p<u>eu</u>, d<u>eu</u>x)
eau	– *oh* (cout<u>eau</u>)
ou	– *oo* (gen<u>ou</u>, c<u>ou</u>sc<u>ou</u>s)

> **BON À SAVOIR!**
> Two words you will often hear – **oui** (*yes*) and **lui** (*him*)
> are examples of a breathy *w* sound – they're pronounced
> rather like *hwee* and *lwhee*.

French consonants

Most French consonants are pronounced the same as their English
equivalents. Some consonants, however, are pronounced differently
depending on which vowel follows:

c	– *k* as in *keen* when it is followed by **a**, **o** or **u** (<u>c</u>adeau, <u>c</u>outeau, <u>c</u>umin) – note that when a cedilla (**ç**) is added to the **c**, it will sound like *s* in *sit* (<u>ç</u>a, gar<u>ç</u>on, dé<u>ç</u>u)
	– *s* as in *ceiling* when it is followed by **e**, **i** or **y** (séan<u>c</u>e, <u>c</u>itron, <u>c</u>yprès)
ch	– *sh* as in *shop* (<u>ch</u>emise, mou<u>ch</u>oir)
g	– *g* as in *gate* when it is followed by **a**, **o** or **u** (<u>g</u>az, é<u>g</u>outer, ai<u>g</u>u)
	– *s* as in *leisure* when it is followed by **e**, **i** or **y** (ju<u>g</u>e, <u>g</u>ilet, <u>g</u>ym)
gn	– *ni* as in *onion* (oi<u>gn</u>on, campa<u>gn</u>e)
j	– *s* as in *leisure* (<u>j</u>eter, <u>J</u>ules)
q, qu	– *k* as in *keen* (cha<u>qu</u>e, <u>qu</u>estion)
s	– *z* as in *zoo* when it is between vowels (heureu<u>s</u>e, oi<u>s</u>eau)
	– *s* as in *sit* when it isn't (ca<u>ss</u>é, <u>s</u>auce, désa<u>s</u>tre)

th	– *t* as in *take* (ma<u>th</u>s, <u>th</u>ermostat, <u>th</u>éâtre)
t in -tion	– *s* as in *sit* (nata<u>t</u>ion, na<u>t</u>ional)

Some consonants are pronounced differently to English:

h	– when it begins a word, it can be 'silent' (l'<u>h</u>omme, un <u>h</u>ôtel) or 'aspirate' (les <u>h</u>aricots, le <u>h</u>all). When the **h** is silent, the word behaves as though it starts with a vowel and forms a liaison with the preceding word where appropriate (see below). When the **h** is aspirate, no liaison is made.
r	– *rr*: a raspy sound in the back of the throat (<u>r</u>ue, <u>r</u>ouge, ra<u>r</u>e)
ll	– *y* as in *yes* (fi<u>ll</u>e, pai<u>ll</u>e)

> **BON À SAVOIR!**
> Note, however, that **mille** (*one thousand*) is pronounced to rhyme with *peel*.

Stress

In English words, a particular syllable is stressed (*con*cert, *den*tist), whereas in French each syllable has its own length and each is pronounced with the same intensity.

Liaison

Liaison is what happens when a French word ending in a consonant which would usually be silent, for example, **peti<u>t</u>** (*small*), **le<u>s</u>** (*the*), precedes a word starting with a vowel or a 'silent' **h**. The silent consonant is sounded to make the words flow more easily.

petit ami (*boyfriend*) is pronounced puh-tee<u>t</u>-ah-mee (the **t** at the end of **petit** is sounded)

les hôtels (*hotels*) is pronounced la<u>y</u>z-oh-tel (the **s** at the end of **les** sounds like a **z**)

Small talk

Comment ça va? – How are things?

Whether you're going to be working in a French-speaking country or you're going to spend some time with your French-speaking friends, you'll want to be able to chat with people and get to know them better. The phrases in this unit will help you talk naturally to friends, family and colleagues in a number of everyday situations.

■ GREETINGS ■

Just as in English, there are several ways of greeting people in French, depending on who you are addressing, and whether you want to be formal or not. Say **bonjour, madame/mademoiselle/monsieur** if you want to sound polite and just **bonjour** to someone you know a little. If you're on friendly terms with someone, you can say **salut!** (*hi!*).

Hello...

Bonjour.	**Hello**.
Bonjour, madame.	**Good morning**.
Bonjour, Pierre.	**Good afternoon** Pierre.
Salut, Olivier!	**Hi** Olivier!
Bonsoir.	**Good evening**.

BON À SAVOIR!
In French there is no equivalent for *good morning* and *good afternoon* – people just say **bonjour** during the day or **bonsoir** in the evening.

Use **au revoir, madame/mademoiselle/monsieur** to say goodbye to people you don't know well. You can just say **au revoir** to people you know, or use **salut!** (*bye!*) if you are on friendly terms with them.

Goodbye...

Au revoir, monsieur.	Goodbye.
Au revoir, mademoiselle.	Goodbye.
Salut!	Bye!
Bonsoir.	Goodnight.

See you...

À plus tard!	**See you** later!
À demain!	**See you** tomorrow!
À lundi!	**See you** on Monday!

INTRODUCING PEOPLE

You may want to introduce people you know to one another. The simplest way is by saying **voici** (*this is*) when introducing a person. You can also use **je te présente** (*I'd like you to meet*) when addressing someone you know well, or **je vous présente** to be more formal or when speaking to several people.

This is...

Voici mon mari, Richard.	**This is** my husband, Richard.
Voici mes enfants: Andrew, Gordon et Emma.	**These are** my children, Andrew, Gordon and Emma.
Je vous présente Danielle.	**I'd like you to meet** Danielle.
Je te présente Kevin, mon compagnon.	**I'd like you to meet** Kevin, my partner.

BON À SAVOIR!

When you're introduced to someone, you'll want to know how to react. The traditional **enchanté** should only be used in formal or business situations these days, and very often people just say **bonjour**.

In order to get the conversation going, you'll want to be able to talk about yourself – what your name is, what you do and so on. To say what your name is in French, you use the verb **s'appeler** which literally means *to call oneself*. The **s'** (*oneself*) changes to **m'** (*myself*) in **je m'appelle** (*my name is*). For more information on reflexive verbs like **s'appeler**, see page 271.

My name is...

Je m'appelle Jean-Pierre Métayer.	**My name is** Jean-Pierre Métayer.
Je m'appelle Tarik.	**My name is** Tarik.
Il s'appelle André.	**His name is** André.
Elle s'appelle Lara.	**Her name is** Lara.
Vous vous appelez comment?	What**'s your name**?
Moi, c'est Liam.	Hi, **I'm** Liam.

If you want to say how old you are, use **j'ai** followed by your age and **ans** (literally *I have... years*). **ai** comes from the verb **avoir**. For more information on **avoir**, see page 280.

I'm...years old

J'ai trente-sept **ans**.	**I'm** thirty-seven **years old**.
J'ai vingt-deux **ans**.	**I'm** twenty-two.
Mon fils **a** huit **ans**.	My son**'s** eight.
Vous avez quel **âge**?	How **old are you**?

BON À SAVOIR!
If you have to ask **Vous avez quel âge?**, you can always add **sans indiscrétion** (*if you don't mind my asking*).

To talk about who you are and what you do, use **je suis** (*I am*). This comes from the verb **être**. For more information on **être**, see page 282.

Je suis une amie de Paul.	**I'm** a friend of Paul's.
Je suis le frère de Ben.	**I'm** Ben's brother.
Je suis célibataire.	**I'm** single.
Je travaille en tant que programmeur pour l'entreprise Dunier.	**I work as a** programmer for the Dunier company.
Je suis enseignant.	**I'm a** teacher.

BON À SAVOIR!

When you say what you do in French, you don't put an article in front of the job name: *I'm a baker* is **je suis boulanger**. However, you do need an article when you address someone by their title, so *Mrs Chairwoman* is **Madame la Directrice**.

I have...

J'ai deux sœurs.	**I have** two sisters.
J'ai un fils et une fille.	**I have** one son and one daughter.
On a de la famille dans le sud de la France.	**We have** relatives in southern France.
Elle a les yeux bleus.	**She has** blue eyes.
Il a les cheveux châtain.	**He has** brown hair.

I live...

Je vis au pays de Galles.	**I live** in Wales.
Je vis seul.	**I live** alone.
On habite dans un appartement.	**We live** in a flat.

BON À SAVOIR!

If you're female, you'll say **seule** (*alone*) rather than **seul**.

I'm staying...

Je suis descendu à l'hôtel du Palais.	**I'm staying** at the Palace Hotel.
Vous êtes descendu à quel hôtel?	Which hotel **are you staying** at?
Je suis à Paris pour une semaine.	**I'm staying** in Paris for a week.
Je loge chez des amis.	**I'm staying** with friends.

To say that you've done something for a given length of time, use **ça fait...** followed by a time word such as **jour** (*day*), **semaine** (*week*) or **an** (*year*) and the verb in the present tense. For more information on the present tense, see page 272.

I have...for...

Ça fait cinq ans **que je** suis infirmière.	**I've been** a nurse **for** five years.
Ça fait dix ans **que je** vis en France.	**I've lived** in France **for** ten years.
Je suis à Saint-Raphaël **depuis** deux semaines.	**I've been** in Saint-Raphaël **for** two weeks.
J'apprends le français **depuis** 6 mois.	**I've been** learning French **for** 6 months.

ASKING FOR INFORMATION

When you're chatting socially, you will want to ask any number of questions. One simple way of finding out information from someone is to say **parlez-moi** (*tell me*) to someone you don't know very well or **parle-moi** to someone you're on friendly terms with.

Tell me...

Parlez-moi de votre famille.	**Tell me** about your family.
Parlez-moi un peu de vous.	**Tell me** a bit about yourself.
Parle-moi de ton nouveau copain.	**Tell me** about your new boyfriend.
Dis-moi en quoi consiste ton boulot.	**Tell me** what your job involves.

Another handy way of asking for information in spoken French is to put **c'est** at the beginning of the sentence before the question word: **quoi** (*what*), **où** (*where*), **quand** (*when*) and so on.

What...?

C'est quoi ton adresse?	**What's** your address?
C'est quoi le numéro de téléphone d'Olivier?	**What's** Olivier's phone number?
Qu'est-ce que tu fais dans la vie?	**What** do you do?
À quoi elle ressemble?	**What** does she look like?

Where...?

Où est votre bureau?	**Where** is your office?
C'est où cette soirée?	**Where** is the party being held?
Où est-ce que tu travailles?	**Where** do you work?
Où est-ce que tu habites?	**Where** do you live?
Tu viens **d'où**?	**Where** do you come **from**?
Tu loges **où**?	**Where** are you staying?

When...?

C'est quand ton anniversaire?	**When** is your birthday?
Quand est-ce que tu arrives?	**When** will you be here?
Quand est-ce que Laurent doit arriver?	**When** is Laurent supposed to get here?
Quand est-ce que James vient nous rendre visite?	**When** is James coming to visit us?
À quelle heure on se retrouve?	**What time** are we meeting?

If you want to ask how long someone has been doing something, use **Ça fait longtemps que...?** (*How long have you...?*) followed by the present tense. For more information on the present tense, see page 272.

How long have...?

Ça fait longtemps que tu es en France?	**How long have** you been in France?
Ça fait longtemps que tu travailles ici?	**How long have** you been working here?
Ça fait longtemps que vous attendez?	**How long have** you been waiting?

A very versatile way of asking someone socially how something is going or has gone is to use **Ça se passe bien,...?** (*How is...?*) or **Ça s'est bien passé,...?** (*How was...?*).

How...?

Ça s'est bien passé, tes vacances?	**How was** your holiday?
Ça s'est bien passé, votre vol?	**How was** your flight?
Ça se passe bien, à l'université?	**How's** university **going**?

Sometimes you'll want to ask why a friend or acquaintance did or didn't do something. You can use **Pourquoi...?** (*Why...?*) and the past tense to ask. For more information on the past tense, see page 273.

Why...?

Pourquoi est-ce que tu ne m'as pas téléphoné?	**Why** didn't you call me?
Pourquoi est-ce que tu n'y es pas allé?	**Why** didn't you go?
Pourquoi est-ce que tu as déménagé?	**Why** did you move house?
Pourquoi est-ce qu'elle a démissionné?	**Why** did she quit her job?

SAYING WHAT YOU WANT TO DO

When you're talking to friends or colleagues you will often need to be able to talk about what you would like to do. To say what you want to do, use **je voudrais** (*I'd like*). **voudrais** comes from the verb **vouloir**. For more information on **vouloir**, see page 285.

I'd like to...

Je voudrais te remercier de m'avoir aidé.	**I'd like to** thank you for helping me.
Je voudrais parler à M. Gautier, s'il vous plaît.	**I'd like to** speak to Mr Gautier, please.
On voudrait t'inviter à prendre un verre.	**We'd like to** take you out for a drink.
On voudrait te présenter un ami.	**We'd like** you **to** meet a friend.

You can also use **je veux** (*I want*) to talk about what you want to do. If you want to say that you want someone to do something, you use **je veux que** followed by the subjunctive. For more information on the subjunctive, see page 274.

I want to...

Je veux organiser une soirée surprise.	**I want to** organize a surprise party.
Je veux inviter quelques amis pour mon anniversaire.	**I want to** have a few friends over for my birthday.
Je veux que tu viennes avec moi.	**I want** you **to** come with me.
Je veux que la soirée soit réussie.	**I want** the evening **to** be a success.

MAKING SUGGESTIONS

One easy way of making suggestions to your friends and colleagues is to use **on pourrait** (*we could*) followed by the verb in the infinitive. **pourrait** comes from the verb **pouvoir**. For more information on **pouvoir**, see page 284.

We could...

On pourrait demander à Paul de se joindre à nous.	**We could** ask Paul to join us.
On pourrait se voir à un autre moment.	**We could** meet another time.
On pourrait prendre un verre un de ces jours.	**We could** go out for a drink some time.
On pourrait se retrouver au Café de la Poste.	**We could** meet up at the Café de la Poste.

Just as in English you can make a suggestion by simply asking **Pourquoi ne... pas?** (*Why don't…?*). You will notice that French speakers very often omit **ne** to make sentences shorter – this is mainly in spoken French.

Why don't...?

Pourquoi ne pas se donner rendez-vous un de ces jours?	**Why don't** we get together sometime?
Pourquoi pas inviter Fabien et sa copine?	**Why don't** we invite Fabien and his girlfriend?
Pourquoi pas déjeuner avec moi?	**Why don't** you meet me for lunch?
Pourquoi tu **ne** les appelles **pas**?	**Why don't** you phone them?

You can also make a suggestion using the French phrase **Et si...?** (*How about?*) which is followed by a verb in the imperfect tense. For more information on the imperfect tense, see page 272.

How about...?

Et si on les invitait à dîner?	**How about** asking them round for dinner?
Et si tu venais avec nous?	**How about** if you came with us?
Et si je passais te prendre le matin?	**How about** if I picked you up in the morning?

Use **Est-ce que je devrais...?** (*Should I…?*) followed by the verb in the infinitive to ask if you should do something. **devrais** comes from the verb **devoir**. For more information on **devoir**, see page 281.

Should I...?

Est-ce que je devrais inviter Anna?	**Should I** invite Anna?
Est-ce que je devrais la rappeler?	**Should I** call her back?
Est-ce qu'on devrait aller dans un restaurant italien?	**Should we** go to an Italian restaurant?

EXPRESSING OPINIONS

When talking to people in a social or work situation, you may wish to express your opinion of something. In French you can use **je crois** or **je pense** (*I think*). When you use **croire** and **penser** with a negative, as in **je ne pense pas que** or **je ne crois pas que**, the verb which follows is in the subjunctive. For more information on the subjunctive, see page 274.

I think...

Je pense que Sonia a raison.	**I think** Sonia's right.
Je pense vraiment **qu'**il est trop tard pour aller au cinéma.	I really **think** it's too late to go to the cinema.
Je pense qu'on devrait partir à minuit.	**I think** we should leave at midnight.
Je ne pense pas que ça soit le cas du tout.	**I don't think** that's the case at all.
Je crois que c'est une excellente idée.	**I think** it's a great idea.

BON À SAVOIR!

Don't forget to add **que** (*that*) after **croire** and **penser**. It's optional in English, but not in French.

In my opinion...

À mon avis, c'est une bonne proposition.	**In my opinion**, it's a good suggestion.
À mon avis, ça va poser des problèmes.	**In my opinion**, it's going to cause problems.
À mon avis, ce n'est pas vrai.	**In my opinion**, it's not true.
À mon avis, c'est un bon employeur, cette société.	**In my opinion**, it's a great company to work for.

If you want to ask other people what they think of something, use **Qu'est-ce que tu penses de...?** (*What do you think of...?*).

What do you think of...?

Qu'est-ce que tu penses de son dernier film?	**What do you think of** his latest movie?
Qu'est-ce que tu penses de cette idée?	**What do you think of** this idea?
Qu'est-ce que vous diriez de sortir dîner ce soir?	**What do you think about** going out for dinner tonight?
Qu'est-ce que vous en **pensez?**	**What do you think?**

To agree or disagree with what other people say, use **je suis d'accord** or **je ne suis pas d'accord**.

I agree...

Je suis d'accord.	**I agree.**
Je suis d'accord avec Nigel.	**I agree with** Nigel.
Je ne suis pas d'accord avec cette décision.	**I don't agree with** this decision.
Je ne suis pas tout à fait **d'accord avec** Claire.	**I don't** completely **agree with** Claire.
Je suis entièrement **de ton avis!**	I entirely **agree with you!**

You're right...

Tu as raison!	**You're right!**
Je pense que **vous avez raison**.	I think **you're right**.
C'est Matthieu **qui a raison**.	Matthieu**'s right**.
Je crois que **tu as tort**.	I think **you're wrong**.
Tu as tort de ne pas l'écouter.	**You're wrong not to** listen to her.

BON À SAVOIR!

Where we use the verb *to be* in English in the phrases *to be right* or *to be wrong*, French speakers use **avoir** (*to have*): **avoir raison** (*to be right*), **avoir tort** (*to be wrong*).

TALKING ABOUT YOUR PLANS

When talking to your colleagues and friends you will want to tell them about your plans. In French, as in English, the present is very often used to talk about plans, especially for things that have been arranged and that are definite. For more on the present tense, see page 272.

I'm seeing...

Je vois Philippe jeudi.	**I'm seeing** Philippe on Thursday.
Je la **vois** cet après-midi.	**I'm seeing** her this afternoon.
On va au cinéma ce soir.	**We're going** to the cinema tonight.
Nous allons déjeuner ensemble vendredi prochain.	**We're** going for lunch next Friday.

In English, when we talk about the future we often say *I'm going to*. French works the same way. To say that you're going to do something, use **je vais** (*I'm going to*) or **on va** (*we're going to*) before a verb in the infinitive. **vais** and **va** come from the verb **aller**. For more information on **aller**, see page 279.

I'm going to...

Je vais lui téléphoner.	**I'm going to** phone him.
Je vais le prévenir que je ne peux pas venir.	**I'm going to** let him know I can't come.
Je vais leur dire de venir un peu plus tard.	**I'm going to** tell them to come a little later.
On va sortir au restaurant demain soir.	**We're going to** go out for dinner tomorrow night.
On va se revoir.	**We're going to** see each other again.

Are you going to...?

Est-ce que tu vas lui annoncer la nouvelle aujourd'hui?	**Are you going to** tell him the news today?
Est-ce que vous allez le revoir?	**Are you going to** see him again?
Tu vas aller à cette soirée?	**Are you going to** go to this party?
Tu vas acheter une maison?	**Are you going to** buy a house?

When talking about what you intend to do, you can use **j'ai l'intention de** or **je compte** (*I intend to*) followed by a verb in the infinitive.

I intend to...

J'ai l'intention de l'inviter à prendre un verre.	**I intend to** ask her out for a drink.
J'ai l'intention d'aller les voir cet été.	**I intend to** go and see them this summer.
On a l'intention de l'inviter pendant les vacances.	**We intend to** invite him during the holidays.
Je compte régler ce problème le plus vite possible.	**I intend to** sort out this problem as quickly as possible.

Do you intend to...?

Est-ce que tu as l'intention d'aller au mariage d'Yves et Julie?	**Do you intend to** go to Yves and Julie's wedding?
Est-ce que vous avez l'intention de les contacter?	**Do you intend to** get in touch with them?
Qu'**est-ce que vous avez l'intention de** dire?	What **do you intend to** say?
Tu comptes rester dans la région?	**Do you intend to** stay in this area?
Comment **est-ce que tu comptes** lui annoncer la nouvelle?	How **do you intend to** tell him the news?

MAKING ARRANGEMENTS

When making arrangements with someone, use **Est-ce que ça vous va si...?** or **Est-ce que ça te va si...?** to ask someone if something suits them. **va** comes from the verb **aller**. For more information on **aller**, see page 279.

Will it suit you if...?

Est-ce que ça te va si on dîne à neuf heures?	**Does it suit you if** we have dinner at nine?
Est-ce que ça vous va si je vous appelle la semaine prochaine?	**Will it suit you if** I phone you next week?
Ça t'irait comme arrangement?	**Would** this arrangement **suit you**?

To ask somebody if they would prefer something, use **Est-ce que tu préférerais que...?** or **Est-ce que vous préféreriez que...?** (*Would you prefer it if...?*), which comes from the verb **préférer** in the conditional. The conditional is very useful to make polite requests or offers. You can find out more about it on page 274. For more information on **-er** verbs like **préférer**, see page 270.

Would you prefer it if...?

Est-ce que tu préférerais qu'on se donne rendez-vous en ville?	**Would you prefer it if** we met in town?
Est-ce que vous préféreriez qu'on se retrouve au restaurant?	**Would you prefer it if** we met at the restaurant?
Tu préférerais que je passe te chercher?	**Would you prefer it if** I came to collect you?

Is it better to...?

Est-ce qu'il vaut mieux inviter aussi les conjoints?	**Is it better to** invite partners as well?
Est-ce qu'il vaut mieux t'appeler le soir?	**Is it better to** ring you in the evening?
Est-ce qu'il vaut mieux vous prévenir avant de passer?	**Is it better to** let you know before we call in?

If you want to confirm an arrangement with somebody, you can use **Est-ce qu'on est d'accord sur...?** (*Are we agreed on...?*).

Are we agreed on...?

Est-ce qu'on est d'accord sur la date?	**Are we agreed on** the date?
Est-ce qu'on est d'accord sur le lieu du rendez-vous?	**Are we agreed on** where to meet?
Tu es d'accord?	**Do you agree**?
D'accord!	**Agreed!**

BON À SAVOIR!
D'accord is used to accept offers or to agree: **On y va ensemble? – D'accord!** (*Shall we go together? – OK!*).

Here are some key phrases which you are likely to hear in conversation.

Vous êtes déjà allé à Lille?	Have you ever been to Lille?
Vous restez combien de temps à Rouen?	How long are you staying in Rouen?
Ça vous plaît, Rouen?	How do you like Rouen?
Vous apprenez le français depuis combien de temps?	How long have you been learning French?
Ça va, tu arrives à suivre?	Are you following the conversation?
Vous parlez bien français.	Your French is very good.
Est-ce que je parle trop vite?	Am I speaking too fast?
Vous préférez que je parle anglais?	Would you prefer it if I spoke English?
Vous voulez que je répète?	Would you like me to say it again?
Vous voulez que je parle moins vite?	Do you want me to speak more slowly?
Tu peux me tutoyer.	You can call me tu.
On se tutoie?	Shall we call each other tu?
Vous êtes marié?	Are you married?
Vous avez des enfants?	Have you got any children?
Tu viens souvent ici?	Do you come here often?

Lifestyle Tips

• The polite *you* (**vous**) is used to address people whom you don't know. It's also a way of showing respect to someone who's older than you, or, at work, to someone who's higher up in the hierarchy. People who work together on a daily basis usually say **tu** to each other, (**se tutoyer** – *to say* **tu** *to each other*) but it is safer to wait a little before taking that step. Many people do not like to be addressed as **vous**, because they think it's too formal. They will usually suggest you call them **tu**, saying **tu peux me tutoyer** or **on peut se tutoyer**. You can make the first move and ask **On se tutoie?**, if you think that the other person will be more comfortable using the **tu** form.

• When meeting someone for the first time, you usually shake hands (**serrer la main à quelqu'un**), whether it's a man or a woman. In business relations, at business appointments or at negotiations, shaking hands is very common. Men who are on friendly terms usually shake hands, while women kiss on both cheeks (**se faire la bise**). Men also kiss female friends and in some cases other men, for instance when they belong to the same family. Bear in mind that habits may be different depending on where you are in France, which is why French people themselves often get confused; for instance, the number of kisses you give someone to say hello varies from one area to another!

• The words **ami** and **copain** (and the feminine forms **amie** and **copine**) can either mean *friend* or *boyfriend/girlfriend*. If someone uses **mon copain** for instance, they could be either be talking about a male friend or their boyfriend. The expressions **petit(e) ami(e)** and **petit(e) copain/copine** can also be used to mean *boyfriend* and *girlfriend*. To say *my partner*, use **mon compagnon** for a man and **ma compagne** for a woman.

• French people socialize in cafés and restaurants as British people do, but it is probably more common in France than in Britain to invite people, be it for coffee (**pour prendre le café**), for the apéritif (**pour prendre l'apéritif** or, more informally **l'apéro**) or for dinner (**pour le dîner**). Traditionally, **le café** or **l'apéritif** are ways of getting to know people more, while **le dîner** (and lunch, **le déjeuner**) are an opportunity for people who already know each other well, or families, to spend time together.

Getting there

Bon voyage! – Have a good trip!

If you're going to be travelling to and around French-speaking countries and cities, the phrases in this unit will help you ask for directions, find out how to get to places and buy tickets in easy, everyday French.

TALKING ABOUT YOUR PLANS

When you're travelling around, you will probably want to talk about what you're going to do. Use **je vais** (*I'm going to*) or **on va** (*we're going to*) before the verb. These come from the verb **aller**. For more information on **aller**, see page 279.

I'm going to...

Je vais passer une journée à Avignon.	**I'm going to** spend a day in Avignon.
Je vais prendre le train de sept heures.	**I'm going to** take the seven o'clock train.
On va passer deux nuits à Argelès.	**We're going to** spend two nights in Argelès.
Ensuite, **on va** aller à Grenoble.	Then **we're going to** go to Grenoble.
Normalement, **on va** d'abord à Strasbourg.	If all goes well, **we'll be going** to Strasbourg first.

BON À SAVOIR!
Use **normalement** or **si tout va bien** (*if all goes well*) at the beginning of a sentence to talk about a plan that might have to be changed.

I'll...

Je vais t'emmener à la gare.	**I'll** take you to the station.
Ne t'en fais pas, **je vais** prendre le bus.	Don't worry, **I'll** get the bus.
On va t'appeler un taxi.	**We'll** call you a taxi.
On va venir te chercher à la gare.	**We'll** come and pick you up at the railway station.

If you want to talk about what your plans are, you can use **j'ai l'intention de** (*I'm planning to*).

I'm planning to...

J'ai l'intention de louer une voiture.	**I'm planning to** hire a car.
J'ai l'intention d'aller au Maroc.	**I'm planning to** go to Morocco.
On a l'intention de suivre la route côtière.	**We're planning to** drive along the coast.
Je compte passer deux jours à Santiago.	**I intend to** spend two days in Santiago.

I hope to...

J'espère aller en Alsace cette année.	**I hope to** go to Alsace this year.
J'espère voir la Bibliothèque François Mitterrand.	**I hope to** see the François Mitterrand Library.
On espère pouvoir tout visiter.	**We hope** we can visit everything.

If you want to say that you have to do something in French, such as buy a ticket, catch a train and so on, you use **il faut que** (*I have to*) or **il faudrait que** (*I ought to*) followed by the subjunctive. For more information on the subjunctive, see page 274.

I have to...

Il faut que j'achète mon billet demain.	**I have to** buy my ticket tomorrow.
Il faut d'abord **que** je prenne le Train Express Régional jusqu'à Niort.	**I have to** take the local train to Niort first.
Il faut qu'on y soit avant 8 heures.	**We have to** be there by 8 o'clock.

I ought to...

Il faudrait que je fasse le plein.	**I ought to** fill up the tank.
Il faudrait que je confirme mon vol.	**I ought to** confirm my flight.
Il faudrait qu'on soit à la gare à sept heures.	**We ought to** be at the station at seven.
Il faudrait qu'on prenne plus de carburant.	**We ought to** get some more petrol.

Another way of saying what you have to do is to use **je dois** (*I must*) followed by the infinitive.

I must...

Je dois aller chercher la voiture avant trois heures.	**I must** collect the car before three.
Je dois prendre le bus à 5h30 demain matin.	**I must** catch the bus at 5.30 tomorrow morning.
Vous devez présenter votre permis de conduire.	**You must** show your driving licence.
Vous devez imprimer votre billet électronique.	**You must** print out your e-ticket.

SAYING WHAT YOU WANT TO DO

When you are using some kind of transport in France, you may well need to say what you would like to do in French. You can use **je voudrais** (*I'd like*) with the infinitive. This comes from the verb **vouloir**. For more information on **vouloir**, see page 285.

I'd like to...

Je voudrais louer un vélo.	**I'd like to** hire a bike.
Je voudrais prendre le train.	**I'd like to** take the train.
Mon ami voudrait signaler la perte de ses bagages.	**My friend would like to** report his luggage missing.

The most direct way of saying what you want to do is using **je veux** (*I want*) or **je souhaite** (*I wish*) with the infinitive. **veux** is from the verb **vouloir** and **souhaite** is from the verb **souhaiter**. For more information on **vouloir** and **-er** verbs like **souhaiter**, see pages 285 and 269.

I want to...

Je veux aller à Marseille.	**I want to** go to Marseilles.
Je veux descendre à Nancy.	**I want to** get off at Nancy.
On veut partir demain matin.	**We want to** leave tomorrow morning.
Je souhaite échanger mon billet.	**I want to** change my ticket.
Je ne souhaite pas voyager en première classe.	**I don't want to** travel first class.

If you want to say that you feel like doing something, say **j'ai envie de** (*I feel like*). This is slightly stronger than **j'ai bien envie de** (*I quite fancy*). **ai** comes from the verb **avoir**. For more information on **avoir**, see page 280.

I feel like...

J'ai envie de passer par Annecy.	**I feel like** going via Annecy.
J'ai envie de faire le voyage en plusieurs fois.	**I feel like** breaking the journey.
On n'a pas envie de passer six heures dans le train.	**We don't feel like** spending six hours on the train.
J'ai bien envie d'aller à Port-Vendres.	**I quite fancy** going to Port-Vendres.

MAKING SUGGESTIONS

You may wish to make a suggestion to your colleagues or friends in French. One way of doing this is to use **on pourrait** (*we could*). This comes from the verb **pouvoir**. For more information on **pouvoir**, see page 284.

We could...

On pourrait y aller demain.	**We could** go there tomorrow.
On pourrait faire étape à Agen.	**We could** break our journey at Agen.
On peut y aller à pied, **si tu préfères**.	**We can** walk, **if you prefer**.

BON À SAVOIR!
If you want to ask someone what they think of a particular suggestion, use **Qu'est-ce que tu en dis?** or **Qu'est-ce que vous en dites?** (*What do you say?*).

I can... if you like

Je peux te déposer, **si tu veux**.	**I can** give you a lift, **if you like**.
Je peux te retrouver à l'aéroport, **si tu veux**.	**I can** meet you at the airport, **if you like**.
On peut demander au contrôleur, **si vous voulez**.	**We can** ask the ticket inspector, **if you like**.

If you want to ask someone if they would like to do something, use **Tu veux...?**, or **Tu voudrais...?** (*Would you like…?*) if you know the person well or **Vous voulez...?** if you're talking to several people. These all come from the verb **vouloir**. For more information on **vouloir**, see page 285.

Would you like to...?

Tu veux aller te baigner?	**Would you like to** go for a swim?
Tu veux te reposer un peu?	**Would you like to** have a little rest?
Est-ce que tu veux prendre le volant?	**Would you like to** drive?
Vous voulez y aller à pied?	**Would you like to** walk there?
Est-ce que vous voulez qu'on s'arrête ici?	**Would you like to** stop here?

Another way of making suggestions in French is to ask **Pourquoi ne pas...?** (*Why don't…?*), which is often shortened to **Pourquoi pas...?** in spoken French.

Why don't...?

Pourquoi ne pas louer une voiture?	**Why don't we** hire a car?
Pourquoi ne pas prendre le métro?	**Why don't we** take the underground?
Pourquoi pas demander au chauffeur?	**Why don't we** ask the driver?

How about...?

Et si on prenait par la petite route?	**How about** taking the B road?
Et si on prenait le bateau pour y aller?	**How about** going there by boat?
Et si on passait par Biarritz?	**How about** going via Biarritz?

When you are travelling around in a French-speaking country or city, you will often need to find out some information to help you get to where you want to go. When you are asking for information you may need to get someone's attention in order to ask them a question. To do this you can use either **excusez-moi** or **pardon**.

I'm looking for...

Excusez-moi, **je cherche** la gare maritime, s'il vous plaît.	Excuse me, **I'm looking for** the harbour station.
Excusez-moi, **je cherche** l'écomusée du Beaujolais, s'il vous plaît.	Excuse me, **I'm looking for** the Beaujolais heritage centre.
Pardon, le bureau des réclamations, **s'il vous plaît**?	Excuse me, **I'm looking for** the complaints office.

BON À SAVOIR!

Remember to say **merci** or **merci beaucoup** when you get the information. If someone hasn't been able to help you, you can still thank them by saying **merci quand même** (*thanks all the same*).

If you want to ask a general question in French, you can use **C'est...?** or **Est-ce que c'est...?** (*Is it...?*).

Is it...?

C'est par là?	**Is it** this way?
C'est près d'ici?	**Is it** near here?
Est-ce que c'est loin, s'il vous plaît?	**Is it** far?
Est-ce que c'est le train pour Angoulême?	**Is this** the train for Angoulême?
Est-ce que c'est le bon arrêt pour le musée, s'il vous plaît?	**Is this** the right stop for the museum?
Est-ce que cette place **est** libre?	**Is** this seat free?

Is there...?

Il y a une station-service près d'ici, s'il vous plaît?	**Is there** a petrol station near here, please?
Il y a une station de métro près d'ici?	**Is there** an underground station near here?
Il y a des restaurants près d'ici?	**Are there** any restaurants around here?
Est-ce qu'il y a des tarifs étudiants?	**Is there** a student discount?

BON À SAVOIR!

You can see that both *there is* and *there are* are **il y a** in French.

In order to get more specific information, you may want to ask, for example, **Où...?** (*Where...?*), **Quel...?** (*Which...?*), or **À quelle heure...?** (*What time...?*).

Where...?

Où est la consigne?	**Where**'s the left-luggage office?
Où est la station de taxis la plus proche, s'il vous plaît?	**Where**'s the nearest taxi rank, please?
Où sont les toilettes?	**Where** are the public toilets?

Which...?

Je dois prendre **quelle ligne**, s'il vous plaît?	**Which line** do I take, please?
Quels bus vont en centre-ville?	**Which buses** go to the town centre?
De quel quai part le train pour Sarlat?	**Which platform** does the train for Sarlat leave **from**?
Excusez-moi, **c'est quelle direction** pour Brest, s'il vous plaît?	Excuse me, **which way** do I go for Brest, please?
C'est quelle direction pour aller au Stade de France, s'il vous plaît?	**Which way is it** to the Stade de France, please?

What time...?

On embarque **à quelle heure**?	**What time** are we boarding?
Le train part **à quelle heure**?	**What time** does the train leave?
À quelle heure est-ce qu'on arrive à Bruxelles?	**What time** do we get to Brussels?
Le départ **est bien à** sept heures?	The departure **is at** seven, **isn't it**?
Le bus **arrive bien à** neuf heures trente?	The bus **arrives at** nine thirty, **doesn't it**?

BON À SAVOIR!

When you're not sure about something, you can ask for confirmation by adding **bien** after the verb in your question.

If you want to ask how often something happens, how long it takes or how much it costs, you can use a phrase with **combien**.

How often...?

Il y a un bus pour Genève **tous les combien**?	**How often** is there a bus for Geneva?
Il y a un vol pour Londres **tous les combien**?	**How often** is there a flight to London?
Il faut faire le plein **tous les combien** de kilomètres?	**How often** do you have to fill up the tank?

How long...?

Ça prend combien de temps?	**How long does it take**?
Ça prend combien de temps pour aller à la gare?	**How long does it take** to get to the railway station?
Ça prend combien de temps pour aller de Lille à Paris?	**How long does it take** to get from Lille to Paris?
Le voyage **prend combien de temps**?	**How long does** the journey **take**?
On va mettre combien de temps pour y aller?	**How long will it take us** to get there?

How much is...?

Combien coûte un ticket pour Lyon?	**How much is** a ticket to Lyon?
Combien coûte le péage entre Paris et Orléans?	**How much is** the motorway toll between Paris and Orléans?
Combien est-ce que ça coûte de laisser une valise à la consigne?	**How much does it cost** to leave a case in left-luggage?
Combien est-ce que ça coûterait de louer une voiture pour deux jours?	**How much would it cost** to hire a car for two days?

Use **Est-ce que je peux...?** (*Can I...?*) or **Est-ce qu'on peut...?** (*Can we...?*) to ask whether you can do something. These are from the verb **pouvoir**. For more information on **pouvoir**, see page 284.

Can I...?

Est-ce que je peux payer par carte bleue?	**Can I** pay by debit card?
Est-ce que je peux louer une voiture pour la journée?	**Can I** hire a car for the day?
Est-ce qu'on peut fumer dans le train?	**Is** smoking **allowed** on the train?
Est-ce qu'on peut y aller à pied?	**Can you** walk there?
Est-ce qu'il est possible de changer son billet par Internet?	**Can you** change your ticket online?

ASKING FOR THINGS

When asking for something, you can use **Est-ce que je peux avoir...?** (*Can I have...?*) or **Est-ce que je pourrais avoir...?** (*Could I have...?*). These come from the verb **pouvoir**. For more information on **pouvoir**, see page 284.

Can I have...?

Est-ce que je peux avoir un plan du métro, s'il vous plaît?	**Can I have** a map of the underground, please?
Est-ce que je peux avoir une carte à la semaine, s'il vous plaît?	**Can I have** a weekly pass, please?
Est-ce que je pourrais avoir les horaires des trains, s'il vous plaît?	**Could I have** a train timetable, please?

When you want to find out if something is available or if someone has something, use **Est-ce que vous avez…?** or **Vous avez…?** (*Do you have…?*). **avez** comes from the verb **avoir**. For more information on **avoir**, see page 280.

Do you have…?

Est-ce que vous avez les horaires des bus?	**Do you have** any bus timetables?
Vous avez un plan d'accès, s'il vous plaît?	**Do you have** a map that shows how to get there, please?
Vous avez des voitures plus petites en location?	**Do you have** smaller cars to hire?
Est-ce qu'il vous reste des places côté couloir?	**Do you have** any aisle seats **left**?

When you ask for something, you can simply name what you want, but make sure you finish your question with **s'il vous plaît**, or your request might sound rather like an order!

A…, please

Un aller simple, **s'il vous plaît**.	**A** single, **please**.
Une place côté fenêtre, **s'il vous plaît**.	**A** window seat, **please**.
Trois billets retours pour Montréal, **s'il vous plaît**.	**Three** returns to Montreal, **please**.

If you are asking someone if they can do something for you, you should use **Est-ce que vous pouvez…?** (*Can you…?*).

Can you…?

Est-ce que vous pouvez nous emmener à l'hôtel Saint-Antoine, s'il vous plaît?	**Can you** take us to the Saint-Antoine hotel, please?
Est-ce que vous pouvez me prévenir quand on arrivera à l'arrêt du musée?	**Can you** tell me when we're near the museum stop?
Vous pouvez me déposer ici, s'il vous plaît?	**Can you** drop me here, please?
Vous pouvez nous montrer où ça se trouve sur la carte?	**Can you** show us where it is on the map?

Would you mind...?

Est-ce que ça vous dérangerait de m'écrire l'adresse?	**Would you mind** writing down the address for me?
Est-ce que ça vous dérangerait de me déposer à mon hôtel?	**Would you mind** dropping me at my hotel?
Est-ce que ça vous dérangerait de nous montrer où c'est?	**Would you mind** showing us where it is?

SAYING WHAT YOU LIKE, DISLIKE, PREFER ▆▆▆▆▆▆

You will want to be able to discuss what you like and dislike with your French-speaking acquaintances. To say what you like, use **j'aime bien** (*I like*), which is not as strong as **j'aime** (*I love*). To say what you don't like, just use **je n'aime pas** (*I don't like*). These come from the verb **aimer**. For more information on **aimer**, see page 275.

I like...

J'aime bien ces routes de campagne.	**I like these** country roads.
J'aime bien voyager en train.	**I like** travelling by train.
J'aime beaucoup cette voiture.	**I like** this car **a lot**.
J'aime l'avion.	**I love** flying.

I don't like...

Je n'aime pas les voitures automatiques.	**I don't like** automatics.
Je n'aime pas conduire à droite.	**I don't like** driving on the right.

Do you like...?

Tu aimes bien cette région?	**Do you like** this area?
Tu aimes bien voyager seul?	**Do you like** travelling by yourself?
Est-ce que vous aimez conduire de nuit?	**Do you like** driving at night?
Est-ce que vous aimez bien les voyages organisés?	**Do you like** package tours?

If you want to say what you prefer, use **je préfère** (*I prefer*) or **je préférerais** (*I'd prefer*). These come from the verb **préférer**. For more information on **-er** verbs like **préférer**, see page 270.

I prefer to...

Je préfère dormir à l'hôtel.	**I prefer to** sleep in a hotel.
Je préfère prendre l'autoroute.	**I prefer to** take the motorway.
Je préférerais ne pas laisser ma voiture ici.	**I'd prefer** not **to** leave my car here.

I'd rather...

J'aimerais mieux faire le voyage par beau temps.	**I'd rather** make the journey in good weather.
J'aimerais mieux être assise côté fenêtre.	**I'd rather** sit next to the window.
On aimerait mieux faire la route de jour.	**We'd rather** drive in the daytime.

LISTEN OUT FOR

Here are some key phrases you are likely to be hear when you're travelling around.

Prochain arrêt:...	Next stop:...
Le train pour Nice part du quai numéro trois.	The train for Nice leaves from platform three.
Votre billet, s'il vous plaît.	Ticket, please.
Je peux m'asseoir ici?	Do you mind if I sit here?
Continuez tout droit jusqu'aux feux.	Go straight on till you get to the traffic lights.
Prenez la deuxième à gauche.	Take the second turning on the left.
C'est en face de la cathédrale.	It's opposite the cathedral.
C'est tout près.	It's very near.
On peut y aller à pied.	It's within walking distance.
C'est à trois arrêts d'ici.	It's three stops from here.

Lifestyle Tips

• If you're behind the wheel of a car, be ready to produce your driving licence if asked for it by the police. If you've left it behind, you may well be fined. The police officer might ask you: **votre permis de conduire, s'il vous plaît** (*your driving licence, please*). French drivers also have to be able to produce their **carte grise** (*car registration document*) and their **attestation d'assurance** (*car insurance certificate*).

• Motorways are not free in France. When you go onto the motorway, you get a **ticket de péage** or **ticket d'entrée**. When you come off the motorway this will show how many kilometres you've driven and how much you have to pay.

• At motorway tolls, some toll booths are manned, some are automatic (using bank cards), and some are reserved for drivers using the **télépéage** system which makes it possible to pay the toll via a sensor inside the car (with monthly bills sent to your address). It is best to stay clear of these lanes which are marked with a yellow "T" sign, as the drivers equipped with such sensors don't take kindly to tourists holding up their fast lane!

• Over the past years, **covoiturage** (*car sharing*) has become quite popular in France. It can be a cheap and convenient way of getting around, especially for short distances. There are many places where you can find offers for **covoiturage**, but local papers, and ad boards in shops are probably your best bet.

• If you're asked to produce your **titre de transport** on the bus, the train or the underground, it means that you have to show your ticket to the inspector.

• Make sure you punch your ticket before you get on the train or bus. If you have forgotten to do so, it is advisable to go and see **le contrôleur** (*the ticket inspector*) as soon as possible or you might be fined.

• If you're in a hurry, you can hop on the train and buy a ticket for a small amount extra directly from a ticket inspector - go and see him or her as soon as you're on the train or you might be suspected of **resquillage** (*fare-dodging*).

• Queues tend to be informal in French-speaking countries. So if you're trying to get to an information desk and don't know if it's your turn, just ask **C'est à moi?** or **C'est mon tour?** (*Am I next?*). If you want to let someone in before you, you can say **après vous** (*after you*).

Home
from home

Dors bien! – Sleep well!

If you're going to stay in a French-speaking country, the phrases in this unit will provide you with the language you need to help you find the sort of accommodation you want (hotel, hostel, self-catering accommodation or a flat to rent) and ensure that everything is to your satisfaction when you're there. We'll also give you a few tips on what the receptionist or your landlord or landlady may say to you.

ASKING FOR THINGS

To say what kind of accommodation you want in French, use **je voudrais** or **je souhaite** (*I'd like*). **voudrais** comes from the verb **vouloir** and **souhaite** comes from the verb **souhaiter**. For further information on **vouloir** and **-er** verbs like **souhaiter**, see pages 285 and 269.

I'd like...

Je voudrais une chambre avec un balcon.	**I'd like** a room with a balcony.
Je voudrais réserver une chambre double pour deux nuits.	**I'd like to** book a double room for two nights.
On voudrait un dortoir de six personnes.	**We'd like** a six-bed dorm.
Je souhaite rester trois nuits.	**I'd like to** stay three nights.
Je souhaite louer votre gîte pendant deux semaines.	**I'd like to** book your gîte for two weeks.

je veux is a slightly more direct way of saying what you want.

I want...

Je veux un appartement bien éclairé.	**I want** a well-lit flat.
Je veux changer de chambre; celle que vous m'avez donnée est humide.	**I want to** change rooms; the one you gave me is damp.
Je veux qu'on me rembourse.	**I want** a refund.
On ne veut pas de chambre côté rue.	**We don't want** a room overlooking the road.

Use **je tiens à** to say that you insist on something. **tiens** comes from the verb **tenir**.

I insist on...

Je tiens vraiment **à** avoir vue sur la mer.	I absolutely **insist on** having a view of the sea.
Je tiens à ne pas être dérangé.	**I insist on** not being disturbed.
On tient à être dans le centre-ville.	**We insist on** staying in the centre of town.

When you want to find out if something is available, use **Est-ce que vous avez...?** (*Do you have...?*) or **Est-ce que vous auriez...?** (*Would you have...?*). These come from the verb **avoir**. For more information on **avoir**, see page 280.

Do you have...?

Est-ce que vous avez des informations sur le logement?	**Do you have** any information about accommodation?
Est-ce que vous avez des chambres de libre?	**Have you got** any rooms free?
Vous avez Internet?	**Have you got** internet access?
Est-ce que vous auriez des serviettes, s'il vous plaît?	**Would you have** any towels, please?

Can I have...?

Est-ce que je peux avoir la clé de ma chambre, s'il vous plaît?	**Can I have** the key to my room, please?
Est-ce que je peux avoir un reçu, s'il vous plaît?	**Can I have** a receipt, please?
Est-ce qu'on peut avoir une liste des logements disponibles?	**Can we have** a list of available accommodation?
Est-ce que je pourrais avoir deux serviettes en plus?	**Could I have** two more towels?

If you are asking someone whether they can do something for you, use **Est-ce que pouvez...?** (*Can you...?*) and **Est-ce que vous pourriez...?** (*Could you...?*). They both come from the verb **pouvoir**. For more information on **pouvoir**, see page 284.

Can you...?

Est-ce que vous pouvez me confirmer la réservation par e-mail?	**Can you** confirm the booking by email?
Est-ce que vous pouvez m'appeler pour me réveiller à sept heures, s'il vous plaît?	**Can you** give me an alarm call at seven o'clock, please?
Est-ce que vous pourriez changer les serviettes, s'il vous plaît?	**Could you** change the towels, please?
Vous pourriez me montrer la chambre, s'il vous plaît?	**Could you** show me the room, please?

Would you mind...?

Est-ce que ça vous dérangerait de me montrer comment marche la cuisinière?	**Would you mind** showing me how the cooker works?
Est-ce que ça vous dérangerait de m'appeler un taxi?	**Would you mind** calling a taxi for me?
Ça vous dérangerait de monter mes valises à ma chambre?	**Would you mind** taking my suitcases up to my room?

TALKING ABOUT YOURSELF

When you are enquiring about somewhere to stay you will need to give information about yourself. Use **je suis** (*I am*) to talk about yourself and **on est** (*we are*) to include the people who are with you. These come from the verb **être**. For more information on **être**, see page 282.

I'm...

Je suis étudiante.	**I'm** a student.
Je suis canadien.	**I'm** Canadian.
Je suis du sud de l'Angleterre.	**I'm** from the south of England.
On est en vacances.	**We're** on holiday.
Nous sommes les propriétaires.	**We're** the owners.

My name is...

Je m'appelle Brian Gallagher.	**My name is** Brian Gallagher.
Je m'appelle Olivia Gauthier.	**My name is** Olivia Gauthier.
Je m'appelle Madame Smith. J'ai réservé une chambre double pour cette nuit.	**My name is** Mrs Smith. I've booked a double room for tonight.
Mon nom de famille c'est Morris...	**My surname is** Morris...
...et **mon prénom c'est** Emma.	...and **my first name is** Emma.
Ça s'écrit M-O-R-R-I-S.	**It's spelt** M-O-R-R-I-S.

BON À SAVOIR!
Remember that the French alphabet is pronounced differently from the English alphabet. For more information on how to say letters of the alphabet in French, see page 203.

When you want to obtain some information about your accommodation, an easy way to ask questions is just to put **est-ce que** before what you want to know. Alternatively, you can simply make your voice go up at the end of the sentence. This sounds more informal than using **est-ce que**.

Is it...?

Est-ce que c'est cher?	**Is it** expensive?
Est-ce que c'est un hôtel moderne?	**Is it** a modern hotel?
C'est loin?	**Is it** far?
Le petit déjeuner **est** inclus dans le prix?	**Is** breakfast included in the price?
Est-ce que toutes les charges **sont** comprises dans le loyer?	**Are** all the bills included in the rent?

You can use **Il y a...?** in French to ask both *Is there...?* or *Are there...?*.

Is there...?

Est-ce qu'il y a un endroit où manger près d'ici?	**Is there** anywhere near here where we can get something to eat?
Est-ce qu'il y a un interphone?	**Is there** an intercom?
Est-ce qu'il y a vue sur la mer?	**Is there** a sea view?
Est-ce qu'il y a le chauffage central dans l'appartement?	**Is there** central heating in the apartment?
Il y a des toilettes handicapés?	**Are there** any disabled toilets?

Use **je cherche** (*I'm looking for*) or **on cherche** (*we're looking for*) to ask where something is. **cherche** comes from the verb **chercher**. For more information on **-er** verbs like **chercher**, see page 269.

I'm looking for...

Excusez-moi, **je cherche** le camping.	Excuse me, **I'm looking for** the campsite.
Je cherche une chambre d'hôte pour ce soir.	**I'm looking for** a B&B for tonight.
On cherche l'hôtel du Nord.	**We're looking for** the hôtel du Nord.

To get more specific information you may need to ask **Quel...?** (*What...?*), **Où...?** (*Where...?*) or **À quelle heure...?** (*What time...?*).

What...?

Quel est le nom de l'hôtel?	**What**'s the name of the hotel?
Quel est le numéro de l'agence immobilière?	**What**'s the number for the letting agency?
Quelle est l'adresse du propriétaire?	**What**'s the address of the landlord?
Quels sont vos tarifs?	**What** are your rates?

BON À SAVOIR!

Remember to use **quel** with a masculine word and **quelle** with a feminine word.

Where...?

Où est le bar?	**Where**'s the bar?
Où est la salle de fitness?	**Where**'s the gym?
Où sont les ascenseurs?	**Where** are the lifts?
Où est-ce que je peux brancher mon portable?	**Where** can I plug in my laptop?

What time...?

À quelle heure est le dîner?	**What time**'s dinner?
À quelle heure vous fermez les portes le soir?	**What time** do you lock the doors at night?
Il faut libérer la chambre **avant quelle heure**?	**What time** do we have to vacate the room **by**?
Vous servez le petit déjeuner **jusqu'à quelle heure**?	**What time** do you serve breakfast **till**?

You are very likely to want to ask how much something costs. To do this, use a phrase containing **combien**.

How much...?

C'est combien pour une nuit en chambre double?	**How much is** a double room per night?
C'est combien pour la pension complète?	**How much is** full board?
Combien ça coûterait de louer un gîte pour tout le mois de juillet?	**How much would it be** to rent a gîte for the whole of July?

How many...?

Il vous reste **combien de** chambres avec salle de bains?	**How many** en-suite rooms have you got left?
Il y a **combien de** lits dans la chambre familiale?	**How many** beds are there in the family room?

ASKING FOR PERMISSION

Often when you are staying in a hotel or other accommodation you will need to be able to ask whether you can do something or not. Use **Est-ce que je peux...?** (*Can I...?*) or **Est-ce que nous pouvons...?** (*Can we...?*) to ask if you can do something. These come from the verb **pouvoir**. For more information on **pouvoir**, see page 284.

Can I...?

Est-ce que je peux voir la chambre?	**Can I** see the room?
Est-ce que je peux laisser mes valises ici cinq minutes?	**Can I** leave my suitcases here for five minutes?
Est-ce que je peux fumer dans la chambre?	**Can I** smoke in the room?
Est-ce qu'on peut utiliser la piscine?	**Can we** use the pool?
Est-ce qu'on peut camper ici?	**Can we** camp here?

Do you mind if...?

Ça vous dérange si je gare ma voiture dehors un instant?	**Do you mind if** I park my car outside for a moment?
Ça vous dérange si je paye par carte de crédit?	**Do you mind if** I pay by credit card?
Ça te dérange si on prend la chambre du haut?	**Do you mind if** we take the upstairs bedroom?

If you want to ask someone if you may do something, use **Vous permettez que...?** (*Am I allowed to...?*) followed by a verb in the subjunctive. For more information on the subjunctive, see page 274.

Am I allowed to...?

Vous permettez que je reçoive des invités?	**Am I allowed to** have guests?
Vous permettez que je me serve de la machine à laver?	**Am I allowed to** use the washing machine?
Vous permettez qu'on utilise le téléphone?	**May we** use the phone?
On a le droit de se servir du barbecue?	**Are we allowed to** use the barbecue?
On a le droit d'emmener notre chien?	**Are we allowed to** bring our dog?

SAYING WHAT YOU LIKE, DISLIKE, PREFER

When talking about what you like, use **j'aime bien** (*I like*), which is not as strong as **j'aime** or **j'adore** (*I love*). To say what you don't like, just use **je n'aime pas** (*I don't like*). These come from the verb **aimer**. For more information on **aimer**, see page 275.

I like...

J'aime bien les petits hôtels.	**I like** small hotels.
J'aime bien les campings de montagne.	**I like** campsites in the mountains.
J'adore cette pension de famille.	**I love** this guest house.

I don't like...

Je n'aime pas cet hôtel.	**I don't like** this hotel.
On n'aime pas tout prévoir à l'avance.	**We don't like** to plan everything in advance.
Je déteste cette décoration.	**I hate** this decor.

If you want to say what you prefer, use **je préfère** (*I prefer*) or **je préférerais** (*I'd prefer*). To say that you prefer A to B, use **je préfère A à B**. These come from the verb **préférer**. For more information on **-er** verbs like **préférer**, see page 270.

I prefer...

Je préfère cet hôtel.	**I prefer** this hotel.
Je préfère loger chez l'habitant.	**I prefer** to stay with a family.
Je préférerais ne pas attendre pour réserver un hôtel.	**I'd prefer not to** wait to book a hotel.
On préfère l'auberge de jeunesse **au** camping.	**We prefer** youth hostels **to** campsites.

I'd rather...

J'aimerais mieux être dans le centre ville.	**I'd rather** be in the town centre.
J'aimerais mieux être en colocation **que de** vivre seul.	**I'd rather** share a flat **than** live on my own.
On aimerait mieux vivre à la campagne **que d'**avoir un appartement en ville.	**We'd prefer to** live in the country **than** have a flat in town.

EXPRESSING OPINIONS

You may well be asked what you think of your accommodation. Whether it's perfect or not up to scratch, you can use **je trouve** to say what you think. This comes from the verb **trouver**. For more information on **-er** verbs like **trouver**, see page 269.

I think...

Je trouve la chambre un peu petite.	**I think** the bedroom's a bit small.
Je trouve la maison très accueillante.	**I think** the house is very welcoming.
J'ai trouvé le service excellent.	**I thought** the service was excellent.
Je trouve qu'il y a trop de bruit la nuit.	**I find that** there's too much noise at night.

In my opinion...

À mon avis, c'est trop cher pour ce que c'est.	**In my opinion**, it's too expensive for what it is.
À mon avis, c'est parfait pour ce dont on a besoin.	**In my opinion**, it's perfect for our needs.
À mon avis, la chambre est trop petite.	**In my opinion**, the room is too small.
À mon avis, c'est complètement inacceptable.	**In my view**, it's completely unacceptable.

MAKING SUGGESTIONS

If you would like to suggest that you do something, use **je peux** (*I can*) followed by the infinitive and **si vous voulez** (*if you like*) – or **si tu veux** for a person you know well – at the end. **peux** comes from the verb **pouvoir**. For more information on **pouvoir**, see page 284.

I can... if you like

Je peux confirmer les dates demain, **si vous voulez.**	**I can** confirm the dates tomorrow, **if you like**.
Je peux vous envoyer un acompte, **si vous voulez**.	**I can** send you a deposit, **if you like**.
On peut chercher un autre hôtel, **si tu veux**.	**We can** look for another hotel, **if you like**.

If you wish to ask what someone would like you to do, you can use **Vous voulez que je...?** (*Would you like me to...?*) followed by a verb in the subjunctive, which you can find out more about on page 274.

Would you like me to...?

Vous voulez que je vous paye en liquide?	**Would you like me to** pay cash?
Vous voulez que je vous montre ma réservation?	**Would you like me to** show you my booking?
Tu veux que je prenne le lit du haut?	**Would you like me to** take the top bunk?
Est-ce que vous voulez qu'on vous laisse nos passeports?	**Would you like to** keep our passports?

ASKING FOR SUGGESTIONS

You may want to ask for advice or a recommendation concerning your accommodation. To ask for advice, use **Est-ce que vous me conseillez de...?** (*Would you advise...?*). This comes from the verb **conseiller**. For more information on **-er** verbs like **conseiller**, see page 269.

Would you advise...?

Est-ce que vous me conseillez de réserver à l'avance?	**Would you advise me to** book in advance?
Est-ce que vous nous conseillez d'amener des sacs de couchage?	**Would you advise us to** bring sleeping bags?
Vous me conseillez d'amener de quoi manger?	**Would you advise me to** bring something to eat?

Would you recommend...?

Est-ce que vous recommandez cet hôtel?	**Would you recommend** this hotel?
Est-ce que vous recommandez cette agence immobilière?	**Would you recommend** this estate agency?
Est-ce que vous nous recommandez de louer à la semaine?	**Would you recommend that we** rent by the week?
Vous nous recommandez de prendre un appartement en ville?	**Would you recommend us to** take a flat in town?

If you want to say that you have to do something with regard to your accommodation in French, you use **il faut que je** (*I have to*) or **il faudrait que je** (*I ought to*) and then the verb in the subjunctive, which you can find out about on page 274.

I have to...

Il faut que je passe à la réception pour payer.	**I have to** go to the reception to pay.
Il faut que je note l'adresse de l'hôtel.	**I have to** write down the address of the hotel.
Il faut qu'on parte à six heures demain matin.	**We have to** leave at six tomorrow morning.

I ought to...

Il faudrait que je fasse une lessive.	**I ought to** do a load of washing.
Il faudrait que je décharge la voiture.	**I ought to** unload the car.
Il faudrait qu'on se lève avant sept heures.	**We ought to** be up by seven am.
Il faudrait qu'on ait le double des clefs.	**We ought to** have a spare set of keys.

Alternatively, you can use **je dois** (*I must*), from the verb **devoir**. For more information on **devoir**, see page 281.

I must...

Je dois me lever tôt demain.	**I must** get up early tomorrow.
Je dois rendre les clés au propriétaire.	**I must** give the keys back to the owner.
On doit absolument trouver un logement avant la fin du mois.	**We** absolutely **must** find accommodation by the end of the month.

In French you can tell somebody what you need by using **j'ai besoin de** (*I need*).

I need...

J'ai besoin d'un lit d'enfant.	**I need** a cot.
J'ai besoin de téléphoner en Écosse.	**I need** to call Scotland.
Nous avons besoin d'une chambre au rez-de-chaussée.	**We need** a room on the ground floor.

You can use **Est-ce qu'il faut que...?** (*Do I have to...?*) followed by the verb in the subjunctive to ask about what you have to do. For more information on the subjunctive, see page 274.

Do I have to...?

Est-ce qu'il faut que je laisse la clef à la réception quand je sors?	**Do I have to** leave the key at the reception when I go out?
Est-ce qu'il faut qu'on emmène des sacs de couchage?	**Do we need to** bring sleeping bags?
Est-ce qu'il faut vous prévenir quand on quitte l'hôtel?	**Do we have to** let you know when we leave the hotel?
Qu'est-ce qu'il faut que j'emmène?	**What do I need** to bring?
Quand est-ce qu'il faut qu'on libère la chambre?	**When do we have to** vacate the room?

Alternatively, you can use **Est-ce que je dois...?** (*Do I need to...?*)

Do I need to...?

Est-ce que je dois faire le ménage dans l'appartement avant de partir?	**Do I need to** clean the flat before leaving?
Est-ce que je dois réserver?	**Do I need to** book?
Est-ce qu'on doit laisser un pourboire à la femme de chambre?	**Do we need to** leave a tip for the housekeeper?

When you are talking about your plans for where you're going to stay, in French, as in English, the present tense is very often used to talk about things that have been arranged and are definite. For more on the present tense, see page 272.

I'm staying...

Je loge en auberge de jeunesse la première semaine.	**I'm staying** in a youth hostel the first week.
Je loge chez l'habitant le premier soir.	**I'm staying** with a host family the first night.
... ensuite **je dors** à l'hôtel.	... then **I'm staying** in a hotel.

Alternatively, you can use the future tense in French, as in English.

I'll...

Je serai à l'hôtel à dix-sept heures.	**I'll be** at the hotel at five pm.
Je paierai le loyer à l'avance.	**I'll pay** the rent in advance.
On arrivera dans la soirée.	**We'll arrive** in the evening.

In English we often say *I'm going to* to talk about the future. French works the same way. To say that you're going to do something, put **je vais** (*I'm going to*) or **on va** (*we're going to*) before the verb. **vais** and **va** come from the verb **aller**. For more information on **aller**, see page 279.

I'm going to...

Je vais loger à Biarritz.	**I'm going to** stay in Biarritz.
Je vais louer un chalet à la montagne.	**I'm going to** rent a chalet in the mountains.
On va faire du camping.	**We're going to** camp.

If you want to say that you intend to do something, you can use **j'ai l'intention de** or **je compte** (*I intend to*).

I intend to...

J'ai l'intention de louer un appartement.	**I intend to** rent a flat.
J'ai l'intention de trouver un gîte.	**I intend to** find a gîte .
Je compte rester jusqu'à vendredi.	**I intend to** stay until Friday.
On compte partir demain après le petit déjeuner.	**We intend to** leave after breakfast tomorrow.

COMPLAINING

Unfortunately the service you get in your accommodation may not always be perfect. A very simple way of complaining is to say what the problem is using **il y a**, which means both *there is* and *there are* or **il n'y a pas de** which means *there isn't* or *there aren't*.

There's...

Il y a trop de bruit.	**There's** too much noise.
Il y a une fuite au plafond.	**There's** a leak in the ceiling.
Il y a des cafards dans l'appartement.	**There are** cockroaches in the apartment.

There isn't...

Il n'y a pas d'eau chaude.	**There isn't** any hot water.
Il n'y a pas de serviettes propres dans la chambre.	**There aren't** any clean towels in the room.
La chambre **n'a pas de** balcon.	The room **doesn't have** a balcony.
L'appartement **n'a pas** la climatisation.	The apartment **doesn't have** air-conditioning.

You can also use the verb **être** (*to be*) to describe what the problem is.

It's...

L'appartement **est** sale.	The apartment**'s** dirty.
L'eau de la piscine **n'est pas** très propre.	The water in the swimming pool **isn't** very clean.
Cet hôtel **est** trop bruyant.	This hotel**'s** too noisy.
Il fait trop chaud ici.	**It's** too hot in here.

LISTEN OUT FOR

Here are some phrases you are likely to hear when you're looking for somewhere to stay.

Vous cherchez quel type de logement?	What type of accommodation are you looking for?
La réservation est à quel nom?	Whose name is the booking in?
Pour combien de nuits?	For how many nights?
Pour combien de personnes?	For how many people?
Le petit déjeuner est inclus dans le prix.	Breakfast is included in the price.
Je peux voir votre passeport, s'il vous plaît?	Can I see your passport, please?
Nous sommes complets.	We're full.
Il y a une caution de 300 euros.	There's a 300 euro deposit.
Vous êtes joignable à quel numéro?	What number can we contact you on?
Les chiens ne sont pas admis.	We don't allow dogs.
Vous voulez régler comment?	How would you like to pay?
Remplissez ce formulaire, s'il vous plaît.	Please fill in this form.
Signez ici, s'il vous plaît.	Please sign here.
Vous pouvez épeler votre nom, s'il vous plaît?	Can you spell your name for me, please?

Lifestyle Tips

• The proportion of **propriétaires** (*homeowners*) in France is much lower than it is in Britain. People tend to rent a lot more. Long-term rented accommodation is usually unfurnished; **locataires** (*tenants*) often even have to supply their own **appareils ménagers** (*white goods*) and **meubles de cuisine** (*kitchen units*).

• It is not as common for professionals to share a flat – **être en colocation** – in France as it is in Britain, although high rents have changed this over the past few years, especially in cities.

• If you're flat-hunting in France, you will hear flats described as **F1**, **F2**, **F3** and so on. These refer to the number of rooms in a flat, not including the bathroom and kitchen. A **studio** is a studio, an **F1** is a one-room flat, an **F2** is a two-room flat, and so on.

• One good way of getting to know an area and its locals is to stay in a **gîte rural** – a cottage or apartment in the country. Some offer self-catering facilities, but others give you the chance to stay in an apartment within the house of the host family.

• The equivalent of B&Bs in France are **chambres d'hôte**, usually a room in someone's house. Some of these places also offer **table d'hôte**, which means that they will provide a meal using local produce, or even food grown on the farm. If there aren't any vacancies you will see a **"Complet"** (*"Full"*) sign.

• When staying in a **camping** (*campsite*), you will have to pay **des arrhes** (*a deposit*) which is part of the full amount you will pay at the end of your stay. When renting accommodation you may also have to pay **une caution** (*a security deposit*).

Wining and dining

Bon appétit! – Enjoy your meal!

If you're going out for a meal in France either in a local café or in a fancy restaurant, the phrases in this unit will give you the confidence to talk to the waiter and chat with your French friends in easy, natural French. We'll also give you some tips on getting advice about what to order, and a few key phrases the waiters are likely to use.

MAKING ARRANGEMENTS

If you want to make arrangements such as where and when to meet when you go out for a meal with French-speaking people, you can ask **Où est-ce que...?** (*Where...?*) or **À quelle heure...?** (*What time...?*).

Where...?

Où est-ce qu'on se retrouve?	**Where** shall we meet?
Où est-ce que tu veux que je vienne te prendre?	**Where** do you want me to pick you up?
Où est-ce qu'on pourrait aller manger?	**Where** shall we go to eat?

What time...?

À quelle heure est-ce qu'on se retrouve?	**What time** shall we meet?
À quelle heure est-ce qu'elle va arriver?	**What time** is she going to get here?
Tu as réservé une table **pour quelle heure**?	**What time** did you book the table **for**?
Vous servez **jusqu'à quelle heure**?	**What time** do you serve **till**?
On peut arriver **à partir de quelle heure**?	**How early** can we come?

If you want to check that the arrangements suit your friends or colleagues, you can use **Ça te va si...?** or **Ça vous va si...?** (*Will it be all right if...?*).

Will it be all right if...?

Ça te va si on va au restaurant demain soir?	**Will it be all right if** we go to the restaurant tomorrow night?
Ça te va si on se retrouve à sept heures?	**Will it be all right if** we meet up at seven pm?
Ça vous va si on vous rejoint là-bas?	**Will it be all right if** we meet you there?

Is it better to...?

Est-ce qu'il vaut mieux réserver?	**Is it better to** book?
Est-ce qu'il vaut mieux arriver en avance?	**Is it better to** arrive early?
Est-ce qu'il vaudrait mieux changer notre réservation?	**Would it be better to** change our reservation?
Est-ce que ça t'irait mieux samedi soir?	**Would** Saturday evening **suit you better**?

It would suit me best to...

Ça m'arrangerait de vous retrouver sur place.	**It'd suit me best to** meet you there.
Ça m'arrangerait d'y aller à huit heures.	**It'd suit me best to** be there for eight.
Ça nous arrangerait d'y aller en voiture.	**It'd be better for us to** go there by car.

ASKING FOR INFORMATION

When you're going out for a meal you'll need to ask for various pieces of information, such as where things are and how much they cost. To ask where something is, you can use **Où se trouve...?** (*Where is...?*), and to ask how much it costs, use **C'est combien...?** (*How much is...?*).

Where's...?

Où se trouve le restaurant?	**Where is** the restaurant?
Où se trouve le coin change-bébé?	**Where's** the baby changing area?
Excusez-moi, **où se trouvent** les toilettes?	Excuse me, **where are** the toilets?

How much...?

C'est combien une bouteille de blanc du pays?	**How much is** a bottle of local white wine?
C'est combien une petite salade?	**How much is** it for a side salad?
Il est à combien, le menu?	**How much is** the set menu?

What...?

Qu'est-ce qu'il y a comme dessert?	**What** is there for dessert?
Qu'est-ce qu'il y a dans le cassoulet?	**What** is in a "cassoulet"?
Qu'est-ce qu'il y a comme garniture?	**What** does it come with?

Many of the questions you will be asking can be answered by *yes* or *no*. You can either put **est-ce que** before what you want to know or alternatively you can raise the tone of your voice at the end of the sentence – this will make you sound more informal.

Is it...?

Est-ce que c'est un plat typique de la région?	**Is it** a local dish?
Est-ce que c'est compris dans le menu à 15 euros?	**Is it** included in the 15 € set menu?
Est-ce qu'il est cher, ce restaurant?	**Is it** an expensive restaurant?
Ça convient aux végétariens?	**Is it ok for** vegetarians?

When you're out in a French restaurant you will need to be able to ask for what you want. If you want to ask for something in French, use **je voudrais** (*I'd like*) or **on voudrait** (*we'd like*). **voudrais** and **voudrait** come from the verb **vouloir**. For more information on **vouloir**, see page 285.

I'd like...

Je voudrais du pain, s'il vous plaît.	**I'd like** some bread, please.
Je voudrais une carafe d'eau, s'il vous plaît.	**I'd like** a jug of water, please.
On voudrait une autre bouteille de vin.	**We'd like** another bottle of wine.
Une table pour deux personnes, **s'il vous plaît**.	A table for two, **please**.

When the waiter approaches and you want to say that you're not ready to order, use **je n'ai pas encore décidé**. Alternatively, if your order has already been taken, you can say **on a déjà commandé, merci** (*someone's already taken our order, thanks*).

I'll have...

Comme entrée, **je vais prendre** la terrine de lapin.	As a starter, **I'll have** the rabbit terrine.
Comme plat principal, **je vais prendre** le saumon.	For the main course, **I'll have** salmon.
Je vais prendre la mousse au chocolat comme dessert.	For dessert, **I'll have** the chocolate mousse.
Comme boisson, **nous allons prendre** une bouteille d'eau pétillante.	**We'll have** sparkling water to drink.
Je ne sais pas quoi **prendre**.	I don't know what **to have**.

When you want to find out if something is available, use **Est-ce que vous avez...?** or **Vous avez...?** (*Have you got...?*). **avez** comes from the verb **avoir**. For more information on **avoir**, see page 280.

Have you got...?

Est-ce que vous avez un menu enfants?	**Have you got** a children's menu?
Est-ce que vous avez une table en terrasse?	**Do you have** a table outside?
Vous avez une carte des vins?	**Do you have** a wine list?
Vous avez une chaise pour bébé?	**Have you got** a high chair?

If you want to ask someone, for example the waiter, for something in French, use **Je peux avoir...?** (*Can I have...?*) or **Je pourrais avoir...?** (*Could I have...?*). **peux** and **pourrais** come from the verb **pouvoir**. For more information on **pouvoir**, see page 284.

Can I have...?

Je peux avoir une autre fourchette, s'il vous plaît?	**Can I have** another fork, please?
Je peux avoir la carte des desserts, s'il vous plaît?	**Can I have** the dessert menu, please?
On peut avoir du pain, s'il vous plaît?	**Can we have** some bread, please?
Je pourrais avoir l'addition, s'il vous plaît?	**Could I have** the bill, please?
Est-ce que je pourrais avoir de la moutarde, s'il vous plaît?	**Could I have** some mustard, please?

If you want to ask someone such as a friend or a close colleague to do something for you, use **Tu pourrais...?** (*Could you...?*). When you're talking to the waiter, use **Vous pourriez...?** instead. **pourrais** and **pourriez** come from the verb **pouvoir**. For more information on **pouvoir**, see page 284.

Could you...?

Tu pourrais me passer le sel, s'il te plaît?	**Could you** pass me the salt, please?
Tu pourrais me donner du pain, s'il te plaît?	**Could you** give me some bread, please?
Vous pourriez prendre notre commande, s'il vous plaît?	**Could you** take our order, please?
Est-ce que vous pourriez nous apporter notre café, s'il vous plaît?	**Could you** bring us our coffee, please?
Est-ce que vous pourriez revenir dans cinq minutes?	**Could you possibly** come back in five minutes?

Would you mind...?

Est-ce que ça vous ennuierait de prendre ma veste?	**Would you mind** hanging up my jacket?
Est-ce que ça vous ennuierait de fermer la fenêtre?	**Would you mind** closing the window?
Est-ce que ça t'ennuierait de changer de place avec moi?	**Would you mind** swapping seats with me?

If you want to say what you'd like to do when you're eating out, use either **je voudrais** or **j'aimerais** (*I'd like*) followed by the infinitive. They come from the verbs **vouloir** and **aimer**. For more information on **vouloir** and **aimer**, see pages 285 and 275.

I'd like to...

J'aimerais commander, s'il vous plaît.	**I'd like to** order, please.
J'aimerais voir la carte des desserts.	**I'd like to** see the dessert menu.
Je voudrais réserver une table, s'il vous plaît.	**I'd like to** book a table, please.
Nous voudrions commander du vin, s'il vous plaît.	**We'd like to** order some wine, please.
Nous aimerions payer par carte.	**We'd like to** pay by card.

You can also say what you feel like doing in French, by using **j'ai envie de** (*I feel like*) with the infinitive.

I feel like...

J'ai envie de prendre la fondue savoyarde.	**I feel like** having the cheese fondue.
J'ai envie de manger chinois, pour changer.	**I feel like** having Chinese food for a change.
Je n'ai pas envie de prendre d'entrée.	**I don't feel like** a starter.
Tu as envie de goûter ma glace?	**Would you like** to try my ice cream?

SAYING WHAT YOU LIKE, DISLIKE, PREFER ▊

When you're out wining and dining you will probably want to talk about what you like or dislike, especially when it comes to food. To say what you like, you can use **j'aime bien** (*I like*), which is not as strong as **j'aime** or **j'adore** (*I love*). If you want to say that you don't like something, you can use **je n'aime pas**.

I like...

J'aime bien le fromage.	**I like** cheese.
J'aime bien les asperges.	**I like** asparagus.
J'adore les fruits de mer.	**I love** seafood.
Tu aimes les artichauts?	**Do you like** artichokes?
Vous aimez la cuisine thaïlandaise?	**Do you like** Thai food?

I don't like...

Je n'aime pas les olives.	**I don't like** olives.
Je n'aime pas trop la cuisine mexicaine.	**I'm not too keen on** Mexican food.
J'ai horreur des abats.	**I can't stand** offal.
Tu n'aimes pas les champignons?	**Don't you like** mushrooms?

In French when you talk about things that you like in general, you need to say **j'aime bien le fromage** (*I like the cheese*), **je n'aime pas les olives** (*I don't like the olives*) instead of *I like cheese, I don't like olives*.

I'd rather...

Je préfère goûter un plat typique d'ici.	**I'd rather** try a local dish.
Je préfère qu'on partage l'addition.	**I'd rather** we split the bill.
Je préfère prendre une entrée **plutôt qu'**un dessert.	**I'd rather** have a starter **than** a dessert.
Est-ce que tu préférerais aller ailleurs?	**Would you rather** go somewhere else?

If you have special dietary needs, you can bring these into the conversation by using **je suis** (*I'm*).

I'm...

Je suis allergique aux œufs.	**I'm** allergic to eggs.
Je suis végétarien.	**I'm** a vegetarian.

ASKING FOR SUGGESTIONS

If you want to ask the waiter or other people at your table to recommend something, you can use **Qu'est-ce que vous me conseillez?** or **Qu'est-ce que tu me conseilles?** (*What do you recommend?*).

What do you recommend...?

Qu'est-ce que vous me conseillez comme entrée?	**What do you recommend** as a starter?
Qu'est-ce que vous nous conseillez comme vin?	**Which** wine **do you recommend**?
Qu'est-ce que tu me conseilles de prendre?	**What would you recommend me** to have?
Est-ce que vous pouvez me recommander un plat de la région?	**Can you recommend** a local dish?

If you want to ask whether you should do something, use **Tu crois que je devrais...?** or **Vous croyez que je devrais...?** (*Do you think I should...?*).

Do you think I should...?

Tu crois que je devrais prendre la tarte?	**Do you think I should** have the tart?
Tu crois que je devrais goûter les escargots?	**Do you think I should** try the snails?
Vous croyez que je devrais prendre du vin rouge avec ce plat?	**Do you think I should** have red wine with this dish?
Tu crois qu'on devrait laisser un pourboire?	**Do you think we should** leave a tip?

MAKING SUGGESTIONS ████████████

You may wish to make a suggestion to your colleagues or friends in French. One way of doing this is to use **on pourrait** (*we could*). This comes from the verb **pouvoir**. For more information on **pouvoir**, see page 284.

We could...

On pourrait se mettre ici.	**We could** sit here.
On pourrait juste prendre une salade.	**We could** just have a salad.
On pourrait se mettre dehors, **si vous voulez**.	**We could** sit outside, **if you prefer**.

If you want to make a suggestion using *let's*, you can use the **nous** form of the imperative in French. For more information on the imperative, see page 273.

Let's...

Asseyons-nous dehors.	**Let's** sit outside.
Prenons la fondue.	**Let's** have the fondue.
Ne prenons pas d'entrée.	**Let's not** bother with a starter.

If you are asking someone whether they feel like having or doing something, use **Ça te dit de...?** (*Do you fancy...?*).

Do you fancy...?

Ça te dit de prendre un café?	**Do you fancy** a coffee?
Ça te dit de goûter ma soupe? Elle est délicieuse.	**Do you fancy** trying my soup? It's delicious.
Ça vous dit de prendre un dessert?	**Do you fancy** some dessert?
Ça vous dit de commander une deuxième bouteille?	**Do you fancy** ordering a second bottle?

You can have...

Prends une entrée, si tu veux.	**You can have** a starter, if you like.
Prenez un digestif, si vous voulez.	**You can have** a liqueur, if you like.
Prenez le menu à 20 euros, si vous préférez.	**You can have** the 20 € set menu, if you like.

Another very simple way of making suggestions is to ask a question starting with **on** and followed by a verb in the present tense. This is a fairly informal way of making a suggestion. For more information on the present tense, see page 272.

How about...?

On prend un apéritif?	**How about** having a drink first?
On commande une autre bouteille?	**How about** we order another bottle?
On demande l'addition?	**How about** asking for the bill?

LISTEN OUT FOR

Here are some key phrases you are likely to hear when you're eating out.

Tu veux que je vienne te prendre?	Do you want me to pick you up?
Tu es libre samedi?	Are you busy on Saturday?
Vous avez réservé?	Have you got a reservation?
Je suis désolé, nous sommes complets.	Sorry, we're full.
Par ici, s'il vous plaît.	This way please.
Suivez-moi, s'il vous plaît.	Follow me please.
Voici la carte des vins.	Here's the wine list.
Le plat du jour est écrit au tableau.	Today's special is on the board.
Je vous recommande la *tarte tatin*.	I'd recommend the *tarte tatin*.
C'est une spécialité de la région.	It's a local speciality.
Vous avez choisi?	Are you ready to order?
Désirez-vous un apéritif?	Would you like a drink first?
Et comme boisson?	What will you have to drink?
Désirez-vous du fromage ou un dessert?	Would you like the cheese board or a dessert?
Vous désirez autre chose?	Would you like anything else?
Je suis à vous dans un instant.	I'll be right with you.
Je vous l'apporte tout de suite.	I'll bring it right away.
C'est moi qui vous invite.	It's on me.
C'est offert par la maison.	This is on the house.

Lifestyle Tips

• To attract the waiter's attention, you just need to say **s'il vous plaît?** or **monsieur/mademoiselle/madame, s'il vous plaît?**. The word **Garçon!** that most people will have learnt at school is considered rude and offensive by waiters now and shouldn't be used.

• You'll always be served **du pain** (*bread*) with your meal, and you won't be charged for it. Most French people wouldn't contemplate having a meal without bread.

• While service charges are usually included on restaurant bills, it is still very common to leave **un pourboire** (*a tip*) of a few euros in a restaurant, especially if the service has been good. In bars, people tend to leave a few cents (**centimes d'euro**) in small change when buying drinks.

• Children are welcome in French restaurants, even in the evening. If you need a high chair, you can ask **Est-ce que vous avez une chaise haute?**. Many restaurants will have **un menu enfant** (*a children's menu*).

• When serving you your food waiters will often say **Bon appétit!** (*Enjoy your meal!*) at the start of the meal, and sometimes **Bonne continuation!** when bringing the second course. You should reply **Merci!**. If people you are eating with or other diners in the restaurant say this to you, the correct response is: **Merci, vous aussi!** (*The same to you!*).

Hitting the town

Amusez-vous bien! – Enjoy yourselves!

This unit will help you to feel confident in all kinds of social situations in French. Whether you are going to a concert, the theatre or cinema, going to watch a sports match, going to a bar, or throwing or being invited to a party, these phrases will ensure that your French sounds natural.

MAKING SUGGESTIONS

When you're planning to go out with French-speaking friends or colleagues you may want to suggest what you could do. One good way of making a suggestion is to use **on peut** (*we can*) or **on pourrait** (*we could*). These are from the verb **pouvoir**. For more information on **pouvoir**, see page 284.

We can...

On peut aller boire un verre, **si tu veux**.	**We can** go and have a drink, **if you like**.
On peut aller au théâtre, **si vous voulez**.	**We can** go to the theatre, **if you like**.
On pourrait aller à un concert, **si tu veux**.	**We could** go to a concert, **if you like**.

Another way of making a suggestion is by using **on va** (*let's*) followed by the infinitive.

Let's...

On va prendre un verre?	**Let's** go out for a drink.
On va voir si on peut avoir des billets pour le match de samedi?	**Let's** see if we can get tickets for the match on Saturday.
On va s'asseoir?	**Shall we** go and sit down?
On commande une autre bouteille de vin?	**Let's** order another bottle of wine.

You can also ask someone what they would like to do by asking **Tu veux...?** or **Vous voulez...?** (*Do you want to...?*).

Do you want to...?

Tu veux aller prendre un café samedi après-midi?	**Do you want to** go for a coffee on Saturday afternoon?
Tu veux aller au café après le cinéma?	**Do you want to** go to a bar after the movie?
J'organise une soirée. **Tu veux** venir?	I'm having a party. **Do you want to** come?
Vous voulez nous retrouver au café demain soir?	**Do you want to** meet us in the bar tomorrow night?
Vous voulez venir manger chez nous demain soir?	**Do you want to** come for dinner tomorrow night?

BON À SAVOIR!

When talking about *tonight* and *tomorrow night*, use **ce soir** and **demain soir**.

Do you fancy...?

Ça te dirait d'aller boire un pot?	**Do you fancy** going for a drink?
Ça te dirait d'aller au cinéma?	**Do you fancy** going to the cinema?
Ça vous dirait d'aller prendre un café quelque part?	**Do you fancy** going for a coffee somewhere?
Ça vous dirait d'aller voir un match de foot?	**Do you fancy** going to a football match?

BON À SAVOIR!

The French expressions for *going for a drink* are **boire un verre** or **boire un pot**. These expressions are quite informal, and are used with friends and people you know well.

TALKING ABOUT YOUR PLANS

If you want to talk about the plans you've made for social activities, you can say **je vais** (*I'm going to*) or **on va** (*we're going to*).

I'm going to...

Je vais inviter des amis pour mon anniversaire.	**I'm going to** have some friends over for my birthday.
Je vais aller à la soirée de Laurent samedi prochain.	**I'm going to** Laurent's party next Saturday.
On va dîner chez des amis ce soir.	**We're going to** have dinner at our friends' house tonight.

Are you going to...?

Vous allez inviter beaucoup de personnes?	**Are you going to** invite many people?
Tu vas aller à la soirée de Susie?	**Are you going to** Susie's party?
Quand est-ce que **tu vas pouvoir** venir?	When **will you be able to** come?

Perhaps I'll...

Je vais peut-être y aller.	**Perhaps I'll** go.
Je vais peut-être reprendre un dernier verre.	**Perhaps I'll** have another drink.
Je vais peut-être organiser une soirée.	**I may** have a party.

ASKING FOR INFORMATION ▮▮▮▮▮▮▮▮▮▮▮▮▮▮

When you're planning to go out socially, you will need to ask for some information about what's available or what's on. To ask questions that can be answered *yes* or *no*, just put **est-ce que** before what you want to know.

Is there...?

Est-ce qu'il y a un cinéma ici?	**Is there** a cinema here?
Est-ce qu'il y a des concerts gratuits ce week-end?	**Are there** any free concerts on this weekend?
Est-ce qu'il y a un match de rugby cet après-midi?	**Is there** a rugby match on this afternoon?
Est-ce qu'il y a des réductions pour les étudiants?	**Is there** a discount for students?

BON À SAVOIR!
Both *Is there...?* and *Are there...?* are translated by **Est-ce qu'il y a...?**.

To ask someone whether they have something, for example, in a bar or at the theatre, use **Est-ce que vous avez...?** (*Do you have...?*).

Do you have...?

Est-ce que vous avez une carte des cocktails?	**Do you have** a cocktail menu?
Est-ce que vous avez des programmes?	**Do you have** any programmes?
Est-ce que vous avez de la bière pression?	**Do you have** beer on draught?

To obtain specific information, for example, what time something starts or finishes or how much it costs, you can use phrases such as **À quelle heure...?** (*What time...?*) and **Combien coûte...?** (*How much...?*).

What...?

Ils jouent **quel** genre de musique?	**What** kind of music do they play?
Tu vas dans **quel** bar?	**What** bar are you going to?
Tu as des billets pour **quelle** séance?	**What** showing have you got tickets for?
Qu'est-ce qu'il passe au cinéma en ce moment?	**What**'s on at the cinema at the moment?

What time...?

À quelle heure commence le film?	**What time** does the film start?
À quelle heure finit le concert?	**What time** does the concert finish?
On a commandé le taxi **pour quelle heure**?	**What time** is the taxi ordered for?

How much...?

Combien coûte l'entrée?	**How much** does it cost to get in?
Combien coûte un billet pour la représentation de ce soir?	**How much** is a ticket for this evening's performance?
Combien coûte le programme?	**How much** is it for a programme?

How long...?

Combien de temps dure l'opéra?	**How long** does the opera last?
Vous allez être dans ce bar pendant **combien de temps**?	**How long** are you going to be in this bar?
On met **combien de temps** pour aller au stade?	**How long** does it take to get to the stadium?

ASKING FOR THINGS

When you're asking for things, the easiest way to say what you want is to use **je voudrais** (*I'd like*) or **on voudrait** (*we'd like*). **voudrais** and **voudrait** are from the verb **vouloir**. For more information on **vouloir**, see page 285.

I'd like...

Je voudrais une vodka orange, s'il vous plaît.	**I'd like** a vodka and orange, please.
Je voudrais deux tickets pour « Saint Laurent ».	**I'd like** two tickets for 'Saint Laurent'.
Je voudrais un billet pour le match Rouen-Cherbourg.	**I'd like** a ticket for the Rouen-Cherbourg match.
On voudrait payer, s'il vous plaît.	**We would like** to settle the bill, please.
J'aimerais une place à l'orchestre.	**I'd like** a seat in the stalls.

I'll have...

Je vais prendre un thé au lait.	**I'll have** a cup of tea.
Je vais prendre un gin tonic.	**I'll have** a G & T.
On va prendre une autre bouteille de vin blanc de la maison.	**We'll have** another bottle of house white.

To ask someone for something, use **Est-ce que je peux avoir...?** (*Can I have...?*).

Can I have...?

Est-ce que je peux avoir une carafe d'eau?	**Can I have** a jug of water?
Est-ce que je peux avoir un billet pour le spectacle?	**Can I have** a ticket for the show?
Est-ce qu'on peut avoir l'addition?	**Can we have** the bill?

SAYING WHAT YOU LIKE, DISLIKE, PREFER

When you're out socializing you will probably want to say what you like or dislike. To say what you like, you can use **j'aime bien** (*I like*) which isn't as strong as **j'aime** or **j'adore** (*I love*). If you want to say that you don't like something, use **je n'aime pas** (*I don't like*).

I like...

J'aime bien les films d'horreur.	**I like** horror films.
J'aime bien la techno.	**I like** techno music.
J'adore l'opéra.	**I love** opera.

I don't like...

Je n'aime pas aller au théâtre.	**I don't like** going to the theatre.
J'ai horreur du pastis.	**I can't stand** pastis.

To talk about what you prefer, use **je préfère** (*I prefer*). **préfère** comes from the verb **préférer**. For more information on **-er** verbs like **préférer**, see page 270.

I prefer...

Je préfère les films d'art et d'essai.	**I prefer** arthouse films.
Je préfère aller voir un film **plutôt qu'**un concert.	**I'd rather** see a film **than** go to a concert.
Je préfère le vin **à** la bière.	**I prefer** wine **to** beer.
Je préfère y aller un autre jour.	**I'd rather** go another day.
Tu préfères les films français **ou** américains?	**Do you prefer** French **or** American films?

If you want to ask other people what they like, use **Tu aimes...?** (*Do you like...?*) for someone you know well, and **Vous aimez...?** for someone you do not know well, or for more than one person.

Do you like...?

Tu aimes les comédies musicales?	**Do you like** musicals?
Vous aimez aller au cinéma?	**Do you like** going to the cinema?
Tu n'aimes pas le football?	**Don't you like** football?

If you want to ask someone whether they enjoyed a play, film and so on, you can ask **Ça t'a plu?** (*Did you enjoy it?*).

Did you enjoy it?

Ça t'a plu?	**Did you enjoy it**?
Ça m'a vraiment **plu**.	I really **enjoyed it**.
Ça ne m'a pas plu du tout.	**I didn't enjoy it** at all.

EXPRESSING OPINIONS

If you want to express your opinion of something you've seen or of somewhere you've been, you can use the verbs **croire** and **penser** to say what you think.

I think...

Je pense que ça va te plaire.	**I think** you'll like it.
Je pense qu'ils vont gagner.	**I think** they'll win.
Tu ne penses pas que la pièce était un peu longue?	**Don't you think** the play was a bit long?
Je crois que c'est une actrice formidable.	**I think** she is a fantastic actress.
Je crois que c'est un bon film.	**I think** it's a good film.

BON À SAVOIR!
Remember that you have to use **que** (*that*) in French, even though it's optional in English.

In my opinion...

À mon avis, Spielberg est un metteur en scène formidable.	**In my opinion**, Spielberg is a wonderful director.
À mon avis, cette salle de concert est sans pareille.	**In my opinion**, this concert hall is second to none.
À mon avis, la fin laissait vraiment à désirer.	**In my view**, the ending was very weak.

What do you think of…?

Qu'est-ce que vous pensez de ses films?	**What do you think of** his films?
Qu'est-ce que tu penses du rap?	**What do you think of** rap music?
Qu'est-ce que tu en dis, de ce café?	**What do you make of** this bar?

If you want to agree or disagree with someone, you can say **je suis d'accord** (*I agree*) or **je ne suis pas d'accord** (*I don't agree*).

I agree…

Je suis d'accord.	**I agree.**
Je suis d'accord avec toi.	**I agree** with you.
Je suis totalement **d'accord** avec ce que vous dites.	I totally **agree** with what you say.
Non, **je ne suis pas d'accord.**	No, **I don't agree.**
Je ne suis pas du tout **d'accord.**	**I don't agree** at all.

ASKING FOR PERMISSION

When you're out, you may want to ask someone if it's OK for you to do something. One useful way of asking for permission is to use **Est-ce que je peux…?** (*Can I…?*) or **Est-ce qu'on peut…?** (*Can we…?*). **peux** and **peut** are from the verb **pouvoir**. For more information on **pouvoir**, see page 284.

Can I…?

Est-ce que je peux m'asseoir n'importe où?	**Can I** sit anywhere?
Est-ce que je peux payer par carte?	**Can I** pay by card?
Est-ce que je peux prendre cette chaise?	**Can I** take this chair?
Est-ce qu'on peut s'installer en terrasse?	**Can we** sit outside?
Est-ce qu'on peut fumer en terrasse?	**Can we** smoke on the terrace?

Do you mind...?

Ça vous dérange si je fume?	**Do you mind** if I smoke?
Ça vous dérange si on s'asseoit ici?	**Do you mind** if we sit here?
Vous permettez que je me joigne à vous?	**Do you mind** if I join you?

LISTEN OUT FOR ████████████████████

Here are some key phrases you are likely to hear when you're going out.

Où voulez-vous vous asseoir?	Where would you like to sit?
Vos billets, s'il vous plaît.	Can I see your tickets, please?
Voulez-vous acheter un programme?	Would you like to buy a programme?
Ça vous dérange d'échanger de place avec moi?	Would you mind swapping places?
Tu es libre demain?	Are you free tomorrow?
Je ne suis pas libre la semaine prochaine.	I'm busy next week.
Quand est-ce que ça t'arrange?	When would be a good time for you?
Je t'offre un verre.	Let me get you a drink.
C'est moi qui offre.	This is on me.
Tu as passé une bonne soirée?	Did you have a good time tonight?
Merci de m'avoir invité.	Thank you for inviting me.
Merci, vous n'auriez pas dû.	Thank you, you shouldn't have.
Qu'est-ce que je vous sers?	What can I get you?

Lifestyle Tips

In a café or bar:

• You generally don't need to go to the bar to be served. The waiter will come to you. In small towns, the waiter will just leave **l'addition** (*the bill*) on your table, and you pay when you're ready. In busy places, they might ask you to pay as soon as you get your drinks.

• If you ask for **un café**, you will be given an espresso. You need to specify if you want a large coffee **un grand café** or **un café allongé**. A white coffee is **un café au lait**.

• You need to specify that you want your tea with milk, otherwise it will be served black or with lemon. Ask for **un thé au lait**.

• The price of drinks is cheaper at the bar than sitting inside, which in turn is less expensive than sitting outside (**en terrasse**).

• Expressions for *Cheers!* in French include **À votre santé!** (shortened to **Santé!**), **À la vôtre!** and **Tchin-tchin!** To one person you know well, you will say **À ta santé!** or **À la tienne!**

At somebody's house:

• You may be invited for **le dîner** (*dinner*), **le déjeuner** (*lunch*), or sometimes just **l'apéritif** – a drink before a meal. If you don't know someone very well (new neighbours for example), it's a good way of getting to know them without having to spend too long with them!

• When invited to someone's house for dinner, French people usually bring flowers or chocolates rather than wine as a present. If a French-speaking person brings you a gift, you can always say **merci, tu n'aurais pas dû** (*thank you, you shouldn't have*).

At the cinema:

• New films come out on a Wednesday (**mercredi**) in France (because French school kids are usually off on a Wednesday afternoon).

Closing times:

• Times may vary a little depending on the area of France you're in, but usually **bars** close around 1 am – **à une heure du matin**. **Les boîtes de nuit** (*clubs*) tend to close between 3 and 5.

Museums, monuments and much more

Passez une bonne journée! – Have a nice day!

If you're planning to see the sights in a French-speaking city or country, the phrases in this unit will give you the confidence to ask where you can go, what you can do there and how much it will cost using natural French.

SAYING WHAT YOU WANT TO DO

You may need to be able to say what you'd like to do in French. To do this, you can use **je voudrais** (*I'd like*). **voudrais** comes from the verb **vouloir**. For more information on **vouloir**, see page 285.

I'd like to...

Je voudrais monter au clocher.	**I'd like to** go up the church tower.
Je voudrais prendre des photos de ce tableau, si c'est possible.	**I'd like to** take some pictures of this painting, if that's OK.
On voudrait aller à la cathédrale en bus.	**We'd like to** take the bus to the cathedral.
On voudrait visiter l'exposition de peintures.	**We'd like to** see the art exhibition.

You may also want to show your enthusiasm about doing something. To say *I'd love to*, you can use **j'aimerais vraiment**, or **ça me plairait vraiment de** followed by a verb in the infinitive.

I'd love to...

J'aimerais vraiment voir la grotte de Lascaux.	**I'd love to** see the cave paintings of Lascaux.
J'aimerais vraiment emmener les enfants au parc Astérix.	**I'd love to** take the kids to the Astérix theme park.
Elle aimerait vraiment voir le Mont Saint-Michel.	**She'd love to** see the Mont Saint-Michel.
Ça me plairait vraiment de faire un baptême de parapente.	**I'd love to** try paragliding.

TALKING ABOUT YOUR PLANS

It is very likely that you will want to talk about what you are planning to do on your trip. In English we often say *I'm going to* to talk about the future. French works the same way. To say that you're going to do something, use **je vais** (*I'm going to*) or **on va** (*we're going to*) followed by a verb. **vais** and **va** come from the verb **aller**. For more information on **aller**, see page 279.

I'm going to...

Je vais visiter le château de Versailles.	**I'm going to** visit the Palace of Versailles.
Je vais téléphoner pour savoir si c'est ouvert le dimanche.	**I'm going to** phone to find out if it's open on Sundays.
On va emmener les enfants avec nous.	**We're going to** take the kids with us.
Est-ce que tu vas faire toute la visite guidée?	**Are you going to** do the whole guided tour?

You can use both **je compte** and **j'ai l'intention de** to talk about what you intend to do.

I intend to...

Je compte y aller avec un guide de haute montagne.	**I intend to** go with a mountain guide.
On compte faire le tour des volcans d'Auvergne cet été.	**We intend to** do the Auvergne volcano trail this summer.
Est-ce que vous comptez y passer beaucoup de temps?	**Do you intend to** spend much time there?
J'ai l'intention de retourner au musée d'Art et d'Industrie la prochaine fois.	**I intend to** go back to the musée d'Art et d'Industrie next time.
Qu'est-ce que **vous avez l'intention de** visiter en premier?	What **do you plan to** visit first?

If you want to talk about the plans that have been made, you can use **je dois** followed by the infinitive, which is the equivalent of *I'm to*. **dois** comes from **devoir**. For more information on **devoir**, see page 281.

I'm to...

Je dois retrouver le groupe à quatre heures.	**I'm to** meet up with the group at four.
On doit passer la nuit dans un refuge et atteindre le sommet le lendemain.	**We're to** spend the night in a mountain hut and reach the summit the following day.
On doit visiter les jardins l'après-midi.	**We're to** visit the grounds in the afternoon.
À quelle heure **est-ce qu'on doit** arriver?	What time **are we supposed to** get there?

MAKING SUGGESTIONS

You may wish to make a suggestion to your colleagues or friends in French. One way of doing this is to use **je propose de** (*I suggest*) followed by the verb in the infinitive. **propose** comes from the verb **proposer**. For more information on **–er** verbs like **proposer**, see page 269.

I suggest…

Je propose de visiter l'écomusée.	**I suggest** we visit the heritage centre.
Je propose de pique-niquer dans le parc.	**I suggest** we have a picnic in the park.
Je propose de reporter la visite du zoo à lundi.	**I say** we postpone the trip to the zoo until Monday.
Qu'est-ce que vous nous **proposez** comme activité?	**What do you suggest** we do?

> **BON À SAVOIR!**
> Don't worry, you won't be proposing to anyone by using **je propose**! The French expression for *to propose to somebody* is **demander quelqu'un en mariage**.

You can make a suggestion using the phrase **Pourquoi ne pas…?** (*Why don't…?*). You will notice that French speakers very often omit **ne** to make sentences shorter.

Why don't…?

Pourquoi ne pas faire le tour de la vieille ville à pied?	**Why don't** we walk round the old town?
Pourquoi tu **ne** prends **pas** des photos depuis la tour?	**Why don't** you take some pictures from the tower?
Pourquoi pas louer une carriole pour voir la ville?	**Why don't** we hire a horse-drawn carriage to see the town?
Pourquoi tu prends **pas** le métro pour aller à Montmartre?	**Why don't** you take the underground to go to Montmartre?

Another way of making suggestions is to say **on devrait** (*we should*). **devrait** comes from the verb **devoir**. For more information on **devoir**, see page 281.

We should...

On devrait monter en téléphérique.	**We should** take the cable car to the top.
On devrait revenir demain pour voir le reste.	**We should** come back tomorrow to see the rest.
Tu devrais aller voir le spectacle son et lumière ce soir.	**You should** go to the sound and light show tonight.
Vous devriez louer un vélo pour faire le tour de l'île.	**You should** hire a bike to cycle round the island.

ASKING FOR INFORMATION

If you need some information, many of the questions you will be asking can be answered by *yes* or *no*. You can either put **est-ce que** before what you want to know or alternatively you can raise the tone of your voice at the end of the sentence – this will make you sound more informal.

Is...?

Est-ce que le château **est** intéressant?	**Is** the castle interesting?
Est-ce que la visite **est** guidée?	**Is** it a guided tour?
L'entrée du musée **est** gratuite ou est-ce qu'il faut payer?	**Is** the museum free or do you have to pay?
Est-ce que c'est une balade difficile?	**Is it** a difficult walk?
Est-ce que c'est accessible aux personnes handicapées?	**Is there** easy access for disabled people?

You may also need to ask if something is available in the place you're visiting. Use **Est-ce qu'il y a...?** to ask both *Is there...?* and *Are there...?*

Is there...?

Est-ce qu'il y a un office de tourisme dans cette ville?	**Is there** a tourist information office in this town?
Est-ce qu'il y a quelque chose à voir à Montauban?	**Is there** anything to see in Montauban?
Est-ce qu'il y a des prix pour les seniors?	**Is there** a discount for pensioners?
Est-ce qu'il y a des momies dans le musée?	**Are there** any mummies in the museum?
Qu'est-ce qu'il y a à voir à Lille? Ça mérite d'être visité?	**What is there** to see in Lille? Is it worth a visit?

In order to obtain more specific information, you can use **quel** (*what*) for a masculine noun and **quelle** (*what*) for a feminine noun.

What...?

Quel est le meilleur moment pour y aller?	**What**'s the best time to go?
Quelle est la station la plus proche de l'Arc de Triomphe?	**What** is the nearest station to the Arc de Triomphe?
Quelles sont les heures d'ouverture?	**What** are the opening hours?
C'est **quel** genre de peinture?	**What** type of painting is it?
Le dépliant est écrit **en quelle** langue?	**What** language is the leaflet written **in**?

What time...?

À quelle heure est-ce qu'on se retrouve au bus?	**What time** do we meet at the bus?
À quelle heure ferme le parc d'attractions?	**What time** does the theme park close?
À quelle heure est la prochaine visite guidée?	**What time** is the next guided tour?
À quelle heure est-ce qu'on arrive?	**What time** do we get there?

To ask how much something is, use **Combien coûte...?** (*How much is...?*). To ask how much it costs to do something, use **Ça coûte combien de...?** and then the verb in the infinitive. These come from the verb **coûter**. To find out more about –er verbs like **coûter**, see page 269.

How much is...?

Combien coûte cette carte postale, s'il vous plaît?	**How much is** this postcard, please?
Combien coûte un ticket au tarif étudiant?	**How much is** a student ticket?
Combien coûte la traversée en bateau?	**How much is** the ferry crossing?
Ça coûte combien de faire une excursion à Pérouges?	**How much is it** to take a trip to Pérouges?
Ça coûte combien d'y aller en avion?	**How much is it** to fly there?

How long...?

Combien de temps dure la visite?	**How long** does the tour last?
Combien de temps dure la promenade en bateau?	**How long** does the boat trip last?
Combien de temps ça prend pour y aller?	**How long** does it take to get there?

To ask how you do something, you can use **Comment est-ce qu'on...?** (*How do you...?*) followed by the verb in the present tense or **Comment est-ce qu'on fait pour...?** followed by the verb in the infinitive. For more information about the present tense, see page 272.

How do you...?

Comment est-ce qu'on va dans la vieille ville?	**How do you** get to the old town?
Comment est-ce qu'on accède au deuxième étage?	**How do you** get to the second floor?
Comment est-ce qu'on fait pour choisir la langue du commentaire?	**How do you** choose which language the commentary's read in?
Comment est-ce qu'on fait pour acheter des tickets?	**How do you** buy tickets?

ASKING FOR THINGS

When you're out and about in a French-speaking city or country, you will want to be able to ask for things in French. Use **Est-ce que je peux avoir...?** (*Can I have...?*) or **Est-ce que je pourrais avoir...?** (*Could I have...?*).

Can I have...?

Est-ce que je peux avoir deux entrées pour le musée, s'il vous plaît?	**Can I have** two tickets for the museum, please?
Est-ce que je peux avoir le programme du concert de ce soir?	**Can I have** the programme for this evening's concert?
Est-ce que je pourrais avoir un casque pour le commentaire?	**Could I have** some headphones to hear the commentary?
Est-ce que je pourrais avoir un plan du musée?	**Could I have** a map of the museum?

Very often you will want to say that you need something in particular. To do this use **il me faut** or **il me faudrait** (*I need*) – remember that **faudrait** sounds more polite than **faut**.

I need...

Il me faut l'adresse du musée.	**I need** the address of the museum.
Il lui faut deux tickets de plus.	**She needs** two more tickets.
Il me faudrait un plan de la ville.	**I need** a street map of the city.
Il nous faudrait un guide qui parle anglais.	**We need** a guide who can speak English.

If you want to find out if something is available, use **Est-ce que vous avez...?** or **Est-ce que vous auriez...?** (*Do you have...?* or *Would you have...?*). **avez** and **auriez** are from the verb **avoir**. For more information on **avoir**, see page 280.

Do you have...?

Est-ce que vous avez des dépliants en anglais?	**Do you have** any brochures in English?
Est-ce que vous avez des audioguides dans d'autres langues?	**Do you have** any audio guides in other languages?
Vous avez un journal local, s'il vous plaît?	**Have you got** a local newspaper, please?
Vous auriez de la documentation sur les circuits touristiques de la région?	**Would you have** any information on trips in this area?

When you want to ask if someone can do something for you, use **Est-ce que vous pouvez...?** or **Est-ce que vous pourriez...?** (*Can you...?* or *Could you...?*). These come from the verb **pouvoir**, about which you can find out more on page 284.

Can you...?

Est-ce que vous pouvez nous prendre en photo?	**Can you** take a picture of us?
Est-ce que vous pouvez me dire quels sont les horaires de visite?	**Can you** tell me what the opening hours are?
Est-ce que vous pourriez me faire passer par la vieille ville?	**Could you** take me through the old town?
Est-ce que vous pourriez m'aider, s'il vous plaît?	**Could you** help me, please?

ASKING FOR PERMISSION

There may be occasions where you want to ask for permission to do something. To do this, use **Est-ce que je peux...?** (*Can I...?*) or **Est-ce que je pourrais...?** (*Could I...?*). **peux** and **pourrais** come from the verb **pouvoir**. For more information on **pouvoir**, see page 284.

Can I...?

Est-ce que je peux prendre des photos?	**Can I** take pictures?
Est-ce que je peux entrer avec mon sac?	**Can I** take my bag in?
Est-ce qu'on peut garer la voiture ici?	**Can we** park our car here?
Est-ce que je pourrais vous emprunter votre guide une seconde?	**Could I** borrow your guidebook for a second?

Another way of asking for permission is to use **Est-ce que ça vous dérange si...?** (*Do you mind if...?*).

Do you mind if...?

Est-ce que ça vous dérange si j'entre avec mon sac?	**Do you mind if** I take my bag inside with me?
Est-ce que ça vous dérange si on s'asseoit dans l'herbe?	**Do you mind if** we sit on the grass?
Est-ce que ça vous dérange si je laisse la poussette ici?	**Do you mind if** I leave the pushchair here?

Is it a problem if...?

Est-ce que ça pose un problème si je fume?	**Is it a problem if** I smoke?
Excusez-moi, **est-ce que ça pose un problème si** je prends des photos?	Excuse me, **is it a problem if** I take pictures?
Est-ce que ça vous pose un problème si je paye par carte bleue?	**Is it a problem for you if** I pay by card?

If you want to talk about what you like, use **j'aime bien** (*I like*) which is not as strong as **j'aime** or **j'adore** (*I love*). You can also substitute **bien** with **beaucoup** (*a lot*), **vraiment** (*really*) and **assez** (*quite*). To say what you don't like, just use **je n'aime pas**. These come from the verb **aimer**. For more information on **aimer**, see page 275.

I like...

J'aime bien visiter les galeries d'art moderne.	**I like** visiting modern art galleries.
J'aime bien les feux d'artifice.	**I like** firework displays.
J'aime beaucoup cette sculpture.	**I like** this sculpture **a lot**.
J'adore les petits villages de Provence.	**I love** the small villages of Provence.
Tu aimes bien ce genre d'architecture?	**Do you like** this type of architecture?

I don't like...

Je n'aime pas les excursions en bus.	**I don't like** bus tours.
Je n'aime pas les montagnes russes.	**I don't like** roller-coasters.
Je n'aime pas du tout faire la queue.	**I don't like** having to queue **at all**.

If you want to say what you prefer, you can use **je préfère** (*I prefer*). If you want to say that something would suit you better, use **je préférerais** or **j'aimerais mieux** (*I'd rather*).

I prefer...

Je préfère les musées **aux** édifices religieux.	**I prefer** museums **to** religious buildings.
Je préfère éviter ce quartier.	**I prefer to** avoid that area.
On préfère y aller à pied **que** de prendre le bus.	**We'd rather** walk **than** take the bus.

I'd rather...

J'aimerais mieux passer toute la semaine à Marseille.	**I'd rather** spend the whole week in Marseilles.
Je préférerais prendre le funiculaire.	**I'd rather** take the funicular railway.
On aimerait mieux rejoindre le groupe plus tard.	**We'd rather** meet up with the group later.
On préférerait profiter du beau temps et aller au musée un autre jour.	**We'd rather** enjoy the nice weather and go to the museum another day.

COMPLAINING

You may have to complain about something which you're unhappy with. To do this, you can say **excusez-moi** or **pardon, je voudrais me plaindre** (*excuse me, I wish to complain*) and go on to describe what you're unhappy about.

I'm not happy...

Je ne suis pas content de notre guide.	**I'm not happy with** our guide.
Je ne suis pas content d'avoir payé si cher pour ça.	**I'm not happy that** I had to pay so much for it.

I'm disappointed...

Je suis déçu de notre sortie.	**I'm disappointed with** our trip.
Je suis déçu de la façon dont on nous a traités.	**I'm disappointed with** the way we were treated.
Les enfants **sont déçus de** ne pas avoir vu les clowns.	The children **were disappointed that** they didn't get to see the clowns.

To say what you think of something, use **je trouve que**. The verb **trouver** on its own means *to find*, but when it is followed by **que** it means *to think*. Don't forget to add **que** (*that*) after **trouver**. It's optional in English, but not in French. For more information on **-er** verbs like **trouver**, see page 269.

I think...

Je trouve que c'est un peu cher pour ce que c'est.	**I think** it's a bit expensive for what it is.
On trouve que le guide ne donne pas assez d'explications.	**We think that** the guide doesn't explain things clearly enough.
Je trouve que ce n'est pas très bien organisé.	**I don't think** it's very well organized.
Je n'ai pas trouvé le musée très intéressant.	**I didn't think** the museum was very interesting.

Another way of expressing your disappointment is to use **c'est dommage que** (*it's a shame that*). The verb that follows is in the subjunctive, which you can find out more about on page 274.

It's a shame that...

C'est dommage qu'il n'y ait rien pour les enfants.	**It's a shame that** there's nothing for children.
C'est dommage que le dépliant ne soit qu'en français.	**It's a shame that** the leaflet is only in French.
C'est dommage que le bâtiment principal ne soit pas ouvert.	**It's a shame that** the main building isn't open.

There's...

Il y a très peu d'information sur l'histoire de ce lieu.	**There's** very little information about the history of this place.
Il y a beaucoup de bruit dans le musée.	**There's** a lot of noise in the museum.
Il n'y a pas d'aménagements pour les handicapés.	**There are no** facilities for the disabled.

BON À SAVOIR!
Remember that **il y a** translates as both *there is* and *there are*.

LISTEN OUT FOR

Here are some key phrases you're likely to hear when you're sightseeing.

En quelle langue est-ce que vous voudriez avoir les informations?	What language would you like the information in?
Voici un dépliant en anglais.	Here's a leaflet in English.
Vous avez une carte d'étudiant?	Do you have a student card?
Le musée est ouvert de neuf heures à trois heures.	The museum's open from nine to three.
La galerie est fermée le dimanche.	The gallery's closed on Sundays.
La prochaine visite guidée est à dix heures.	The next guided tour's at ten.
Combien de tickets est-ce que vous voudriez?	How many tickets would you like?
C'est huit euros par personne.	It's eight euros each.
Les photos sont interdites.	You're not allowed to take pictures.
Est-ce que je peux fouiller votre sac?	Can I search your bag?
Laissez votre sac et votre manteau au vestiaire.	Please leave your bag and coat in the cloakroom.
Est-ce que ça vous a plu?	Did you enjoy it?

Lifestyle Tips

• The **Journées du Patrimoine** are two days (at the weekend) in mid-September during which you can visit monuments and museums for free. You can find useful information about this event on the website of the French Ministry of Culture (**le ministère de la Culture**) at the following address: http://www.culture.gouv.fr.

• Another French cultural event is **la Fête de la musique**. It is a music festival held on the first day of summer (21 June). Throughout France, amateur and professional musicians perform for free in parks, streets and squares.

• In the high season there is often a lot going on; local newspapers are a good way of keeping you informed about social and cultural events and telling you what there is to see in a given area. Remember to have a look at the **marchand de journaux** (*newsagent's*) – you may even find some local newspapers in English!

• If you're planning to go to a French museum or art gallery on a Monday or Tuesday, check that it will be open first, as many of them have their **fermeture hebdomadaire** (*weekly day off*) on these days.

• Unlike many museums in Britain, which are free, French ones are mostly not. A lot of public museums and galleries are free for everyone on the first Sunday of every month (**le 1er dimanche du mois**), however expect long queues!

Retail therapy

Je peux vous aider? – Can I help you?

Whether you're planning to shop for clothes or household items, get in your groceries or just pick up a postcard, this unit will help give you the confidence to find the best bargains and shop till you drop using typical natural French.

ASKING FOR THINGS

When you're shopping in a French-speaking country, you may be asked **On s'occupe de vous?** (*Are you being attended to?*). If you're just browsing, say **je regarde seulement** (*I'm just browsing*), or if someone else is already serving you, you can say **on s'occupe de moi, merci.** (*I'm already being served, thanks*). Alternatively, if you know what you want, use **je voudrais** (*I'd like*). **voudrais** is from the verb **vouloir** (*to want*). For more information on **vouloir**, see page 285.

I'd like...

Je voudrais deux kilos de pommes de terre, s'il vous plaît.	**I'd like** two kilos of potatoes, please.
Je voudrais une carte mémoire pour mon appareil photo numérique.	**I'd like** a memory card for my digital camera.
Je voudrais un melon bien mûr, s'il vous plaît.	**I'd like** a melon that's nice and ripe, please.
Je voudrais essayer ces chaussures en 38.	**I'd like** to try a 38 in these shoes.
J'en **veux** deux de plus, s'il vous plaît.	**I want** two more of these, please.

Could I have...?

Est-ce que je pourrais avoir un kilo d'oranges, s'il vous plaît?	**Could I have** a kilo of oranges, please?
Est-ce que je pourrais avoir un carnet de timbres?	**Could I have** a book of stamps?
Est-ce que je pourrais avoir un sac, s'il vous plaît?	**Could I have** a carrier bag, please?

You can also say what you are looking for by using **je cherche** or **je suis à la recherche de** (*I'm looking for*).

I'm looking for...

Je cherche de la coriandre fraîche.	**I'm looking for** fresh coriander.
Je cherche du tofu.	**I'm looking for** tofu.
Je cherche un short pour mon fils qui a dix ans.	**I'm looking for** shorts for my ten-year-old son.
Je suis à la recherche d'un cadeau pour un tout-petit.	**I'm looking for** a present for a toddler.

At the market or in shops where an assistant is serving you, you can ask for something by saying **donnez-moi** (*give me*) followed by the amount that you want and **s'il vous plaît**. This comes from the verb **donner** (*to give*) in the imperative. For more information on the imperative, see page 273.

Give me...

Donnez-moi une baguette bien cuite, s'il vous plaît.	**Give me** one well-fired baguette, please.
Donnez-moi deux bouteilles de pineau, s'il vous plaît.	**Give me** two bottles of pineau, please.
Donnez-moi cinq cent grammes de marrons.	**Give me** half a kilo of chestnuts.
Mettez-moi deux douzaines d'huîtres, s'il vous plaît.	**Give me** two dozen oysters, please.

When you've chosen what you want to buy, you can say **je vais prendre**, (*I'll take*). If you haven't made up your mind, say **je ne suis pas encore décidé** (*I haven't decided yet*).

I'll take...

Je vais prendre ces deux cartes postales**.**	**I'll take** these two postcards.
Je vais prendre les bleues à la place des marron.	**I'll take** the blue ones instead of the brown ones.
Je vais prendre le sac que vous m'avez montré en premier.	**I'll take** the bag you first showed me.
Je ne vais pas prendre le jean finalement.	**I won't take** the jeans after all.

SAYING WHAT YOU HAVE TO DO

Shopping isn't always what you'd choose to do, is it? To say that you have to buy something or that you have to do something in French, you can use **il faut que** (*I have to*) and then the verb in the subjunctive. For more information on the subjunctive, see page 274.

I have to...

Il faut que j'achète de nouvelles chaussures.	**I have to** buy some new shoes.
Il faut que je passe à la boulangerie.	**I have to** stop at the baker's.
Il faut que tu demandes à la vendeuse pour essayer.	**You have to** ask the shop assistant if you want to try things on.
Il faut qu'on achète un nouvel aspirateur.	**We have to** buy a new vacuum cleaner.

I must...

Je dois trouver une robe pour la fête de samedi.	**I must** find a dress for the party on Saturday.
Je dois trouver un cadeau d'anniversaire pour ma sœur.	**I must** find a birthday present for my sister.
Je dois acheter un costume pour mon entretien.	**I must** buy a suit for the interview.

To talk about things you need, use **il me faut** or **il me faudrait** (*I need*).

I need...

Il me faut des lunettes de ski.	**I need** some ski goggles.
Il me faut des croissants. Il vous en reste?	**I need** some croissants. Do you have any left?
Il me faudrait des piles pour mon réveil.	**I need** some batteries for my alarm clock.
Qu'**est-ce qu'il te faut** pour les vacances?	What **do you need** for your holidays?

TALKING ABOUT YOUR PLANS ▬▬▬▬▬▬▬

You may want to talk about what you're thinking of buying or where you're thinking of going. French uses the phrase **je pense** (*I'm thinking*) followed by a verb in the infinitive.

I'm thinking of...

Je pense aller au marché demain.	**I'm thinking of** going to the market tomorrow.
Je pense faire les boutiques à Paris.	**I'm thinking of** going shopping in Paris.
On ne pense pas aller en ville ce week-end.	**We don't think we'll** go into town this weekend.
Tu penses passer au supermarché en rentrant?	**Do you think you'll** stop at the supermarket on your way home?

I'm going to...

Je vais acheter un nouveau maillot de bain.	**I'm going to** buy a new swimming costume.
Je vais faire les soldes ce week-end.	**I'm going to** go to the sales this weekend.
On va acheter un nouveau lit.	**We're going to** buy a new bed.

I hope to…

J'espère trouver quelque chose à moins de 20 euros.	**I hope to** find something for under 20 euros.
J'espère trouver un canapé à moitié prix pendant les soldes.	**I hope to** get a half-price sofa in the sales.
On espère trouver un cadeau pour Laurent et Mélanie.	**We hope to** find a present for Laurent and Mélanie.

EXPRESSING OPINIONS

As you look at items for sale, you may well want to make comments to a French-speaking friend or to the shop assistant. To give your opinion, use **je trouve** (*I think*). This comes from the verb **trouver**. For more information on **–er** verbs like **trouver**, see page 269.

I think…

Je trouve cette armoire vraiment belle.	**I think** this wardrobe is really beautiful.
Je trouve ce magasin beaucoup trop cher.	**I think** this shop is far too expensive.
Je trouve que ce pull n'est pas assez chaud.	**I don't think** this jumper is warm enough.
Comment est-ce que tu trouves cette chemise?	**What do you think of** this shirt?

In my opinion…

À mon avis, cette robe est un peu trop longue.	**In my opinion**, this dress is a bit too long.
À mon avis, ce rouge à lèvres est légèrement trop foncé.	**In my opinion**, this lipstick is slightly too dark.
À votre avis, lequel de ces deux pantalons me va le mieux?	**In your opinion**, which of these two pairs of trousers suits me better?
J'ai besoin de **ton avis sur** des appareils photos numériques.	I need **your opinion on** some digital cameras.

You can use **je dirais que** (*I'd say that*) to give your opinion about something. **dirais** comes from the verb **dire**. Here, it is in the conditional, which can be used to say things in a less categorical way.

I'd say...

Je dirais que c'est un peu serré pour moi.	**I'd say** it's a bit tight for me.
Moi, je dirais que ce cadeau va lui plaire.	**I'd say that** she's going to like this present.
Je dirais que c'est une affaire.	**I'd say that** it's a bargain.
Qu'est-ce que tu dis de cette lampe?	**What do you think of** this lamp?

If you want to ask for someone's opinion or advice, you can use **Vous me conseillez de...?** (*Do you think I should...?*). For more information on **-er** verbs like **conseiller**, see page 269.

Do you think I should...?

Vous me conseillez de prendre le bleu ou le rouge?	**Do you think I should** take the blue one or the red one?
Lequel **est-ce que tu me conseilles d'**acheter?	Which **do you think I should** buy?
Qu'**est-ce que vous me conseilleriez**?	What **would you recommend**?

If you're in a strange town, you may want to ask for some information, for example if there is a particular shop in the area. Simple! Both *Is there…?* and *Are there…?* are **Est-ce qu'il y a…?** in French.

Is there…?

Est-ce qu'il y a un supermarché près d'ici?	**Is there** a supermarket near here?
Est-ce qu'il y a un parking près du marché?	**Is there** a car park near the market?
Est-ce qu'il y a un rayon bio?	**Is there** an organic food section?
Est-ce que qu'il y a une garantie?	**Is there** a guarantee?
Il y a des caddies?	**Are there** any trolleys?

Is this…?

C'est le seul modèle que vous avez?	**Is this** the only model you stock?
C'est la plus grande taille que vous avez?	**Is this** the biggest size you have?
C'est tout ce que vous avez comme couleurs?	**Are these** the only colours you have?
C'est le prix à la pièce ou au kilo?	**Is this** the price for one or per kilo?

To find out if something's available, you'll need to use the question **Est-ce que vous avez…?** (*Do you have…?*) or **Est-ce que vous auriez…?** (*Would you have…?*). **avez** and **auriez** are from the verb **avoir**. For more information on **avoir**, see page 280.

Do you have…?

Est-ce que vous avez d'autres modèles?	**Do you have** any other models?
Est-ce que vous l'avez en plus petit?	**Do you have it** in a smaller size?
Est-ce que vous l'auriez dans une autre couleur?	**Would you have it** in another colour?
Est-ce que vous faites le même modèle en vert?	**Do you do** the same model in green?
Est-ce que vous faites des vêtements pour enfants?	**Do you do** children's clothes?

In order to obtain specific information, for example, where something is, which item you should buy or when something will happen, you may want to ask **Où...?** (*Where...?*), **Quel...?** (*Which...?*) or **Quand...?** (*When...?*).

Where...?

Où est le distributeur le plus proche, s'il vous plaît?	**Where**'s the nearest cash point, please?
Où est la caisse, s'il vous plaît?	**Where**'s the cash desk, please?
Est-ce que vous pouvez me dire **où** est le rayon cosmétiques, s'il vous plaît?	Can you tell me **where** the cosmetics department is, please?
Vous pouvez me dire **où** se trouve l'accueil, s'il vous plaît?	Can you tell me **where** customers services are, please?
Où est-ce qu'on peut trouver des lunettes de soleil?	**Where** can I find sunglasses?

Which...?

Quelle marque **est-ce que** vous conseillez?	**Which** brand do you recommend?
Quelles piles **est-ce qu'**il faut que j'achète pour mon appareil photo?	**Which** batteries do I need to buy for my camera?
À quel étage est le rayon vêtements pour hommes?	**Which** floor is the menswear department **on**?
Le marché se tient **quel jour**?	**What day**'s market day?
Lequel est-ce que tu vas prendre?	**Which one** are you going to get?
Laquelle de ces deux webcams est la moins chère?	**Which one** of these two webcams is the cheapest?

BON À SAVOIR!

To say *which one* use **lequel** for masculine singular nouns and **laquelle** for feminine singular things. To say *which ones* use **lesquels** for masculine plural things and **lesquelles** for feminine plural things.

When...?

Quand est-ce que vous fermez pour la pause déjeuner?	**When** do you close for lunch?
Quand est-ce que les soldes commencent?	**When** do the sales start?

What time...?

À quelle heure est-ce que vous ouvrez le matin?	**What time** do you open in the morning?
À quelle heure est-ce que vous arrivez sur le marché?	**What time** do you arrive on the market?

To be able to ask the price of something you can use either **Combien coûte...?** or **À combien est...?** (*How much is...?*). If you're asking about more than one thing, use **Combien coûtent...?** or **À combien sont...?** (*How much are...?*).

How much is...?

Combien coûte une bouteille de jus d'orange?	**How much is** a bottle of orange juice?
Combien coûtent les figues, s'il vous plaît?	**How much are** the figs, please?
À combien est cet abat-jour?	**How much is** this lamp shade?
À combien sont les cerises au kilo?	**How much are** cherries per kilo?
Je vous dois **combien**?	**How much** do I owe you?

To ask whether you can do something, use **Est-ce que je peux...?** (*Can I...?*).

Can I...?

Est-ce que je peux payer par carte?	**Can I** pay by credit card?
Est-ce que je peux avoir un paquet-cadeau?	**Can I** have it gift-wrapped?
Est-ce que vous pouvez me faire un prix?	**Can you** give me a discount?

SAYING WHAT YOU LIKE, DISLIKE, PREFER

To say that you like something, you can say **ça me plaît** (literally, *this pleases me*). You use **me plaît** with singular words and **me plaisent** with plural ones.

I like...

Cette boutique **me plaît**.	**I like** this shop.
Ces chaussures **me plaisent** beaucoup.	**I like** these shoes very much.
Achète-le, si **ça te plaît**.	Get it if **you like it**.
J'aime bien les antiquaires.	**I like** antique shops.
J'adore faire les soldes avec une copine.	**I love** going to the sales with a friend.

I don't like...

Ce style **ne me plaît pas**.	**I don't like** this style.
Ces gants **me plaisent moins**.	**I don't like** these gloves **as much**.
Je n'aime pas les grands magasins.	**I don't like** big stores.
On n'aime pas faire la queue.	**We don't like** queuing.

Of course you might not just want to say what you like and what you don't like when out shopping, you may also want to talk about what you prefer. To say that you prefer A to B, use **je préfère A à B**. For more information on **à** followed by **le** or **les**, see page 252.

I prefer...

Je préfère le vert.	**I prefer** the green one.
Je préfère les petites boutiques **aux** supermarchés.	**I prefer** small shops **to** supermarkets.
On préfère les produits frais **aux** surgelés.	**We prefer** fresh produce **to** frozen.
Je préfère faire mes achats en ligne **plutôt que d'**aller dans les magasins.	**I prefer to** buy online **rather than** go to the shops.

I'd rather...

J'aimerais mieux quelque chose de plus classique.	**I'd rather** go for something more classic.
J'aimerais mieux du café équitable.	**I'd rather** have fairtrade coffee.
J'aimerais mieux essayer avant d'acheter.	**I'd rather** try before I buy.
On aimerait mieux n'acheter que des produits locaux.	**We'd rather** buy only local produce.

MAKING SUGGESTIONS

On shopping expeditions you may well want to make suggestions about what to choose or what to do next. You can do this by putting **Et si...?** (*How about...?*) at the beginning of a sentence. The verb that follows is in the imperfect. You can find out more about the imperfect on page 272.

How about...?

Et si on faisait les boutiques une autre fois?	**How about** we go shopping another time?
Et si on essayait cette nouvelle librairie?	**How about** trying that new bookshop?
Et si on l'achetait sur Internet?	**How about** we buy it online?

To suggest what you and your friends could do, you can use **on pourrait** (*we could*).

We could...

On pourrait aller voir dans un autre magasin.	**We could** have a look in another shop.
On pourrait leur demander de nous le commander.	**We could** ask them to order it for us.
Tu pourrais leur demander un rabais.	**You could** ask them for a discount.

Another simple way of making suggestions is to raise the tone of your voice at the end of a sentence. This will make you sound slightly more informal.

Shall I...

Je prends du pain?	**Shall I get** some bread?
J'achète un gâteau pour ce soir?	**Shall I get** a cake for tonight?
On achète des timbres?	**Shall we buy** some stamps?
On va au supermarché?	**Shall we go** to the supermarket?

When offering to do something, you can say **laisse-moi** or **laissez-moi** (*let me*). It's followed by a verb in the infinitive.

Let me...

Laisse-moi payer.	**Let me** pay for this.
Laisse-moi porter les paquets.	**Let me** carry the shopping.
Laissez-moi vous aider.	**Let me** help you.

ASKING FOR PERMISSION

To ask if you can do something, such as try on an item of clothing, use **Est-ce que je peux...?** (*Can I...?*) or **Est-ce que je pourrais...?** (*Could I...?*). These come from the verb **pouvoir**. For more information on **pouvoir**, see page 284.

Can I...?

Est-ce que je peux essayer cette jupe?	**Can I** try on this skirt?
Est-ce que je peux garder le cintre?	**Can I** keep the hanger?
Je peux les essayer?	**Can I** try them on?
Je pourrais réfléchir encore quelques minutes?	**Could I** think about it for another few minutes?

I'll… if you don't mind

Je vais réessayer l'autre pantalon, **si ça ne vous dérange pas**.	**I'll** try the other trousers on again, **if you don't mind**.
Je vais regarder les autres modèles, **si ça ne vous dérange pas**.	**I'll** have a look at the other models, **if you don't mind**.
Je vais repasser samedi, **si ça ne vous fait rien**.	**I'll** come back on Saturday, **if you don't mind**.

To ask for permission, you can use **Est-ce que vous permettez que…** (*May I…?*) followed by the verb in the subjunctive. You can find out more about the subjunctive on page 274.

May I…?

Est-ce que vous permettez que je regarde de plus près?	**May I** have a closer look?
Vous permettez que je goûte une de vos oranges?	**May I** try one of your oranges?
Vous permettez qu'on sorte le réveil de son emballage?	**May we** take the alarm clock out of its box?
Vous permettez que ma fille essaie la veste qui est en vitrine?	**Can my daughter** try on the jacket that's in the window?

LISTEN OUT FOR

Here are some key phrases you may hear when out shopping.

On s'occupe de vous?	Are you being served?
Est-ce que je peux vous aider?	Can I help you?
Vous faites quelle taille?	What size are you?
Vous avez besoin d'une plus petite taille?	Do you need a smaller size?
Vous voulez que j'aille chercher la taille au-dessus?	Shall I look for a larger size for you?
Vous l'aimeriez en quelle couleur?	What colour would you like it in?
Vous pensiez mettre combien?	How much were you thinking of spending?
On n'en a pas en rayon pour l'instant.	We don't have any in stock just now.
Et avec ceci?	Anything else?
C'est pour offrir?	Is it a present for someone?
Je vous fais un paquet-cadeau?	Shall I giftwrap it for you?
Malheureusement, on n'accepte que les espèces.	It's cash only, I'm afraid.
Je regrette, mais on ne prend pas les cartes de crédit.	I'm afraid we don't take credit cards.
Tapez votre code, s'il vous plaît.	Your PIN number, please.

Lifestyle Tips

• When entering and leaving a shop in France, you usually say **Bonjour/Au revoir, monsieur/madame/messieurs-dames** (*hello/goodbye*) to the shopkeeper and the people in the shop, especially in small towns and villages where there is less anonymity.

• In an attempt to be more environmentally-friendly, many supermarkets have stopped providing plastic bags and expect their customers to re-use those they have at home. If you forget yours, you can still buy one from the cashier. You can ask for **un sac réutilisable** (*a reusable shopping bag*).

• You may have to take a ticket to get a place in the queue at the meat or cheese counters in some supermarkets. If you can't see where to get your ticket from, try asking **Où est-ce qu'on prend son ticket?** (*Where do I get my ticket?*).

• At the market and in the countryside, you might hear people use an old weight unit called **la livre**, which means half a kilo (**une livre de tomates, s'il vous plaît**).

• Most sellers on vegetable stalls at French markets will give you **un bouquet de persil** (*a bunch of parsley*) with the fruit and vegetables you buy.

• If you're looking for bargains at the market, your best bet is to go at around noon, when **les marchands** (*sellers*) begin to clear their stalls. They often have goods that won't keep and that they'll be happy to sell you for next to nothing.

• In independent shops selling gift items and in most shops around Christmas, you may be asked whether your item is a present for someone (**C'est pour offrir?**) and if you want it gift-wrapped (**Je vous fais un paquet-cadeau?**).

Service with a smile

Service irréprochable! – Excellent service!

The phrases in this unit will help you make sure you communicate your needs when you're in a French-speaking country in natural French.
You could be at the bank or police station, the hairdresser's, looking for insurance or seeking advice on any other kind of service – the language you need is covered here.

GREETINGS

It is crucial if you want to sound natural in French that you greet people correctly. Say **bonjour, monsieur/madame/mademoiselle** to someone you've never met; to someone you know a little, you can just say **bonjour**. Note that there is no equivalent in French for *good morning*, or *good afternoon* to say hello – French-speaking people just say **bonjour** during the day and **bonsoir** in the evening.

Have a good...!

Bonne journée!	**Have a good** day!
Bon week-end!	**Have a good** weekend!
Bon après-midi!	**Good** afternoon!
Bonne fin de journée!	**Good** afternoon!
Bonne soirée!	**Good** evening!

BON À SAVOIR!
When entering public places or shops, especially in smaller towns and villages, it's quite common to acknowledge the shopkeeper and/or the customers and say **bonjour, messieurs-dames** (*if both male and female*) or **bonjour, messieurs** (*to gents*) or **bonjour, mesdames** (*to ladies*), depending on who is there.

When you want to say *goodbye*, use **au revoir**. To say *See you…!*,
use **à** followed by **demain** (*tomorrow*), **plus tard** (*later*), **ce soir**
(*tonight*) and so on.

See you...!

À demain!	**See you** tomorrow!
À plus tard!	**See you** later!
À ce soir!	**See you** tonight!
À lundi!	**See you** on Monday!
À dans deux semaines!	**See you** in two weeks!

TALKING ABOUT YOURSELF

Very often you will need to give personal details and some
information about where you're staying and so on. To say what
your name is, use **je m'appelle** (*my name is*) and then your name.
appelle comes from the verb **appeler**. For more information on
–er verbs like **appeler**, see page 270.

My name is...

Je m'appelle Richard Davidson.	**My name is** Richard Davidson.
Je m'appelle Mary Rogers.	**My name is** Mary Rogers.
Mon mari s'appelle Olivier Dauga.	**My husband's name is** Olivier Dauga.

I'm staying...

Je loge à l'hôtel.	**I'm staying** at a hotel.
Je loge chez l'habitant.	**I'm staying** with a host family.
On loge dans une maison de location.	**We're staying** in a rented house.
Je réside en France.	**I live** in France.

My address is...

Mon adresse en France, **c'est** 7, rue de la Boule, 17000 la Rochelle.	**My address** in France **is** 7 rue de la Boule, 17000 La Rochelle.
Mon adresse fixe, **c'est** 29, Kelvin Close, L3 0QT Liverpool.	**My** permanent **address is** 29 Kelvin Close, L3 0QT Liverpool.
L'adresse de mon hôtel, **c'est** Hôtel des Rois, 7, avenue Foch à Aix.	**The address of** my hotel **is** Hôtel des Rois, 7 avenue Foch in Aix.

To say where you're from and how long you're staying, you can use **je suis**. **suis** comes from the verb **être**. For more information on **être**, see page 282.

I am...

Je suis anglais.	**I'm** English.
Je suis d'Aberdeen en Écosse.	**I'm from** Aberdeen in Scotland.
Je suis en vacances.	**I'm** on holiday.
On est ici pour trois semaines.	**We're** here for three weeks.

SAYING WHAT YOU HAVE TO DO

When you're dealing with one kind of service or another, you may want to say that you have to do something in French. To do this, you use **il faut que** (*I have to*) and then the subjunctive, which you can find out more about on page 274.

I have to...

Il faut que je passe au pressing.	**I have to** call in at the dry-cleaner's.
Il faut que je prenne les références de ce produit.	**I have to** take down the details of this product.
Il va falloir que je recharge mon portable.	**I'm going to have to** charge my phone.
Je ne suis pas obligé d'aller à la banque aujourd'hui.	**I don't have to** go to the bank today.

BON À SAVOIR!

To say *I don't have to* use **je ne suis pas obligé de**. Don't use **il ne faut pas que** as it means *I mustn't*.

I need to...

Il faudrait que je passe au pressing.	**I need to** go to the dry cleaner's.
Il faudrait que je me renseigne sur les polices d'assurances.	**I need to** find out about insurance policies.
Il faudrait que je fasse réparer mon appareil photo.	**I need to** have my camera repaired.

You can also say what you have to do using **je dois** (*I must*) and
j'ai besoin de (*I need*) with the infinitive form of the verb. **dois**
comes from the verb **devoir**. For more information on **devoir**,
see page 281.

I must...

Je dois m'arrranger pour faire récupérer mon repassage.	**I must** phone to arrange for my ironing to be picked up.
Je dois trouver un logement.	**I must** find somewhere to live.
On doit passer à l'agence immobilière pour rendre les clefs.	**We must** call at the estate agent's to return the keys.
Il ne faut pas que j'oublie de prendre rendez-vous chez l'esthéticienne.	**I mustn't** forget to make an appointment at the beautician's.

I need...

J'ai besoin d'un conseil.	**I need** a piece of advice.
J'ai besoin de télécharger un document.	**I need to** download a document.
J'ai besoin de faire des photocopies couleur.	**I need to** make some colour photocopies.
Nous avons besoin d'y réfléchir.	**We need to** think about it.

To say what you would like to do in French, use **je voudrais** or **j'aimerais** (*I'd like*). **voudrais** comes from **vouloir** and **aimerais** comes from **aimer**. For more information on these verbs, see page 285 and page 275.

I'd like to…

Je voudrais acheter une carte SIM avec/sans abonnement.	**I'd like to** buy a SIM card with/without a contract.
Je voudrais signaler un problème.	**I'd like to** report a problem.
J'aimerais prendre rendez-vous pour me faire couper les cheveux.	**I'd like to** make an appointment to get my hair cut.
J'aimerais connaître les horaires de train pour Dijon.	**I'd like to** know the train times to Dijon.

je souhaite or **je souhaiterais** (*I wish*) are polite ways of saying what you want to do. They come from the verb **souhaiter**. For more information on –**er** verbs like **souhaiter**, see page 269.

I wish to…

Je souhaite faire un virement.	**I wish to** transfer money.
Je souhaite faire une réclamation.	**I wish to** make a complaint.
Je souhaite parler au directeur de la banque.	**I wish to** speak to the bank manager.

If you want to have something done, put **faire** before the main verb of the sentence; for instance, *I want to have this watch strap replaced* is **je veux faire remplacer ce bracelet de montre**.

I want to have…

Je veux faire remplacer ce bracelet de montre.	**I want to have** this watch strap replaced.
Je veux faire nettoyer ma veste.	**I want to have** my jacket dry-cleaned.

ASKING FOR INFORMATION ███████████████

When you're asking for information about particular services, you can ask someone if they know something by asking **Est-ce que vous savez...?** or **Est-ce que vous sauriez...?** (*Do you know...?*) followed by **où** (*where*), **quand** (*when*), **comment** (*how*) and so on.

Do you know...?

Est-ce que vous savez où je peux faire faire un double de clefs, s'il vous plaît?	**Do you know** where I can have a second key cut?
Vous savez à quel ordre je dois faire le chèque?	**Do you know** who I should make the cheque payable to?
Vous savez quand vous aurez la pièce?	**Do you know** when you'll have the spare part?
Est-ce que vous sauriez où je peux recharger ma carte?	**Do you know** where I can top up my phone?

You can use **Est-ce qu'il y a...?** to ask both *Is there...?* and *Are there...?*

Is there...?

Est-ce qu'il y a un cybercafé dans le quartier?	**Is there** a café with wi-fi in the area?
Est-ce qu'il y a un bon coiffeur en ville?	**Is there** a good hairdresser in town?
Il y a des ordinateurs à la bibliothèque?	**Are there** computers in the library?

Key questions you'll want to ask when finding out about services is how much something costs and how long it will take. Use **combien** to ask these questions.

How much is it...?

C'est combien pour une coupe et un brushing?	**How much is it** for a cut and blow-dry?
C'est combien pour faire débloquer mon téléphone?	**How much is it** to have my phone unlocked?
Il faut compter combien pour faire nettoyer cette veste?	**How much would it be** to have this jacket dry-cleaned?

How long does it take...?

Ça prend combien de temps pour avoir l'argent?	**How long does it take** for the money to come through?
Il vous faut combien de temps pour imprimer ces documents?	**How long does it take you** to print these documents?
Il faut compter combien de temps pour ouvrir un compte en banque?	**How long does it take** to open a bank account?

Use **Comment on fait pour...?** (*How do you...?*) followed by the verb in the infinitive to ask how you do something.

How do you...?

Comment on fait pour ouvrir un compte en banque?	**How do you** open a bank account?
Comment on fait pour agrandir un document?	**How do you** enlarge a document?
Comment on fait pour envoyer de l'argent au Royaume-Uni?	**How do you** send money to the UK?

If you want to ask when something will be ready or available, use **Quand...?** (*When...?*).

When...?

Quand est-ce que les documents seront prêts?	**When** will the documents be ready?
Quand est-ce qu'il faut que je passe prendre le linge?	**When** should I pick up the laundry?
Quand est-ce que vous pouvez nous voir?	**When** are you available to see us?
À quelle heure est-ce que vous fermez?	**When** do you close?

ASKING FOR THINGS

To get something done the way you like it, you'll need to say what you'd like and how you want it done. To say what you'd like, you can use **j'aimerais** or **je voudrais** (*I'd like*) which come from the verbs **aimer** and **vouloir**. For more information on these verbs, see pages 275 and 285.

I'd like...

J'aimerais avoir un formulaire, s'il vous plaît.	**I'd like** an application form, please.
J'aimerais transférer de l'argent.	**I'd like** to transfer some money.
Je voudrais prendre un rendez-vous pour mardi après-midi.	**I'd like** to make an appointment for Tuesday afternoon.
Je voudrais un soin du visage, s'il vous plaît.	**I'd like** a facial, please.

Questions beginning with **Est-ce que...?** tend to sound more polite than simpler ones like **Vous pouvez...?**, so it is better to use them when asking someone to do something for you; for example, **Est-ce que vous pouvez...?** (*Can you…?*) or **Est-ce que vous pourriez...?** (*Could you…?*) followed by the verb in the infinitive. **pouvez** and **pourriez** come from the verb **pouvoir**. For more information on **pouvoir**, see page 284.

Can you...?

Est-ce que vous pouvez me donner un reçu, s'il vous plaît?	**Can you** give me a receipt, please?
Est-ce que vous pouvez m'appeler quand ce sera réparé?	**Can you** ring me when it's fixed?
Vous pouvez me faire un devis?	**Can you** give me an estimate?
Est-ce que vous pourriez jeter un œil à mon appareil photo?	**Could you** have a look at my camera?
Vous pourriez me dire si c'est réparable, s'il vous plaît?	**Could you** tell me if it can be repaired, please?

Would you mind...?

Est-ce que ça vous dérangerait d'attendre pour encaisser le chèque?	**Would you mind** waiting before cashing the cheque?
Est-ce que ça vous dérangerait de me donner une photocopie du contrat?	**Would you mind** giving me a photocopy of the contract?
Est-ce que ça vous dérangerait de me l'envoyer par e-mail?	**Would you mind** sending it to me by email?

Could you possibly...?

Est-ce qu'il vous serait possible de me recevoir cet après-midi?	**Could you possibly** see me this afternoon?
Est-ce qu'il vous serait possible de mettre ces photos sur un CD?	**Could you possibly** put these photos on a CD?
Est-ce qu'il vous serait possible de prolonger la garantie?	**Could you possibly** extend the guarantee?

When you want to find out if something is available, use **Est-ce que vous avez...?** or **Est-ce que vous auriez...?** (*Do you have...?*) to ask someone if they have something. **avez** and **auriez** come from the verb **avoir**. For more information on **avoir**, see page 280.

Do you have...?

Est-ce que vous avez de la documentation sur vos polices d'assurance?	**Do you have** any documentation about your insurance policies?
Est-ce que vous avez une connexion Internet/le Wi-Fi?	**Do you have** an internet connection/Wi-Fi?
Est-ce que vous auriez des piles AA?	**Would you have** any AA batteries?
Est-ce que vous avez de quoi enlever cette tache?	**Do you have something to** remove this stain?

Do you sell...?

Vous vendez des kits mains libres?	**Do you sell** hands-free kits?
Vous vendez des piles?	**Do you sell** batteries?
Est-ce que vous vendez des lentilles jetables?	**Do you sell** disposable contact lenses?

You may want to ask for advice or a recommendation. To ask for suggestions, use **Vous me conseillez de…?** (*Do you think I should…?*). **conseillez** comes from the verb **conseiller**. For more information on **–er** verbs like **conseiller**, see page 269.

Do you think I should…?

Vous me conseillez de changer mon argent à la banque ou au bureau de change?	**Do you think I should** change money at the bank or the bureau de change?
Vous me conseillez d'ouvrir un compte épargne?	**Do you think I should** open a savings account?
Vous nous conseillez de changer les serrures?	**Do you think we should** change the locks?
Qu'est-ce que vous me conseillez?	**What do you think I should do**?

Would you recommend…?

Vous nous **recommandez** ce modèle?	**Would you recommend** this model to us?
Vous recommandez ce produit?	**Would you recommend** this product?
Vous nous recommandez de prendre une assurance tous risques?	**Would you recommend that we** take out comprehensive insurance?

You can use **Est-ce qu'il faut que…?** (*Should I…?*) with the subjunctive to ask whether you should do something. For more information on the subjunctive, see page 274.

Should I…?

Est-ce qu'il faut que j'appelle le plombier?	**Should I** call the plumber?
Est-ce qu'il faut que je prévienne ma banque?	**Should I** advise my bank?
Est-ce qu'il faut demander un devis?	**Do I need to** ask for an estimate?
Qu'est-ce qu'il faut que je fasse?	**What should I do**?

MAKING SUGGESTIONS

Occasionally you might want to make a suggestion with regard to a particular service. To do this you can use **je pourrais** (*I could*).

I could...

Je pourrais contacter ma banque au Royaume-Uni.	**I could** contact my bank in the UK.
Je pourrais remettre le rendez-vous à vendredi.	**I could** change the appointment to Friday.
On pourrait revenir plus tard.	**We could** come back later.

Can we agree on...?

On peut se mettre d'accord sur un prix?	**Can we agree on** a price?
On peut se mettre d'accord sur une heure de rendez-vous?	**Can we agree on** a time to meet up?
On peut se mettre d'accord sur une date?	**Can we agree on** a date?

To ask whether you had better do something, use **Est-ce qu'il vaut mieux que...?** (*Is it better...?*) or **Est-ce qu'il vaudrait mieux que...?** (*Would it be better...?*) followed by the subjunctive, which you can find out more about on page 274.

Is it better...?

Est-ce qu'il vaut mieux que je vienne le matin?	**Is it better if** I come in the morning?
Est-ce qu'il vaut mieux que je m'adresse à un revendeur certifié?	**Is it better if** I go to a certified dealer?
Est-ce qu'il vaudrait mieux appeler l'après-midi?	**Would it better to** phone in the afternoon?

When you're dealing with services, you'll need to make arrangements with people. A simple way of asking someone what suits them, is to use **Ça vous va si...?** (*Is it all right with you if...?*). **va** comes from the verb **aller**. For more information on **aller**, see page 279.

Is it all right with you if...?

Est-ce que ça vous va si je repasse à cinq heures?	**Is it all right with you if** I come back at five pm?
Est-ce que ça vous va si je passe à votre bureau demain?	**Is it all right with you if** I call at your office tomorrow?
Ça vous va si j'envoie le document par e-mail?	**Is it all right with you if** I send the document by email?

To discuss what the best arrangement is, you can use **Est-ce que ça vous arrangerait de...?** (*Would it be better for you if...?*) followed by the verb in the infinitive.

Would it be better for you if...?

Est-ce que ça vous arrangerait d'attendre un peu?	**Would it be better for you if** we waited a little?
Est-ce que ça vous arrangerait de faire un accord écrit?	**Would it be better for you if** we had a written agreement?
Ça vous arrangerait qu'on vous verse un acompte?	**Would it be better for you if** we gave you a deposit?

...would be best for me.

Le mieux pour moi serait dix heures à votre agence.	Ten o'clock in your office **would be best for me**.
Le mieux pour moi serait un rendez-vous dans l'après-midi.	An afternoon appointment **would be best for me**.
Le mieux pour moi serait d'être livré à domicile.	Home delivery **would be best for me**.

TALKING ABOUT YOUR PLANS

In English, we often say *I'm going to* to talk about the future. French works the same way. To say that you're going to do something, put **je vais** (*I'm going to*) or **on va** (*we're going to*) before the verb. **vais** and **va** come from the verb **aller**. For more information on **aller**, see page 279.

I'm going to...

Je vais acheter une nouvelle carte SIM.	**I'm going to** buy a new SIM card.
Je vais me renseigner auprès de ma banque en Grande-Bretagne.	**I'm going to** ask my bank in Britain.
On va vous payer en liquide.	**We're going to** pay you in cash.
Je vois mon banquier cet après-midi.	**I'm going to see** my bank manager this afternoon.
Nous visitons un appartement cette semaine.	**We're visiting** a flat this week.

French speakers often use **je compte** or **j'ai l'intention de** to say *I intend to*. **compte** comes from the verb **compter**, and **ai** comes from **avoir**. For more information on **avoir** and **–er** verbs like **compter**, see pages 280 and 269.

I intend to...

Je compte m'installer définitivement ici.	**I intend to** relocate here permanently.
Je compte ouvrir un nouveau compte.	**I intend to** open a new account.
J'ai l'intention d'investir dans un appareil photo plus perfectionné.	**I intend to** buy a more sophisticated camera.

I'm hoping to...

J'espère recevoir les documents la semaine prochaine.	**I'm hoping to** receive the documents next week.
J'espère terminer les travaux avant décembre.	**I'm hoping to** have the work finished by December.
Nous espérons pouvoir emménager le plus vite possible.	**We're hoping** we can move in as quickly as possible.

You can use **Est-ce que vous allez...?** (*Are you going to…?*) to ask people if they're going to do something. **allez** comes from the verb **aller** (*to go*). For more information on **aller**, see page 279.

Are you going to...?

Est-ce que vous allez changer l'objectif?	**Are you going to** change the lens?
Est-ce que vous allez faire payer la main d'œuvre?	**Are you going to** charge for labour?
Est-ce que vous allez pouvoir enlever cette tache?	**Are you going to** be able to remove this stain?

To ask what someone is going to do, use **Qu'est ce que vous allez...?** (*What are you going to…?*). For questions asking when or how somebody is going to do something, just replace **qu'** with **quand** (*when*), **comment** (*how*), and so on. For more information on **aller**, see page 279.

What are you going to...?

Qu'est-ce que vous allez faire?	**What are you going to** do?
Qu'est-ce que vous allez dire aux assureurs?	**What are you going to** tell the insurance company?
Quand est-ce que vous allez terminer les réparations?	**When are you going to** finish the repair work?
Comment est-ce que vous allez me dédommager?	**How are you going to** compensate me?

SAYING WHAT YOU LIKE, DISLIKE, PREFER

To say what you like, use **j'aime bien** (*I like*). To say what you don't like, just use **je n'aime pas**. These come from the verb **aimer**. For more information on **aimer**, see page 275.

I like...

J'aime bien aller au cinéma.	**I like** going to the cinema.
J'aime bien avoir les cheveux courts.	**I like to** keep my hair short.
J'aime beaucoup me faire faire les ongles.	**I really like** getting my nails done.

I don't like...

Je n'aime pas avoir trop d'argent liquide sur moi.	**I don't like** carrying too much cash on me.
Je n'aime pas trop laisser ma voiture chez le garagiste.	**I don't really like** leaving my car at the garage.
J'ai horreur de cette sonnerie de téléphone.	**I can't stand** this ringtone.

If you want to say what you prefer, use **je préfère** (*I prefer*). To say that you prefer A to B, use **je préfère A à B**. **préfère** comes from the verb **préférer**. For more information on **préférer**, see page 270.

I prefer...

Je préfère un contrat écrit.	**I prefer** a written contract.
Je préfère payer en plusieurs fois.	**I prefer** to pay in instalments.
On préfère ne rien signer pour l'instant.	**We prefer not** to sign **anything** for now.
Je préfère les photos en noir et blanc **aux** photos couleur.	**I prefer** black and white photos **to** colour ones.
Je préfère un abonnement **à** une carte.	**I prefer** a contract **to** a top-up card.

Use **j'aimerais mieux que** (*I'd rather*) followed by the verb in the subjunctive to say that you'd rather someone did something. For more information on the subjunctive, see page 274.

I'd rather...

J'aimerais mieux que vous me remboursiez.	**I'd rather** you refunded me.
J'aimerais mieux que vous m'envoyiez le dossier par e-mail.	**I'd rather** you sent me the file by email.
J'aimerais mieux que vous téléphoniez avant de passer.	**I'd rather** you phoned before calling in.

LISTEN OUT FOR

Here are some key phrases you are likely to hear when dealing with services.

Je peux vous renseigner?	Can I help you?
Ce sera prêt demain.	It'll be ready tomorrow.
Ce n'est pas encore prêt.	It's not ready yet.
Vous avez votre reçu?	Do you have your receipt?
Vous avez besoin d'un reçu?	Do you need a receipt?
Vous avez une pièce d'identité?	Do you have some identification?
Quelle heure vous conviendrait le mieux?	What time of day would suit you best?
Vous avez rendez-vous?	Do you have an appointment?
Veuillez rappeler demain.	Please ring back tomorrow.
Comment voudriez-vous régler?	How would you like to pay?

Lifestyle Tips

• When getting things done, you'll need to know about **horaires d'ouverture** (*opening times*). Shops and businesses such as hairdresser's, dry cleaner's and so on usually open at around nine in the morning and close at seven in the evening in France. In smaller towns, it is common for small shops to close between 12 and 2 for lunch. Except in the bigger towns, most businesses close on Sundays, and many on Mondays too, so that their employees can have a two-day break. As for public services, they tend to close at five at the latest.

• **cartes à puce** (*chip and PIN cards*) have been in use since the early 90s in France, although they were introduced in the UK almost a decade later. You may be asked to **Tapez votre code!** (*Type in your PIN!*).

• Many banks have security doors with an entry bell which the customers ring to be let in. You will probably see the following instructions on such doors: **Sonnez** (*ring*), **Patientez** (*wait*) and **Entrez** (*enter*).

• If you want to make an appointment at the hairdresser's and so forth, the word for an appointment is **rendez-vous**. For instance you could say **je voudrais prendre rendez-vous pour jeudi matin** (*I'd like to make an appointment for Thursday morning*).

Ouch!

Rétablis-toi vite! – Get well soon!

If you happen to be taken ill, have an accident, get toothache or need some other medical advice while in a French-speaking country, the phrases in this unit will give you the confidence to talk to a doctor, dentist or pharmacist to help you get what you need.

DESCRIBING THE PROBLEM

You may find yourself in a situation where you have to describe what the problem is. To do this, you can use **j'ai**. This comes from the verb **avoir**. For more information on **avoir**, see page 280.

I've got a...

J'ai de la fièvre.	**I've got** a temperature.
J'ai des plaques.	**I've got** a rash.
J'ai des palpitations.	**I've been having** palpitations.
Je ne sais pas ce que **j'ai**.	I don't know **what's wrong with me**.
Mon fils **est** cardiaque.	My son **has** a heart condition.
Je fais de l'hypertension.	**I have** high blood pressure.

If you want to say which bit of you hurts, and to talk about aches and pains, you use **j'ai mal à**. Remember that **j'ai mal à** followed by **le** becomes **j'ai mal au**, and **j'ai mal aux** when it is followed by **les**. For more information on **à** followed by **le** and **les**, see page 252.

I've got a... ache

J'ai mal à la tête.	**I've got** a head**ache**.
J'ai mal à l'estomac.	**I've got** stomach**ache**.
Elle a mal aux dents.	**She's got** toothache.
J'ai mal au dos.	**My** back **is sore**.
J'ai mal ici.	**It hurts** here.

I feel...

Je me sens fatigué tout le temps.	**I feel** tired all the time.
Je me sens mieux maintenant.	**I'm feeling** better now.
Je ne **me sens** pas bien du tout.	**I feel** awful.
Je me sentais bien hier.	**I felt** fine yesterday.

I'm...

Je suis allergique à la pénicilline.	**I'm** allergic to penicillin.
Je suis sous antidépresseurs.	**I'm** on antidepressants.
Je suis diabétique.	**I'm** diabetic.
Il est sous analgésiques.	**He's** on painkillers.

SAYING WHAT HAPPENED

If you've had some kind of accident, you will probably need to explain what happened. You can use **j'ai** or **je suis** followed by the form of the verb called the past participle. **ai** and **suis** come from the verbs **avoir** and **être**. For more information on the past tense, see page 269.

I've...

J'ai eu un accident.	**I've had** an accident.
J'ai perdu un plombage.	**I've lost** a filling.
Je suis tombé dans les escaliers.	**I fell down** the stairs.
Je me suis cogné la tête.	**I've bumped** my head.
Elle s'est brûlée sur la cuisinière.	**She burnt herself** on the stove.

I've never...

Je n'ai jamais eu un mal de tête pareil.	**I've never had** such a bad headache.
Il n'a jamais eu d'attaque.	**He's never had** a fit **before**.
Je ne me suis jamais sentie aussi mal.	**I've never felt** so ill.
Ça ne m'est encore jamais arrivé.	**It's never happened to me before**.

You may be unlucky enough to have had a more serious accident. To say that you have broken something, use **je me suis cassé** (*I've broken*).

I've broken...

Je crois que **je me suis cassé** le bras.	I think **I've broken** my arm.
Je me suis cassé la clavicule l'année dernière.	**I broke** my collar bone last year.
Il s'est cassé la jambe.	**He's broken** his leg.
Elle s'est cassé une dent.	**She's broken** a tooth.
Je me suis foulé la cheville.	**I've sprained** my ankle.

> **BON À SAVOIR!**
> French speakers say *I have broken the leg* and so on instead of *I have broken my leg* and so on.

ASKING FOR INFORMATION

When you are asking for information you may need to get someone's attention in order to ask them a question. To do this you can use either **pardon** or **excusez-moi**.

Is there...?

Pardon, **est-ce qu'il y a** un hôpital par ici?	Excuse me, **is there** a hospital nearby?
Est-ce qu'il y a une pharmacie de garde près d'ici?	**Is there** a chemist's open near here?
Est-ce que vous savez s'**il y a** un dentiste par ici?	Do you know if **there's** a dentist in the area?
Pardon, **où est-ce que je peux trouver** un médecin?	Excuse me, **where can I find** a doctor?
Excusez-moi, **où est-ce que je peux trouver** un poste de secours?	Excuse me please, **where can I find** a first-aid post?

> **BON À SAVOIR!**
> You use **Est-ce qu'il y a...?** to ask both *Is there...?* or *Are there...?* in French.

When you need an explanation of what something is exactly, or what it's for, use **Qu'est-ce que c'est que…?** (*What is…?*). For more general questions asking for information, use **quel** before a masculine word or **quelle** before a feminine word.

What's…?

Qu'est-ce que c'est que ce médicament?	**What is** this medicine?
Qu'est-ce que c'est que ces comprimés?	**What are** these tablets?
Quel est le numéro pour avoir une ambulance?	**What's** the number to call for an ambulance?
Quelle est l'adresse de l'hôpital?	**What's** the address of the hospital?
À quoi servent ces comprimés?	**What are** these tablets **for**?

Which…?

Je peux prendre rendez-vous avec **quel** docteur?	**Which** doctor can I get an appointment with?
Dans **quelle** rue est la clinique?	**Which** street is the clinic in?
Est-ce que vous pouvez me dire dans **quelle** salle elle est?	Can you tell me **which** ward she's in?
Quelle est la meilleure clinique?	**Which** clinic is the best?

In order to get more specific information, you may need to ask questions such as **Comment…?** (*How…?*) or **Quand…?** (*When…?*).

How…?

Comment est-ce qu'on prend rendez-vous avec le chiropracteur?	**How** do you make an appointment with the chiropractor?
Comment est-ce qu'on prend ce médicament?	**How** do you take this medicine?
Comment est-ce qu'on s'inscrit à la Sécurité Sociale?	**How** do we register with Social Security?

When...?

Quand est-ce qu'il faut que je me fasse faire ma piqûre?	**When** do I have to have my injection?
Quand est-ce que le médecin va venir?	**When** is the doctor coming?
Quand commencent les visites?	**When** does visiting time start?
Quand est-ce que je dois prendre les comprimés?	**When** do I have to take the tablets?
À quelle heure ouvre le cabinet médical?	**What time** does the doctor's surgery open?

Many of the questions you will be asking can be answered by *yes* or *no*. You can either put **est-ce que** before what you want to know or alternatively you can raise the tone of your voice at the end of the sentence.

Is...?

Est-ce que c'est grave?	**Is it** serious?
Est-ce que l'hôpital **est** loin?	**Is** the hospital far?
Le centre de santé **est** ouvert l'après-midi?	**Is** the health centre open in the afternoon?

ASKING FOR THINGS

When you want to find out if something is available, use
Est-ce que vous avez...? or **Vous avez...?** (*Do you have...?*).
avez comes from the verb **avoir**. For more information on **avoir**,
see page 280.

Do you have...?

Est-ce que vous avez quelque chose contre le mal de tête?	**Do you have** anything for a headache?
Est-ce que vous avez quelque chose contre le rhume des foins?	**Do you have** anything for hay fever?
Vous avez un numéro d'urgence?	**Do you have** an emergency telephone number?
Vous avez du paracétamol pour bébés?	**Do you have** infant paracetamol?

If you want to ask for something in French, use **Est-ce que je peux avoir...?** or **Je peux avoir...?** (*Can I have...?*). **peux** comes from the verb **pouvoir**. For more information on **pouvoir**, see page 284.

Can I have...?

Est-ce que je peux avoir un rendez-vous pour demain, s'il vous plaît?	**Can I have** an appointment for tomorrow, please?
Est-ce que je peux avoir de l'aspirine, s'il vous plaît?	**Can I have** a packet of aspirin, please?
Je peux avoir un pansement de rechange?	**Can I have** a spare bandage?

Can I...?

Est-ce que je peux voir un dentiste ce matin?	**Can I** see the dentist this morning?
Est-ce que je peux parler à un pédiatre tout de suite?	**Can I** talk to a paediatrician right away?
Est-ce que je peux boire de l'alcool avec ce médicament?	**Can I** drink alcohol with this medicine?
Quand **est-ce qu'on peut** passer prendre les résultats?	When **can we** collect the results?

If you are asking someone whether they can do something for you, you should use **Est-ce que vous pouvez...?** (*Can you...?*) or **Est-ce que vous pourriez...?** (*Could you...?*). **pouvez** and **pourriez** come from the verb **pouvoir**. For more information on **pouvoir**, see page 284.

Can you...?

Est-ce que vous pouvez me prescrire quelque chose pour les maux d'oreille, s'il vous plaît?	**Can you** prescribe something for earache, please?
Est-ce que vous pouvez envoyer une ambulance immédiatement?	**Can you** send an ambulance straightaway?
Est-ce que vous pouvez appeler un médecin, s'il vous plaît?	**Can you** call a doctor, please?
Est-ce que vous pouvez me donner quelque chose pour mon bébé qui fait ses dents?	**Can you give me** something for my baby who's teething?

Could you...?

Est-ce que vous pourriez nous emmener à l'hôpital le plus proche?	**Could you** take us to the nearest hospital?
Est-ce que vous pourriez me prendre la tension?	**Could you** check my blood pressure?
Est-ce que ça vous dérangerait de me trouver une infirmière qui parle anglais?	**Would you mind** finding me an English-speaking nurse?
Vous voulez bien me donner un rendez-vous pour une visite de contrôle?	**Would you mind** giving me an appointment for a checkup?

SAYING WHAT YOU WANT TO DO

If you want to say what you'd like to do in French, use either **je voudrais** or **j'aimerais** (*I'd like*). They come from the verbs **vouloir** and **aimer**. For more information on **vouloir** and **aimer**, see pages 285 and 275.

I'd like to...

Je voudrais prendre rendez-vous avec le médecin.	**I'd like to** make an appointment with the doctor.
Je voudrais voir un dentiste tout de suite.	**I'd like to** see a dentist straightaway.
Je voudrais acheter quelque chose contre la toux.	**I'd like to** buy something for a cough.
J'aimerais me faire faire un plombage.	**I'd like to** have a tooth filled.

I'd rather...

J'aimerais mieux aller dans un hôpital privé.	**I'd rather** go to a private hospital.
J'aimerais mieux aller chez un médecin femme **qu'**un médecin homme.	**I'd rather** see a female doctor **than** a male one.
Je préférerais prendre des comprimés **que de** me faire faire une piqûre.	**I'd rather** take tablets **than** have an injection.
On préfère les remèdes naturels.	**We prefer** natural remedies.

In French you can tell somebody what you need by using **j'ai besoin de** (*I need*).

I need...

J'ai besoin de la pilule du lendemain.	**I need** the morning-after pill.
J'ai besoin d'un médecin qui puisse venir ici.	**I need** a doctor who can come here.
On a besoin d'une ambulance de toute urgence.	**We** urgently **need** to call an ambulance.
Est-ce que j'ai besoin d'une ordonnance?	**Do I need** a prescription?

MAKING SUGGESTIONS

You may wish to make a suggestion in French. One way of doing this is to use **on pourrait** (*we could*). This comes from the verb **pouvoir**. For more information on **pouvoir**, see page 284.

We could...

On pourrait demander au pharmacien.	**We could** ask the pharmacist.
On pourrait prendre des analgésiques chez le pharmacien.	**We could** get some painkillers at the chemist's.
On pourrait téléphoner à sa famille.	**We could** phone his family.

Another way of making suggestions in French is to ask **Pourquoi ne pas...?** (*Why don't...?*).

Why don't...?

Pourquoi ne pas appeler un médecin?	**Why don't** we call a doctor?
Pourquoi ne pas demander un rendez-vous avec le cardiologue?	**Why don't** we ask for an appointment with the heart specialist?
Pourquoi pas demander comment se prennent ces antibiotiques?	**Why don't** we ask how the antibiotics should be taken?
Pourquoi tu n'expliques **pas** le problème au médecin?	**Why don't** you explain the problem to the doctor?

BON À SAVOIR!
You may have noticed that **ne** can be (and often is) omitted – this is mainly in spoken French.

LISTEN OUT FOR

Here are some key phrases you are likely to hear at the doctor's or the hospital.

Comment allez-vous?	How are you?
Qu'est-ce qui vous arrive?	What seems to be the problem?
Cela fait combien de temps que vous vous sentez comme ça?	How long have you been feeling like this?
Est-ce que vous avez des problèmes de santé?	Do you have any existing medical conditions?
Est-ce que vous prenez d'autres médicaments?	Are you on any other medication?
Est-ce que vous avez la nausée?	Do you feel sick?
Est-ce que vous avez des vertiges?	Do you feel dizzy?
Où est-ce que vous avez mal?	Where does it hurt?
Ne buvez pas d'alcool tant que vous prenez ce médicament.	Don't drink alcohol while you're taking this medicine.
Remplissez ce formulaire, s'il vous plaît.	Please fill in this form.
Je peux avoir les informations concernant votre assurance maladie?	Can I have your medical insurance details?
Les résultats sont bons.	The results are fine.

Lifestyle Tips

• If you think you need a doctor, you can go to **les urgences** – the A&E department of a hospital.

• You need to pay a fee – **les honoraires** – when you visit the doctor or dentist. Even among state health professionals, some charge more than others. You may be given **une ordonnance** (*a prescription*) to take to **la pharmacie** (*the chemist's*). There isn't a flat fee for medicines, so the price you'll pay will vary according to the medicine you've been prescribed. Unlike in Britain, in France, you can go directly to a specialist without being referred by a GP. Specialists' fees can be higher than GPs'.

• When going to a state health professional (**médecin conventionné**) in France, you will be asked for your **carte européenne d'assurance maladie** – your *European Health Insurance Card*. This card aims to make access to healthcare in any EU country hassle-free for all citizens of EU member states.

• In France, **pharmacies** (*chemists*) are easily recognizable from a distance thanks to the **croix verte** (*green cross*) sign displayed outside them.

• There is always a **pharmacie de garde** (*duty chemist's*) open when other chemists are shut. Its address will be prominently displayed outside all the other local pharmacies as well as in local newspapers.

• The mobile emergency medical service is called **SMUR** or **SAMU**. Its phone number is 15. If you think you need an ambulance in France, call this number and they'll decide what the best course of action is.

• In France when someone sneezes, you can say **À tes souhaits!** (*Bless you!* or literally *To your wishes!*), or **À vos souhaits!** to someone you don't know so well. If the person sneezes a second time, you can then say **À tes** (or **vos**) **amours! (Qu'elles durent toujours)** which literally means *To your love! (May it last forever).*

Help!

Ne vous en faites pas! – Don't worry!

If you find yourself in a situation in France in which you need help, for example if you break down, are involved in an accident or are robbed, or even if you simply can't get the heating to come on, this unit will give the language to help you cope with confidence.

DESCRIBING THE PROBLEM

If you are asking somebody for help of some kind, you will need to be able to describe what the problem is. Use **il y a** to mean both *there is* and *there are*, and **il n'y a pas de** to say *there isn't any* or *there aren't any*.

There is...

Il y a une odeur de gaz dans ma chambre.	**There's** a smell of gas in my room.
Il y a des cafards dans l'appartement.	**There are** cockroaches in the apartment.
Il n'y a pas de savon dans la salle de bain.	**There isn't any** soap in the bathroom.
Il n'y a pas de serviettes dans ma chambre.	**There aren't any** towels in my room.
Il y a eu un accident.	**There's been** an accident.

You may need to explain exactly what the problem is. To do this you can often use **j'ai** (*I've got*) or **je n'ai pas de** (*I haven't got*). **ai** comes from the verb **avoir**. For more information on **avoir**, see page 280.

I've got...

J'ai un problème.	**I've got** a problem.
J'ai un pneu à plat.	**I've got** a flat tyre.
Je n'ai pas de pompe.	**I haven't got** a pump.
On nous a volé et **nous n'avons pas** assez d'argent pour rentrer chez nous.	We've been robbed and **we haven't got** enough money to get back home.

The problem you are having may be because you are not able to do something. In French you can use **je n'arrive pas à** to say what you can't do.

I can't...

Je n'arrive pas à faire démarrer la voiture.	**I can't** get the car to start.
Je n'arrive pas à allumer le chauffe-eau – il est cassé.	**I can't** light the boiler – it's broken.
On n'arrive pas à ouvrir la porte de la chambre.	**We can't** open the door to the bedroom.

It may be the case, however, that you do not know how to do something. In French you would use **je ne sais pas** to talk about what you don't know how to do.

I can't...

Je ne sais pas changer un pneu.	**I can't** change a tyre.
Je ne sais pas conduire.	**I can't** drive.
Je ne sais pas très bien parler français.	**I can't** speak French very well.

If you want to say that you don't understand something, use **je ne comprends pas**.

I don't understand...

Je ne comprends pas ce que vous voulez dire.	**I don't understand** what you mean.
Je suis désolé, mais **je ne comprends pas** le mode d'emploi.	I'm sorry but **I don't understand** the instructions.
On ne comprend pas pourquoi ça ne marche pas.	**We can't understand** why it doesn't work.

SAYING WHAT HAPPENED

You will probably need to explain to somebody what happened. You can use **j'ai** (or sometimes **je suis**) followed by the past participle. **ai** and **suis** come from the verbs **avoir** and **être**. For more information on forming the past tense, see page 269.

I have...

J'ai perdu mon passeport.	**I've lost** my passport.
J'ai eu un accident.	**I've had** an accident.
Nous avons enfermé les clés dans l'appartement.	**We've locked** ourselves out of the apartment.
Ma valise **n'est pas arrivée**.	My case **hasn't arrived**.
On est tombé en panne.	**We've broken down**.
Nous sommes en panne d'essence.	**We've run out** of petrol.

I've been...

J'ai été agressé.	**I've been** mugged.
J'ai été cambriolé.	**I've been** burgled.
Ma voiture **a été** forcée.	My car**'s been** broken into.
On nous a trop fait payer.	**We've been** overcharged.
On m'a arraché mon sac.	My bag**'s been** snatched.

DESCRIBING PEOPLE AND THINGS

If you have some kind of problem in France you may need to be able to give a description of someone or something. To do this you can simply use **est** (*is*) followed by an adjective. **est** comes from the verb **être**. For more information on **être**, see page 282.

It is…

C'est un break noir.	**It's** a black estate car.
C'est un iPhone®.	**It's** an iPhone®.
Ce sont des bijoux de très grande valeur.	**They're** very valuable jewels.
Le sac **est** rouge.	The bag**'s** red.
La valise **est** verte avec des roulettes.	The suitcase **is** green with wheels.
Mon portefeuille **est en** cuir.	My wallet**'s made of** leather.
Il est grand et assez jeune.	**He's** tall and quite young-looking.

You may also be asked to give more details about yourself or somebody else, for example, age, hair colour and so on. To do this, use **il a** or **elle a** (literally *he has* or *she has*). **a** comes from the verb **avoir**. For more information on **avoir**, see page 280.

He's…

Il a cinq **ans**.	**He's** five **years old**.
Elle a huit **ans**.	**She's** eight.
J'ai trente **ans**.	**I'm** thirty.

BON À SAVOIR!

When talking about your or someone else's age, you must say **ans** in French.

He's got…

Il a les cheveux blonds et courts.	**He's got** short blond hair.
Elle a les cheveux bruns.	**She's got** brown hair.
Elle a les yeux verts.	**She's got** green eyes.
Ils ont les yeux marron tous les deux.	**They** both **have** brown eyes.

She's wearing...

Elle porte un jean et un tee-shirt vert.	**She's wearing** jeans and a green T-shirt.
Elle porte une robe orange.	**She's wearing** an orange dress.
Il portait un pull en laine et un pantalon noir.	**He was wearing** a woolly jumper and black trousers.

ASKING FOR INFORMATION

When you are asking for information you may need to get someone's attention in order to ask them a question. To do this you can use either **pardon** or **excusez-moi**.

Is there...?

Excusez-moi, **est-ce qu'il y a** un garage par ici?	Excuse me, **is there** a garage around here?
Pardon, **est-ce qu'il y a** un électricien dans le quartier?	Excuse me, **is there** an electrician in the area?
Est-ce qu'il y a des hôtels à proximité?	**Are there** any hotels nearby?

BON À SAVOIR!
Both *Is there…?* and *Are there…?* are **Est-ce qu'il y a…?** in French.

Which...?

Quel plombier me recommandez-vous?	**Which** plumber do you recommend?
Excusez-moi, il faut faire **quel** numéro pour appeler la police?	Excuse me, **what** number do you dial for the police?
Quels documents est-ce que je dois présenter?	**Which** documents do I need to show?

In order to obtain specific information, for example, how to do something, when something will happen or how much it will cost, you may want to ask **Comment...?** (*How…?*), **Quand...?** (*When…?*) or **Combien...?** (*How much…?*).

How...?

Comment est-ce qu'on fait pour avoir une ligne extérieure?	**How** do I get an outside line?
Comment est-ce qu'on fait pour signaler un vol?	**How** do we report a theft?
Excusez-moi, **comment est-ce qu'**on va au garage?	Excuse me, **how** do we get to the garage?
Est-ce que vous pouvez me dire **comment** récupérer la valise?	Can you tell me **how** we can get the suitcase back?

When...?

Quand est-ce que vous allez venir réparer la climatisation?	**When** will you come to fix the air-conditioning?
Quand est-ce que vous allez livrer la valise?	**When** will you deliver the suitcase?
Quand est-ce que je peux amener la voiture au garage?	**When** can I bring the car to the garage?
Est-ce que vous savez **quand** on pourra voir l'avocat?	Do you know **when** we'll be able to see the lawyer?

How much...?

Combien est-ce que ça va coûter de réparer la voiture?	**How much** will it be to repair the car?
Vous pouvez me dire **combien** va coûter la réparation?	Can you tell me **how much** you will charge me to fix this?
Combien coûtent les frais de dossier?	**How much** are the registration fees?

If you want to ask for something in French, use **Est-ce que je peux avoir...?** or **Je peux avoir...?** (*Can I have...?*). **peux** comes from the verb **pouvoir**. For more information on **pouvoir**, see page 284.

Can I have...?

Est-ce que je peux avoir votre numéro de téléphone?	**Can I have** your phone number?
Est-ce que je peux avoir un autre formulaire?	**Can I have** another form?
Je peux avoir une autre couverture, s'il vous plaît?	**Can I have** another blanket, please?
Est-ce que je peux emprunter votre portable pour passer un coup de fil urgent?	**Can I borrow** your mobile to make an urgent call?

If you want to find out if something is available, use **Est-ce que vous avez...?** (*Do you have...?*).

Do you have...?

Est-ce que vous avez des câbles de démarrage?	**Do you have** jump leads?
Excusez-moi, **est-ce que vous avez** un bureau des objets trouvés?	Excuse me, **do you have** a lost property office?
Pardon, **est-ce que vous avez** ce document en anglais?	Excuse me, **do you have** this document in English?

If you are asking someone whether they can do something for you, you should use **Est-ce que vous pouvez...?** (*Can you...?*) or **Est-ce que vous pourriez...?** (*Could you...?*). **pouvez** and **pourriez** come from the verb **pouvoir**. For more information on **pouvoir**, see page 284.

Can you...?

Est-ce que vous pouvez m'aider, s'il vous plaît?	**Can you** help me, please?
Est-ce que vous pouvez appeler la police?	**Can you** call the police?
Est-ce que vous pourriez recommander un électricien?	**Could you** recommend an electrician?
Est-ce que vous pourriez me montrer comment fonctionne la douche?	**Could you** show me how the shower works?

SAYING WHAT YOU WANT TO DO

You may need to be able to say what you want or what you'd like to do in French. To do this, you can use either **je veux** (*I want*) or **je voudrais** (*I'd like*). **veux** and **voudrais** are both from the verb **vouloir**. For more information on **vouloir**, see page 285.

I'd like to...

Je voudrais signaler un vol.	**I'd like to** report a theft.
Je voudrais téléphoner.	**I'd like to** make a call.
Je voudrais parler à un avocat.	**I'd like to** speak to a lawyer.

I don't want to...

Je ne veux pas rester dans cette chambre.	**I don't want to** stay in this room.
Je ne veux pas laisser ma voiture ici.	**I don't want to** leave my car here.
Nous ne voulons pas aller à l'hôtel sans nos bagages.	**We don't want to** go to the hotel without our luggage.

If you want to say what your preference is, use **j'aimerais mieux** (*I'd rather*).

I'd rather...

J'aimerais mieux faire appel à un avocat qui parle anglais.	**I'd rather** hire a lawyer who can speak English.
J'aimerais mieux être au rez-de-chaussée **qu'**au premier étage.	**I'd rather** stay on the ground floor **than** on the first floor.
On préférerait lire les documents en anglais, si possible.	**We'd rather** read the documents in English, if possible.

SAYING WHAT YOU HAVE TO DO

You may want to say what you have to do in French. Use **il faut que** (*I have to*) with the subjunctive or **j'ai besoin de** (*I need*). For more information on the subjunctive, see page 274.

I have to...

Il faut que j'aille à l'ambassade britannique.	**I have to** go to the British embassy.
Il faut que je recharge la batterie de mon téléphone.	**I have to** charge up my phone.
Il faut que je parle à un avocat.	**I must** speak to a lawyer.

I need...

J'ai besoin d'un pneu neuf.	**I need** a new tyre.
J'ai besoin de téléphoner.	**I need to** make a call.
J'ai besoin d'appeler un électricien.	**I need to** call an electrician.

MAKING SUGGESTIONS

You may wish to make a suggestion to your French-speaking acquaintances. One way of doing this is to use **on pourrait** (*we could*). **pourrait** comes from the verb **pouvoir**. For more information on **pouvoir**, see page 284.

We could...

On pourrait appeler un serrurier.	**We could** call a locksmith.
On pourrait demander le numéro d'un électricien à quelqu'un.	**We could** ask someone for the number of an electrician.
On pourrait toujours aller au bureau des objets trouvés.	**We could** always go to the lost property office.
Si tu préfères, on peut aller voir le gérant et expliquer le problème.	**If you prefer, we could** go to the manager and explain the problem.

You can also use **Et si...?** followed by a verb in the imperfect tense to suggest doing something. For more information on the imperfect, see page 272.

How about...?

Et si on parlait à un avocat?	**How about** talking to a lawyer?
Et si on appelait ton consulat?	**How about** calling your consulate?
Et si on signalait le problème à la réception?	**How about** reporting the fault to reception?

Another way of making suggestions is to ask **Pourquoi est-ce qu'on ne... pas?** (*Why don't...?*).

Why don't...?

Pourquoi est-ce qu'on ne demande **pas** de l'aide aux voisins?	**Why don't we** ask the neighbours for help?
Pourquoi est-ce qu'on n'appelle **pas** la réception?	**Why don't we** call reception?
Pourquoi tu ne vas **pas** au commissariat pour signaler le vol?	**Why don't you** go to the police station to report the theft?

In English we often say *I'm going to* to talk about the future. French works the same way. To say that you're going to do something, use **je vais** (*I'm going to*) or **on va** (*we're going to*) before the verb. **vais** and **va** come from the verb **aller**. For more information on **aller**, see page 279.

I'm going to...

Je vais appeler le garage.	**I'm going to** phone the garage.
Je vais signaler le vol à la police.	**I'm going to** report the theft to the police.
Je vais appeler au secours avec mon portable.	**I'm going to** call for help on my mobile.
On va appeler un électricien pour qu'il répare l'installation électrique.	**We're going to** phone an electrician to fix the wiring.

Are you going to...?

Est-ce que vous allez remorquer notre voiture?	**Are you going to** tow our car back?
Est-ce que vous allez venir aujourd'hui?	**Are you going to** come out today?
Vous allez nous appeler quand ce sera prêt?	**Are you going to** call us when it's ready?

LISTEN OUT FOR

Here are some key phrases you are likely to hear when you have some kind of problem.

Quel est le problème?	What's the problem?
Qu'est ce qui s'est passé?	What happened?
Est-ce que je peux avoir les coordonnées de votre assurance?	Can I have your insurance details?
Qu'est-ce qui a été volé?	What's been stolen?
Est-ce que je peux avoir votre adresse, s'il vous plaît?	Can I have your address, please?
Vous êtes d'où?	Where are you from?
Où est-ce que vous logez?	Where are you staying?
Est-ce que je peux voir votre permis de conduire?	Can I have your driving licence?
Est-ce qu'il y avait des témoins?	Were there any witnesses?
Remplissez ce formulaire, s'il vous plaît.	Please fill in this form.

Lifestyle Tips

• If you have to report a crime to the police in France, you'll need to go to the **commissariat de police** (*police station*) where you'll have to **faire une déclaration** (*file a report*). In a big city, it is likely to be the **police nationale** (*national police*) you go to, though in rural areas it may be the **gendarmerie**, a police branch of the military.

• There are several types of police in France. There's the **police nationale** who are in charge of national security and public order in general. Then, there's the **police municipale** (*municipal police*) who mainly deal with traffic and minor crimes. There is also the **gendarmerie nationale** who look after rural policing and border patrols.

• As in the UK, if you're driving around France, you'll need to be careful where you park if you want to avoid paying a **contravention** (*fine*) or having your car towed away by the **camion-grue** (*tow truck*) and having to get it back at great expense from the **fourrière** (*pound*). Make sure you look at any signs and ask if you don't understand them. You can always ask **Que veut dire ce panneau?** (*What does this sign mean?*).

Getting in touch

Qui est à l'appareil? – Who's calling, please?

Talking on the phone is one of the hardest things to do in a foreign language, because you can't see the person you're speaking to, and therefore you can't rely on body language and facial expressions to help you understand and communicate. This unit gives you the language to overcome this and helps you to sound natural and confident when speaking on the telephone in French. It also covers different means of communication in French: email, texting, social media and the good old post.

MAKING A TELEPHONE CALL

If you want to tell someone that you need to make a phone call, use **je dois** (*I need to*). **dois** comes from the verb **devoir**. For more information on **devoir**, see page 281.

I need to...

Je dois téléphoner.	**I need to** make a call
Je dois téléphoner à ma femme.	**I need to** phone my wife.
Je dois passer un coup de fil à mon pote.	**I need to** give my mate a ring.
N'oublie pas que **tu dois** rappeler ta mère ce soir.	Don't forget **you need to** call your mum back tonight.

> **BON À SAVOIR!**
> The French expressions for calling someone are **téléphoner** (*to phone*) and **passer un coup de fil** (*to ring*). The second one is less formal, just as it is in English.

Many of the questions you may want to ask can be answered by *yes* or *no*. To ask such questions, use **Est-ce que...?** with what you want to know. So, if you want to ask if someone has something, for example a telephone number, use **Est-ce que vous avez...?** (*Do you have...?*)

Do you have...?

Est-ce que vous avez le numéro personnel de Madame Kay, s'il vous plaît?	**Do you have** Mrs Kay's home number, please?
Est-ce que vous avez une adresse e-mail?	**Do you have** an email address?
Est-ce que tu as un numéro de portable?	**Do you have** a mobile number?

You can ask for something such as a telephone number in French by using **Quel est...?** before a masculine noun and **Quelle est...?** before a feminine noun.

What's...?

Quel est son numéro de téléphone?	**What's** her phone number?
Quel est le numéro des renseignements?	**What's** the number for directory enquiries?
Quel est l'indicatif de l'Irlande?	**What's** the dialling code for Ireland?
Je peux prendre **quelle** ligne pour appeler?	**What** line can I use to make a call?
Je dois faire **quel** numéro pour appeler à l'extérieur?	**What** number do I have to dial to get an outside line?

WHEN THE PERSON YOU'RE CALLING ANSWERS

Once you've made the call and someone answers, you will need to say *hello* and tell them who's calling. The French expression **Allô?** is only used when speaking on the phone. You can say this whether you are making or receiving the call, and for any type of call, formal or informal. Always make sure you introduce yourself to the person who picks up the phone using **c'est** (*this is*).

Hello, this is...

Allô, **c'est** Madame Devernois.	**Hello**, **this is** Mrs Devernois.
Allô, Monsieur André, **c'est** Monsieur Ronaldson **à l'appareil**.	**Hello** Mr André, **this is** Mr Ronaldson **speaking**.
Bonsoir, Madame Paoletti, **c'est** Madame Marsh **à l'appareil**.	**Good evening** Mrs Paoletti, **this is** Mrs Marsh **speaking**.
Salut, Tarik, **c'est** Flo.	**Hi** Tarik, Flo **here**.
Bonjour, Stéphanie est là? **C'est de la part de** Marie.	**Hello**, is Stéphanie in? **This is** Marie.

I'm...

Je suis une collègue de Nicole.	**I'm** a colleague of Nicole's.
Je suis un copain d'Émilie.	**I'm** a friend of Émilie's.
Je suis la fille de Monsieur Cadey.	**I'm** Mr Cadey's daughter.
Allô, **je suis** le locataire du 5 rue des Cèdres.	Hello, **I'm** the tenant of 5 rue des Cèdres.

If you want to ask for somebody in particular, use **Est-ce que...
est là?** (*Is...there?*).

Is...there?

Est-ce qu'Olivier **est là**, s'il vous plaît?	**Is** Olivier **there**, please?
Est-ce que tes parents **sont là**?	**Are** your parents **in**?
Est-ce que vous pouvez me dire si Madame Revert **est là**?	Could you tell me whether Mrs Revert **is in**?

BON À SAVOIR!

If the person you want to speak to isn't in, the answer you may
hear is **désolé, il n'est pas là** (*sorry, he's not in*).

Is this...?

Est-ce que je suis bien au commissariat de police?	**Is this the** police station?
C'est bien le numéro de la mairie?	**This is** the number for the town hall, **isn't it**?
Je suis bien au 08 13 76 89 98?	**Is this** 08 13 76 89 98?

BON À SAVOIR!

French telephone numbers are read out in groups of two digits,
so the number above would be read as: **zéro huit**, **treize,
soixante-seize**, **quatre-vingt-neuf**, **quatre-vingt-dix-huit** (*zero
eight, thirteen, seventy-six, eighty-nine, ninety-eight*).

There are several ways of asking whether you may do
something. Starting your question with **puis-je** will make you
sound very formal. **Est-ce que je pourrais...?** (*May I...?*) is much
more frequent in everyday spoken French.

May I...?

Puis-je parler au directeur, s'il vous plaît?	**May I** speak to the manager, please?
Est-ce que je pourrais parler à Cécile, s'il vous plaît?	**May I** speak to Cécile, please?
Est-ce que je pourrais avoir le numéro de l'hôtel Europa?	**May I** have the number of the Europa hotel?

One of the first things you may want to ask when you speak to someone is how they are. The French expressions **Comment ça va?** and **Ça va?** both mean the same thing – *How are you?*. You can also say **Comment vas-tu?** to one person you know well, and **Comment allez-vous?** to several people or to someone you don't know so well.

How are you?

Ça va?	**How are you**?
Comment ça va?	**How are you**?
Ça va bien?	**How are you**?

How's...?

Comment va?	**How's life**?
Comment va ton frère?	**How is** your brother?
Comment vont tes parents?	**How are** your parents?

In response to being asked how you are, you can use several different phrases.

Fine, thanks.

Ça va bien, merci, et vous?	**I'm fine, thanks**, what about you?
Bien, merci, et toi?	**I'm fine, thanks**, and you?
Ça va pas mal, et toi?	**Not bad**. And yourself?
Ça ne va pas fort en ce moment.	**I haven't been great** lately.

SAYING WHY YOU'RE CALLING

In the course of the telephone call you will often want to explain to someone why you are calling or where you're calling from. To do this, you use the verb **appeler**. For more information on **–er** verbs like **appeler**, see page 269.

I'm phoning about...

J'appelle à propos de demain soir.	**I'm phoning about** tomorrow night.
J'appelle à propos de votre annonce dans le journal.	**I'm phoning about** your ad in the paper.
J'appelle pour parler à Marie.	**I'm phoning to** talk to Marie.
J'appelle pour avoir des détails sur vos tarifs.	**I'm phoning to** get further details on your rates.

I'm calling from...

J'appelle d'une cabine.	**I'm calling from** a public phone.
J'appelle de mon portable.	**I'm calling from** my mobile.
Je vous **appelle de** mon travail.	**I'm calling** you **from** work.

If you want to ask whether you can do something, use **Est-ce que je peux...?** (*Can I...?*).

Can I...?

Est-ce que je peux laisser un message?	**Can I** leave a message?
Est-ce que je peux rappeler plus tard?	**Can I** call back later?
Je peux vous laisser un message à lui transmettre?	**Can you** pass on a message, please?

If you are asking someone whether they can do something for you, you should use **Est-ce que vous pouvez...?** (*Can you...?*) or **Est-ce que vous pourriez...?** (*Could you...?*). These come from the verb **pouvoir**. For more information on **pouvoir**, see page 284.

Can you...?

Est-ce que vous pouvez lui dire que Paul a appelé, s'il vous plaît?	**Can you** let him know that Paul rang, please?
Est-ce que vous pouvez me passer Johanna, s'il vous plaît?	**Can you** put me through to Johanna, please?
Tu peux lui faire la commission, s'il te plaît?	**Can you** pass the message on to him, please?
Est-ce que vous pourriez lui transmettre un message?	**Could you** give her a message?
Vous pourriez lui demander de me rappeler?	**Could you** ask her to call me, please?

GIVING INFORMATION

When you make a phone call in French, you may well be asked to give certain pieces of information. To give your phone number or address, use **mon numéro, c'est** (*my number is*) and **mon adresse, c'est** (*my address is*).

My number is...

Mon numéro de portable, **c'est le**...	**My** mobile **number is**...
...et **mon numéro** de fixe, **c'est le**...	...and **my** landline **number is**...
Le numéro de téléphone de mon hôtel, **c'est le**...	**My** hotel **phone number is**...

My address is...

Mon adresse à Paris, **c'est**...	**My address** in Paris **is**...
Mon adresse en Angleterre, **c'est**...	**My address** in England **is**...
J'habite le 6, Maryhill Drive à Cork.	**My address is** 6 Maryhill Drive, Cork.
Je loge à l'Hôtel Méditerranée.	**I'm staying** at the Méditerranée Hotel.

To give details of where you can be contacted, use **vous pouvez me joindre** (*you can contact me*).

You can contact me...

Vous pouvez me joindre au 09 98 02 46 23.	**You can contact me** on 09 98 02 46 23.
Tu peux me joindre sur mon fixe.	**You can contact me** on my landline.
Tu peux la joindre entre midi et deux heures.	**You can get her** between twelve and two.
Tu peux me laisser un message sur le répondeur.	**You can** leave me a message on my answerphone.

ANSWERING THE TELEPHONE

You always answer the telephone with the same French expression **Allô?**. This is only used when speaking on the phone. You can say this whether you are making or receiving the call, and for any type of call, formal or informal.

Hello?

Allô?	**Hello?**
Allô, oui?	**Hello?**
Allô, j'écoute?	**Hello?**

If the person on the other end of the line asks for you, you answer **elle-même** if you are a woman, and **lui-même** if you are a man. This is a formal way of saying *speaking*. If you want to be less formal but still polite, you can simply say **oui, c'est moi**.

Speaking.

Elle-même.	**Speaking**.
Lui-même.	**Speaking**.
Oui, **c'est moi**.	Yes, **it's me**.

When you answer the telephone you often need to ask whether the caller would like to leave a message, call back later and so on. Use **Vous voulez...?** to someone you don't know well, or **Tu veux...?** to someone you know well to say *Would you like to...?*. **voulez** and **veux** both come from the verb **vouloir**. For more information on **vouloir**, see page 285.

Would you like to...?

Vous voulez laisser un message?	**Would you like to** leave a message?
Vous voulez qu'il vous rappelle?	**Would you like** him **to** call you back?
Tu veux rappeler un peu plus tard?	**Would you like to** call back a bit later?

Would you mind...?

Est-ce que ça vous dérangerait de parler plus lentement, s'il vous plaît?	**Would you mind** speaking more slowly, please?
Est-ce que ça vous dérangerait de répéter, s'il vous plaît? Je vous entends mal.	**Would you mind** saying that again, please? I can't hear you very well.
Est-ce que ça vous ennuierait de l'épeler, s'il vous plaît?	**Would you mind** spelling it out, please?
Ça t'ennuierait de me rappeler demain?	**Would you mind** calling me back tomorrow?

ENDING A TELEPHONE CALL

When you end a telephone call in French, you can say goodbye as you normally would face to face. Use **au revoir, madame/mademoiselle/monsieur** to say goodbye to people you don't know well. You can just say **au revoir** to the people you know, or **salut** if you want to sound more informal.

Goodbye!

Au revoir, Laurent!	**Goodbye** Laurent!
Au revoir, Monsieur Blum!	**Goodbye** Mr Blum!
Allez, **salut**, Emma! On se rappelle !	Right, **bye** Emma! Talk to you later!

Have a good...!

Bonne journée!	**Have a good** day!
Bon week-end!	**Have a good** weekend!
Bonne soirée!	**Have a good** evening!

To say *See you...!*, use **à** followed by **demain** (*tomorrow*), **plus tard** (*later*), **ce soir** (*tonight*) and so on.

See you...!

À demain!	**See you** tomorrow!
À plus tard!	**See you** later!
À ce soir!	**See you** tonight!
À bientôt!	**See you** soon!
À plus!	**Later**!

As part of saying your goodbyes, you may want to pass your greetings or best wishes on to other people. To do this, use **passe le bonjour à** (*say hello to*).

Say hello to...

Passe le bonjour à ta famille.	**Say hello to** your family.
Passe le bonjour à ta sœur.	**Say hello to** your sister.
Salue tes parents **de ma part**.	**Say hello to** your parents **for me**.
Lara te **dit bonjour**.	Lara **says hello**.
Mes amitiés à ton père.	**Give** your father **my best wishes**.

BON À SAVOIR!

You may be interested to know that the French for *to hang up on someone* is **raccrocher au nez de quelqu'un** which literally means *to hang up on someone's nose*.

Occasionally you may be forced into finishing a call earlier than you had planned, especially on a mobile phone. To tell someone what the problem is, use **je n'ai...plus de** (*I don't have any...left*).

I don't have any...left

Je n'ai bientôt **plus de** batterie.	**I don't have** much battery **left**.
Je n'ai presque **plus de** crédit.	**I've** almost **no** credit **left**.

BON À SAVOIR!

Of course, the main reason for mobile calls ending suddenly is often that the network coverage isn't adequate. To tell someone that they're breaking up, use **ça va couper**.

LISTEN OUT FOR

Here are some key phrases you may hear when using the telephone.

Qui est à l'appareil?	Who's calling, please?
C'est de la part de qui?	Who shall I say is calling?
Ne quittez pas, s'il vous plaît.	Please hold the line.
Ne quitte pas, je vais le chercher.	Hang on a minute, I'll get him.
Vous n'avez pas fait le bon numéro.	You've got the wrong number.
Vous connaissez le numéro de poste?	Do you have the extension number?
Je transfère votre communication.	I'll put you through.
Le numéro que vous avez composé n'est pas attribué.	The number you have dialled doesn't exist.
Vous êtes bien au 09 73 47 60 21.	You've reached 09 73 47 60 21.
Veuillez laisser un message après le bip.	Please leave a message after the tone.
Cet appel vous sera facturé 1 euro la minute.	This call will cost 1 euro per minute.
Tous nos opérateurs sont en ligne, merci de rappeler ultérieurement.	All our operators are busy, please call back later.
Votre correspondant n'est pas en mesure de prendre cet appel; veuillez laisser votre message sur sa boîte vocale.	Your call is being forwarded to the mobile messaging service.
Ça va couper.	You're breaking up.
Merci d'avoir appelé.	Thanks for calling.

There will be times when you need to send an email or write a letter in French. Here are some useful phrases which you can use to do this. You can also have a look at examples of emails and letters in French.

Starting a personal email or letter

Chère Aurélie,...	Dear Aurélie,...
Ma chère tante,...	My dear aunt,...
Salut Élodie!	Hi Élodie!

Ending a personal email or letter

Cordialement.	Kind regards.
Bien à vous, Marie.	Yours, Marie.
Amitiés, Jean.	Kind regards, Jean.
Je t'embrasse, Naïma.	Love, Naïma.
À bientôt!	See you soon!
Mes amitiés à Fadou.	Send my best wishes to Fadou.
(Grosses) Bises, Charlotte.	Love, Charlotte.

Fichier	Edition	Affichage	Outils	**Composer**	Aide	Envoyer

A: coralie@europost.fr

Nouveau message
Répondre
Répondre à tous
Faire suivre
Fichier joint

Cc:

Copie cachée:

Objet: dîner?

Salut Cécile,

Comment ça va? J'espère que tes vacances se sont bien passées et que tu t'es bien reposée.

On pourrait se retrouver bientôt si ça te dit, soit pour déjeuner en ville, soit chez moi pour dîner. Dis-moi ce que tu en penses.

Bises,

Coralie

Saying your email address
In French, when you tell someone your email address, you say:
coralie arobase europost point ef-ayr

Starting a formal email or letter

Cher M. Provence,...	Dear Mr Provence,...
Madame,...	Dear Madam,...
Madame, Monsieur,...	Dear Sir or Madam,...
Cher Thomas/Chère Océane,...	Dear Thomas/Océane,...

Ending a formal email or letter

Veuillez accepter, Madame, l'expression de mes sentiments distingués.	Yours faithfully/sincerely
Veuillez accepter, Monsieur, l'expression de mes sentiments distingués.	Yours faithfully/sincerely
J'attends votre réponse. Cordialement, Mme Banks.	I look forward to hearing from you. Kind regards, Mrs Banks.
Je vous prie de croire, Monsieur, à l'assurance de mes sentiments distingués.	Yours faithfully/sincerely

BON À SAVOIR!

French formal letters and emails sometimes finish with long-winded standard expressions such as the ones above. You can get away with only writing **cordialement** followed by your name, particularly in emails, but it is slightly less formal.

Addressing an envelope

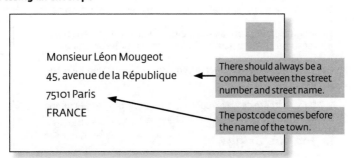

Monsieur Léon Mougeot
45, avenue de la République
75101 Paris
FRANCE

There should always be a comma between the street number and street name.

The postcode comes before the name of the town.

A: administration@stages-france.org

Cc:

Copie cachée:

Objet: logement pour stage d'été

Saying an email address
In French, when you tell someone an email address, you say: *administration arobase stages trait d'union france point org*

Madame, Monsieur,

Je suis très intéressé par votre stage linguistique d'été, dont j'ai trouvé les détails sur votre site Web. Avant de réserver une place, j'aurais voulu savoir si vous pouvez me conseiller un logement à proximité, de préférence dans une famille, pour les deux semaines de stage.

Je vous remercie par avance pour votre réponse.

Cordialement,

James Wilson

When ending a formal email in French, you can sign off with the more informal **Cordialement**, followed by your name.

Joanne Briggs
64 Poplar Drive
Leeds LS1 2HE

Your own name and address

Crèche Everest
15, av. Jean Médecin
06000 Nice

Name and address of the person/company you are writing to

Leeds, le 2 juin 2015

Town/city you are writing from, and the date

Madame, Monsieur,

Actuellement étudiante en dernière année de formation «Voyages et tourisme» à Leeds City College, je suis à la recherche d'un stage d'un mois en France. Votre structure m'a semblé idéale car j'aimerais me spécialiser dans l'encadrement des enfants.

Je vous serais reconnaissante de m'indiquer si vous seriez en mesure de m'accueillir en tant que stagiaire l'été prochain.

Je joins mon CV à cette lettre, en espérant qu'il retiendra votre attention.

Dans l'attente de votre réponse, je vous prie d'agréer, Madame, Monsieur, mes salutations distinguées.

Joanne Briggs

Texting is as important a part of French communication as it is in the UK. If you would like to text (**envoyer un texto** or **SMS**) in French, here are some abbreviations used in French text messaging and emails. You will notice that just as the numbers 2, 4 and 8 are used in English in text messages (*C U 2moro; R U coming 4 Xmas?; Gr8!*), French texts also use 1 for all "in/un/ain/" sounds, 2 for "de/deu" sounds and 6 for "si/sis" sounds.

Texto	French	English
@+	à plus tard	see you later
@2m1	à demain	see you tomorrow
bi1to	bientôt	soon
biz	bisous, bises	kisses
bjr	bonjour	hello
bsr	bonsoir	good evening
c	c'est	it's
cpg	c'est pas grave	it's no big deal
dsl	désolé	I'm sorry
entouk	en tout cas	in any case
G la N	J'ai la haine	I'm gutted
IR	hier	yesterday
je t'M	je t'aime	I love you
ki	qui	who
koi	quoi	what
lol/mdr	mort de rire	rolling on the floor laughing
mr6	merci	thanks
MSG	message	message
p2k	pas de quoi	you're welcome
parske	parce que	because
pk	pourquoi	why
qqn	quelqu'un	someone
ri1	rien	nothing
slt	salut	hi
svp	s'il vous plaît	please
TOK	t'es OK?	are you OK?
TOQP	t'es occupé?	are you busy?
we	week-end	weekend
Xlnt	excellent	excellent

With social media an everyday means of communication, below are some useful phrases and terms to help you.

French	English
un(e) ami(e)	a friend
ajouter à sa liste d'amis	to friend
un blog	a blog
un compte	an account
créer/ouvrir un compte	to create/open an account
faire un commentaire sur	to comment (on)
un fil de discussion	a (discussion) thread
un forum	a forum
un mot-dièse, un hashtag	a hashtag
un message privé, un MP, un message direct	a DM, a direct message
envoyer un message privé or un MP à quelqu'un	to DM somebody
une mise à jour du statut	a status update
un mur	a wall
écrire sur le mur de quelqu'un	to write on somebody's wall
un news feed, un fil d'actualités or de nouvelles	a news feed
une photo du profil	a profile picture
poster quelque chose sur le mur de quelqu'un	to post something on or to somebody's wall
un profil	a profile
retweeter	to retweet
un suiveur, une suiveuse; un(e) abonné(e	a follower
suivre	to follow
arrêter de suivre	to unfollow
un sujet tendance	a trending topic
taguer quelqu'un sur une photo	to tag somebody in a photo
un tweet	a tweet
tweeter (sur)	to tweet (about)

Lifestyle Tips

• It is better to avoid loud ringtones (**sonneries**) and mobile-phone conversations in public places in France, and more particularly on public transport and in restaurants. It is even less accepted than it is in the UK.

• If you really need to send a text message or to make a phone call while in company, it is always better to apologize and explain: **excusez-moi, je dois passer un coup de fil** (*sorry, I need to make a phone call*) or **je dois envoyer un texto** or **SMS** (*I need to send a text message*).

• In France, you might come across special phone numbers called **numéro vert®** with the prefix 0800, **numéro azur®** (0810) and **numéro indigo®** (0820 or 0825). These are fixed-rate numbers, used mainly by companies. **numéros verts®** are free from a landline, **numéros azur®** are at a reduced rate and **numéros indigo®** are charged at local rates.

• As in Britain, the use of a **téléphone portable** (*mobile phone*) is forbidden while driving. The use of **kits mains libres** (*hands-free kits*) however is allowed.

Time, numbers, date

Trois, deux, un... Partez! – Three, two, one... Go!

When communicating in French you'll often need to say and understand numbers, so here's a list to help you.

0	zéro
1	un(e)
2	deux
3	trois
4	quatre
5	cinq
6	six
7	sept
8	huit
9	neuf
10	dix
11	onze
12	douze
13	treize
14	quatorze
15	quinze
16	seize
17	dix-sept
18	dix-huit
19	dix-neuf
20	vingt

BON À SAVOIR!
A little tip: French speakers never use the letter O to refer to **zéro** (*zero*), as we do in English.

In French, the word **un** (*one*) can change its ending. The masculine form **un** becomes **une** before a feminine noun.

one

Combien de DVD as-tu acheté? – Seulement **un**.	How many DVDs did you buy? – Only **one**.
J'ai **un** frère.	I've got **one** brother.
Il ne me reste qu'**une** cigarette.	I've only got **one** cigarette left.
Tu as écrit combien de pages? – **Une**.	How many pages have you written? – **One**.

Although most consonants aren't pronounced at the end of French words, the **–t** in **vingt** is when it is followed by a number.

21	vingt et un(e)
22	vingt-deux
23	vingt-trois
24	vingt-quatre
25	vingt-cinq
26	vingt-six
27	vingt-sept
28	vingt-huit
29	vingt-neuf

Use **et** to form tens ending in one; **vingt et un** (*twenty-one*), **trente et un** (*thirty-one*), **quarante et un** (*forty-one*) and so on, and for **soixante et onze** (*seventy-one*). The exceptions are **quatre-vingt-un** (*eighty-one*) and **quatre-vingt-onze** (*ninety-one*).

30	trente
31	trente et un(e)
40	quarante
42	quarante-deux
50	cinquante
53	cinquante-trois
60	soixante
64	soixante-quatre
70	soixante-dix
71	soixante et onze
75	soixante-quinze
80	quatre-vingts
81	quatre-vingt-un(e)
90	quatre-vingt-dix
91	quatre-vingt-onze
99	quatre-vingt-dix-neuf

Just as the word for *one* can be **un** or **une**, the words for *twenty-one*, *thirty-one*, *forty-one* and so on also change. The masculine forms **vingt et un**, **trente et un** and so forth become **vingt et une**, **trente et une** and so on in the feminine.

twenty-one to sixty-nine

Tu as quel âge? – J'ai **vingt et un** ans.	How old are you? – I'm **twenty-one**.
Il y avait **trente et un** étudiants dans la classe.	There were **thirty-one** students in the class.
Il y a **vingt et une** femmes dans ce service.	There are **twenty-one** women in this department.
Il y a **trente et un** jours en janvier.	There are **thirty-one** days in January.
Il y aura **cinquante et une** personnes dans le groupe.	There'll be **fifty-one** people in the group.

When **quatre-vingts** (*eighty*) is on its own, or when it is not followed by any other number, it is spelt with an **–s** at the end. When it is followed by another number, as in **quatre-vingt-un**, **quatre-vingt-deux**, **quatre-vingt-huit** and so on (*eighty-one*, *eighty-two*, *eighty-eight* and so on), the **–s** is dropped. The **–s** at the end of **quatre-vingts** is pronounced like a "z" when it precedes a word beginning with a vowel, for instance in **quatre-vingts ans**, **quatre-vingts euros** and so on.

eighty

Le billet coûte **quatre-vingt-neuf** euros.	The ticket costs **eighty-nine** euros.
Mon grand-père vient d'avoir **quatre-vingts** ans.	My grandad has just turned **eighty**.

BON À SAVOIR!

French speakers tend to read telephone numbers in tens where possible, so when saying 08 13 76 89 98, you'd say **zéro huit**, **treize**, **soixante-seize**, **quatre-vingt-neuf**, **quatre-vingt-dix-huit** (*o-eight*, *thirteen*, *seventy-six*, *eighty-nine*, *ninety-eight*).

Remember that **soixante-dix** (*seventy* – literally *sixty-ten*) and **quatre-vingt-dix** (*ninety* – literally *eighty-ten*) work differently from the other tens. Logically enough, you have to start from ten when counting up, so that *seventy-one* is **soixante et onze**, *seventy-two* is **soixante-douze** and so on. The same applies to **quatre-vingt-dix** (*ninety*).

seventies and nineties

Il est né en **soixante-dix-sept**.	He was born in **seventy-seven**.
Soixante-quinze est le numéro du département de Paris.	**Seventy-five** is the département number of Paris.
Les bleus ont gagné la coupe du monde de football en **quatre-vingt-dix-huit**.	The French national team won the football World Cup in **ninety-eight**.

BON À SAVOIR!

Just as in English, you can name a year from the last century by the last two digits, for example, **quatre-vingt-dix-huit** ('98). It doesn't apply to the noughties and beyond, however, so for '06 you would say **deux mille six** (*two thousand and six*).

100	cent
101	cent un(e)
150	cent cinquante
200	deux cents
300	trois cent(s)
400	quatre cent(s)
500	cinq cent(s)
600	six cent(s)
700	sept cent(s)
800	huit cent(s)
900	neuf cent(s)

cent (*one hundred*) takes an **–s** when it is preceded by a number and when no number follows it, for example **deux cents** (*two hundred*). When it is followed by another number, as in **deux cent un** (*two hundred and one*), the **-s** is dropped.

hundred

Il y a **cent** centimes dans un euro.	There are **one hundred** cents in a euro.
Vous avez *Les Cent un dalmatiens* en DVD?	Do you have *One hundred and one dalmatians* on DVD?
Ça coûte **cent cinquante** euros.	It costs **one hundred and fifty** euros.
Il doit y avoir plus de **deux cents** personnes.	There must be over **two hundred** people.
Il y avait à peu près **cinq cent cinquante** employés dans le bâtiment.	There were around **five hundred and fifty** employees in the building.

BON À SAVOIR!
Don't translate the *and* in *one hundred and one*, *one hundred and two*, *one hundred and twenty* and so on in French. Just give **cent**, **deux cents**, **cinq cents** and so on, followed immediately by the other number.

In French, a space rather than a comma is used to separate thousands and millions.

1 000	mille
1 001	mille un(e)
1 020	mille vingt
1 150	mille cent cinquante
2 000	deux mille
2 500	deux mille cinq cents
3 400	trois mille quatre cents
100 000	cent mille

one thousand to one hundred thousand

Cette ville existe depuis plus de **mille** ans.	There's been a town here for over **a thousand** years.
Ils se sont mariés en **deux mille deux**.	They got married in **two thousand and two**.
Combien font **cent mille** euros en livres?	How much is **one hundred thousand** euros in pounds?
Ils vont payer **deux cent cinquante-six mille** livres pour leur nouvelle maison.	They're paying **two hundred and fifty-six thousand** pounds for their new house.

1 000 000	un million
1 000 000 000	mille millions
1 000 000 000 000	un milliard

To talk about a million or a billion things, you use **un million de** and **un milliard de**.

one million to one billion

Il a gagné **un million de** livres à la loterie.	He won **a million** pounds on the lottery.
Le gouvernement a déjà dépensé **deux milliards de** livres dans ce projet.	The government has already spent **two billion** pounds on this project.

In French, a decimal **virgule** (*comma*) is used rather than a decimal point.

...point...

zéro **virgule** cinq (0,5)	nought **point** five (0.5)
quatre-vingt-dix-neuf **virgule** neuf (99,9)	ninety-nine **point** nine (99.9)
six **virgule** quatre-vingt-neuf (6,89)	six **point** eighty-nine (6.89)
Ils ont augmenté les taux d'intérêt à quatre **virgule** cinq pour cent. (4,5%)	They've put interest rates up to four **point** five per cent. (4.5%)

To read prices that include both euros and cents, put **euros** in the middle between the euro and the cent figures. The word **centimes** is optional.

euros and cents

Ça fera **dix-huit euros quatre-vingt-dix-neuf centimes**. (18,99 €)	That'll be **eighteen euros and ninety-nine cents**. (€18.99)
Ça m'a coûté **soixante-cinq euros vingt**. (65€20)	It cost me **sixty-five euros twenty**. (€65.20)

BON À SAVOIR!
When you write prices in figures in French, you put the euro symbol after the figure or instead of the comma. Note that although both euros and dollars are divided into cents in English, in French euro cents are mostly called **centimes d'euros**, while dollar cents are **cents**.

kilos and grams

Il me faut **un kilo de** pommes de terre.	I need **a kilo of** potatoes.
Je voudrais **deux cents grammes de** viande hachée.	I'd like **two hundred grams of** mince.
Je peux avoir **une livre de** tomates?	Can I have **half a kilo of** tomatoes?

BON À SAVOIR!
The feminine word **une livre** is used to mean *half a kilo*. It can also mean a *pound sterling*. The masculine word **un livre** means *a book*.

litres

À combien est **le litre de** carburant?	How much is **a litre of** petrol?
Il faut **un demi-litre de** lait pour cette recette.	You need **half a litre of** milk for this recipe.

kilometres, metres and centimetres

Il faisait du **cent quarante kilomètres à l'heure**.	He was doing o**ne hundred and forty kilometres an hour**.
On est à **trente kilomètres de** Saint-Malo.	We're **thirty kilometres from** Saint-Malo.
Je mesure **un mètre soixante-six**.	I'm **one metre sixty-six centimetres** tall.
Ça fait **vingt centimètres de long sur dix de large**.	It's **twenty centimetres long by ten wide**.

percentages

Le taux d'inflation est de **deux virgule cinq pour cent**.	The inflation rate is **two point five per cent**.
Cinquante-cinq pour cent ont voté non au référendum.	**Fifty-five per cent** voted no in the referendum.

temperature

Les températures oscilleront entre **douze** et **quinze degrés**.	The temperatures will vary between **twelve** and **fifteen degrees**.
Il fait **trente degrés**.	It's **thirty degrees**.

There are times when you'll need to use numbers to show the order of things. As in English, there's another set of numbers you use for this. Unlike in English, they are never used in dates, except for **premier** (*first*). In English we can write figures with *-st,- nd*, *-rd*, *-th* on the end as required (*1st, 2nd, 3rd, 4th* and so on). Similarly in French you write the figure followed by **er** or **re** (*feminine*) for 1st or **e** for any other figure. These abbreviations can be given an **-s** in the plural.

1st	premier, première (1er, 1re)
2nd	deuxième, second(e) (2ème, 2e)
3rd	troisième (3ème, 3e)
4th	quatrième (4ème, 4e)
5th	cinquième (5ème, 5e)
6th	sixième (6ème, 6e)
7th	septième (7ème, 7e)
8th	huitième (8ème, 8e)
9th	neuvième (9ème, 9e)
10th	dixième (10ème, 10e)
100th	centième (100ème, 100e)
1000th	millième (1000ème, 1000e)

Once you can count in French, it is very easy to form these numbers; substitute the final **-e** with **-ième** for numbers that end with an **-e** (**onze**, **quinze**, **quarante**, **soixante** and so on). Add **-ième** onto the end of the words that end with a consonant (**trois**, **vingt**, **quatre-vingt-dix**). All you need to memorize is that **cinq** becomes **cinquième** and **neuf** becomes **neuvième**.

first, second, third

Ils fêtent leur **premier** anniversaire de mariage aujourd'hui.	They're celebrating their **first** wedding anniversary today.
C'est la **première** fois qu'il vient ici.	This is the **first** time he's been here.
C'est mon **deuxième** séjour en Provence.	This is my **second** trip to Provence.
Il est arrivé **troisième** de la course.	He came **third** in the race.

1st, 2nd, 3rd

C'est la **1ʳᵉ** porte à droite.	It's the **1st** door on the right.
Il travaille sur la **5ᵉ** avenue.	He works on **5th** Avenue.
Il est arrivé **20ᵉ** au classement.	He's ranked **20th**.

L'HEURE – THE TIME

In French, as in English, you have to use numbers when talking about the time. Use **il est... heures** (*it's... o'clock*) to say what time it is in French. Remember that you can't omit the word **heures** in French as you can in English with *o' clock*, apart from when you use **midi** (*midday*) or **minuit** (*midnight*).

It's...o'clock

Il est une **heure**.	**It's** one **o'clock**.
Il est minuit.	**It's** midnight.
Il est midi.	**It's** midday.
Il est six **heures**.	**It's** six **o'clock**.
Il est trois **heures** du matin.	**It's** three in the morning.
Il est quatre **heures** de l'après-midi.	**It's** four **o'clock** in the afternoon.

BON À SAVOIR!

You use **du matin** to talk about the early hours of the morning. For example, **deux heures du matin** is *two o'clock in the morning*.

The word *past* is usually not translated in French; the minutes follow the hours directly (**une heure cinq** – *five past one*) except for *quarter past* and *half past* where **et** is used: **deux heures et quart** (*quarter past two*), **une heure et demie** (*half past one*) and so on.

It's...past...

Il est une heure vingt-cinq.	**It's** twenty-five **past** one.
Il est six heures cinq.	**It's** five **past** six.
Il est une heure **et** quart.	**It's** quarter **past** one.
Il est cinq heures **et** demie.	**It's** half **past** five.

Put **moins le** before **quart** to say *quarter to*, for example, **il est minuit moins le quart** (*it's quarter to midnight*). For other times using *to*, put **moins** and the number of minutes directly after the hours, for example, **il est midi moins cinq** (*it's five to twelve*).

It's...to...

Il est une heure **moins le** quart.	**It's** quarter **to** one.
Il est une heure **moins** vingt.	**It's** twenty **to** one.
Il est huit heures **moins** dix.	**It's** ten **to** eight.
Il est trois heures **moins** cinq.	**It's** five **to** three.

When you're in a French-speaking country, you may need to find out what the time is or what time something is happening. Except when asking **Quelle heure est-il?** (*What's the time?*), you'll need to ask **À quelle heure...?** (*What time...?*).

What time...?

À quelle heure est le prochain train pour Albi?	**What time**'s the next train for Albi?
À quelle heure ça commence?	**What time** does it start?
On se retrouve **à quelle heure**?	**What time** shall we meet?
Quelle heure est-il?	**What's the time**?
Vous avez **quelle heure**?	**What time** do you make it?

To say what time something is happening at, use **à**: **à une heure** (*at one o'clock*), **à deux heures** (*at two o'clock*), **à trois heures et demie** (*at half past three*) and so on. To say when something is happening by, use **avant**: **avant une heure** (*by one o'clock*), **avant deux heures** (*by two o'clock*), **avant trois heures et demie** (*by half past three*) and so on.

at ...

Ça commence **à** sept heures.	It starts **at** seven o'clock.
Le train part **à** sept heures et demie.	The train leaves **at** seven thirty.
Je te vois **à** trois heures et demie.	I'll see you **at** half past three.
On peut se donner rendez-vous **à** cinq heures et quart.	We can arrange to meet up **at** quarter past five.

by...

Est-ce que tu peux y être **avant** trois heures?	Can you be there **by** three o'clock?
Il faut que nous ayons terminé **avant** une heure moins le quart.	We must be finished **by** quarter to one.

du matin is often used where in English we'd say *am*. **de l'après-midi** and **du soir** are used where we'd say *pm*. It is also quite common to use the 24-hour clock in French in order to distinguish between the morning and the afternoon.

at... am/pm

Je me lève **à huit heures du matin**.	I get up **at eight am**.
Je rentre à la maison **à quatre heures de l'après-midi**.	I go home again **at four pm**.
Je vais au lit **à vingt-trois heures**.	I go to bed **at eleven pm**.
Rendez-vous **à midi pile**.	Let's meet **at 12 noon precisely**.
Nous sommes sortis **vers huit heures**.	We went out **at around eight pm**.

LISTEN OUT FOR

Here are some key phrases you may hear to do with the time and numbers.

Le train de Paris part à 13h55 (treize heures cinquante-cinq).	The train for Paris leaves at 13:55.
Le train de 14h15 (quatorze heures quinze) pour Strasbourg partira de la voie deux.	The 14:15 train to Strasbourg will depart from platform two.
Le vol numéro 307 (trois cent sept) à destination de Londres décollera à 20h45 (vingt heures quarante cinq).	Flight number 307 for London is due to take off at 20:45.
Le vol 909 (neuf cent neuf) en provenance de Paris est à l'heure.	Flight 909 from Paris is on time.
Le bus arrive à Calais à 19h10 (dix-neuf heures dix).	The coach gets in to Calais at 19:10.
Il doit être onze heures à peu près.	It must be about eleven.

LA DURÉE – SAYING HOW LONG

If you want to say that something will happen in so many minutes' time or in so many days' time, use **dans** to mean *in*. Use **en** instead to say how long something takes or took to do.

in...

Je serai de retour **dans** vingt minutes.	I'll be back **in** twenty minutes.
Elle sera ici **dans** une semaine.	She'll be here **in** a week.
Il a fini l'exercice **en** seulement trois minutes.	He completed the exercise **in** only three minutes.
Je peux probablement faire le travail **en** une heure ou deux.	I can probably do the job **in** an hour or two.

To ask how long something lasts, use **Combien de temps...?**
(*How long...?*). The verb **durer** (*to last*) is a useful one to know for
asking such questions.

How long...?

Combien de temps dure le film?	**How long**'s the film?
Combien de temps va durer la visite?	**How long** will the tour take?
Tu en as pour **combien de temps**?	**How long** will you be?
Combien de temps est-ce que ça va te prendre pour peindre le mur?	**How long will it take you to** paint the wall?
Ça va prendre combien de temps pour arriver en Grande-Bretagne?	**How long will it take to** get to Great Britain?
Ça prend combien de temps pour aller dans le centre?	**How long does it take to** get to the centre?

If you want to say how long something takes, use **ça prend** or **ça met** (*it takes*).

It takes...

Ça prend moins de vingt minutes pour aller dans le centre à pied.	**It takes** less than twenty minutes to walk to the town centre.
Ça prend cinq minutes à préparer.	**It takes** five minutes to make.
Ça m'**a pris** deux heures pour aller à pied au village.	**It took** me two hours to walk to the village.
Ça met environ quarante minutes **à** cuire.	**It takes** about forty minutes **to** cook.
Ils mettent longtemps **à** te servir ici.	**They take** a long time **to** serve you here.

LES SAISONS – THE SEASONS

The seasons in French are used in the same way as in English.

le printemps	spring
l'été	summer
l'automne	autumn
l'hiver	winter

To say *in autumn*, *in winter*, *in summer* and so on, use **en automne**, **en hiver**, **en été**, but *in spring* is **au printemps**.

in...

C'est **au printemps** qu'on a le meilleur temps ici.	We get the best weather here **in spring**.
On ne part pas camper **en hiver**.	We don't go camping **in winter**.
Ils se sont mariés **en été** 2013.	They got married **in the summer of** 2013.
Je préfère **le printemps**.	I like **the spring** best.
Je n'aime pas du tout **l'hiver**.	I don't like **winter** at all.

To clarify whether you're talking about *this summer* or *last summer*, *this winter* or *next winter*, you use **cet** (*this*) (or **ce** for **printemps**), **prochain** (*next*) and **dernier** (*last*).

this/last/next...

On va en Bretagne **cet été**.	We're going to Brittany **this summer**.
Je vais à Avoriaz **cet hiver**.	I'm going to Avoriaz **this winter**.
Il a fait assez doux **l'hiver dernier**.	It was quite mild **last winter**.
Elle va avoir son bébé **le printemps prochain**.	She's expecting her baby **next spring**.

LES MOIS DE L'ANNÉE – THE MONTHS OF THE YEAR ■

The months of the year are always written with a small letter in French.

janvier	January
février	February
mars	March
avril	April
mai	May
juin	June
juillet	July
août	August
septembre	September
octobre	October
novembre	November
décembre	December

To say *in January*, *in February* and so on in French you use what you'd expect: **en janvier**, **en février**, and so forth.

in...

Mon anniversaire est **en août**.	My birthday is **in August**.
On partira probablement en vacances **en mai**.	We'll probably go on holiday **in May**.
J'ai rendu visite à des amis à Perpignan **en septembre**.	I visited some friends in Perpignan **in September**.
On va aller à la montagne pour nos vacances **en août**.	We're going to go to the mountains for our holidays **this August**.

last.../next...

Où est-ce que tu as passé tes vacances **en juin dernier**?	Where did you go on holiday **last June**?
J'espère aller en Amérique du Sud **en juillet prochain**.	I'm hoping to go to South America **next July**.

If you want to say that something is happening *at the beginning of* or *at the end of* a month, you can use the expressions **début** and **fin**.

Elle commence à l'université **début** octobre.	She starts university **at the beginning of** October.
Les grandes vacances commencent **fin** juin.	The summer holidays start **at the end of** June.
Ils déménagent **à la mi-**juin.	They're moving house **in the middle of** June.

LES DATES – DATES

To ask what the date is, you can use **Quelle est la date d'aujourd'hui?** (*What's the date today?*). When talking about dates, French speakers use **deux** (*two*), **trois** (*three*), **quatre** (*four*) and so on rather than **deuxième** (*second*), **troisième** (*third*) and so on. For the *first* of the month, however, **premier** is used.

It's the...of...

On est le premier juillet.	**It's the first of** July.
On est le 28 décembre aujourd'hui.	**It's** December **28th** today.
C'est le dix janvier demain.	Tomorrow**'s the tenth of** January.
C'était le 20 novembre hier.	**It was 20th** November yesterday.
On est le jeudi **2** mars.	**It's** Thursday, **2nd** March.

> **BON À SAVOIR!**
> When writing a letter, write the date in the form **lundi 19 mars 2015**.

To say what date something is happening or happened on, use **le** before the number.

on the...of...

Il est né **le quatorze février** 1990.	He was born **on the fourteenth of February**, 1990.
Il est mort **le vingt-trois avril** 1616.	He died **on April the twenty-third**, 1616.
Ils prévoyaient de se marier **le 18 octobre** 2015.	They were planning to get married **on October 18th** 2015.
Où est-ce que tu penses que tu seras **le vingt octobre**?	Where do you think you'll be **on the twentieth of October**?

The days of the week are always written with a small letter in French.

lundi	Monday
mardi	Tuesday
mercredi	Wednesday
jeudi	Thursday
vendredi	Friday
samedi	Saturday
dimanche	Sunday

To say what day it is, just say **on est jeudi** (*it's Thursday*), **on est samedi** (*it's Saturday*). You can also say **c'est jeudi aujourd'hui** (*today's Thursday*) and so on.

It's...

On est quel jour aujourd'hui? – **On est** jeudi.	What day's today? – **It's** Thursday.
On est bien lundi aujourd'hui?	**It's** Monday today, isn't it?
Super! **C'est** samedi aujourd'hui.	Great! **It's** Saturday today.

When making arrangements or saying when something happened you may want to specify the day. In French it's easy. Just use the day in question **lundi**, **vendredi** to mean *on Monday*, *on Friday* and so on.

on...

Je vais à Dublin **lundi**.	I'm going to Dublin **on Monday**.
C'est mon anniversaire **mardi**.	It's my birthday **on Tuesday**.
On les verra **mercredi**.	We'll see them **on Wednesday**.

To say that something regularly happens on a particular day use **le** and the day in question. So **le lundi** means *on Mondays*.

Le samedi on va à la gym.	We go to the gym **on Saturdays**.
On sort toujours **le vendredi**.	We always go out **on Fridays**.
Il est toujours en retard **le lundi**.	He's always late in **on Mondays**.

If you want to specify the time of day, add **matin** (*morning*), **après-midi** (*afternoon*) or **soir** (*evening, night*) after the day.

on... morning/afternoon/evening/night

Je vais chez le garagiste **mardi matin**.	I'm going to the garage **on Tuesday morning**.
Je te verrai **vendredi après-midi**.	I'll see you **on Friday afternoon**.
Il y avait un bon film à la télévision **dimanche soir**.	There was a good film on television **on Sunday evening**.
Qu'est-ce que tu fais **samedi soir**?	What are you doing on **Saturday night**?

You may want to say *every Monday*, *every Sunday* and so on. In French, you say **tous les lundis**, **tous les dimanches** and so forth.

every...

On l'appelle **tous les lundis**.	We ring her **every Monday**.
Il joue au golf **tous les samedis**.	He plays golf **every Saturday**.
Je les voyais **tous les vendredis**.	I used to see them **every Friday**.
On fait le ménage **tous les dimanches matin**.	We do the cleaning **every Sunday morning**.

You may want to say that you do something every other day, week and so on. To say every other use **un... sur deux**.

every other...

Il a les enfants **un week-end sur deux**.	He has the children **every other weekend**.
On joue au foot **un samedi sur deux**.	We play football **every other Saturday**.

You can use **ce** (*this*), **dernier** (*last*) and **prochain** (*next*) to specify a day in particular. You can also use the day of the week on its own, which is an implicit way of saying **ce** (*this*).

this/next/last...

C'est notre anniversaire de mariage **ce vendredi**.	It's our wedding anniversary **this Friday**.
Je pars en vacances **mardi**.	I'm going on holiday **this Tuesday**.
Je t'ai envoyé les photos par e-mail **vendredi dernier**.	I emailed you the photos **last Friday**.
Est-ce que **vendredi prochain** te conviendrait?	Would **next Friday** suit you?
Vendredi de la semaine prochaine, c'est mon anniversaire.	It's my birthday **on Friday week**.
On a décidé de se voir **vendredi de la semaine prochaine**.	We've arranged to meet up **a week on Friday**.

If you want to ask what day something is happening, use **Quel jour...?** (*What day…?*).

What day...?

La réunion est **quel jour**? – Mardi.	**What day**'s the meeting? – Tuesday.
Tu sais **quel jour** il vient? – Il vient mercredi.	Do you know **what day** he's coming? – He's coming on Wednesday.
Tu y es allé **quel jour**? – Mardi je crois.	**Which day** did you go there? – Tuesday, I think.

If you want to talk about the past, the present or the future, you can use a number of phrases in French.

yesterday

hier	**yesterday**
hier matin	**yesterday morning**
hier après-midi	**yesterday afternoon**
hier soir	**yesterday evening**, **last night**
la nuit dernière	**last night** (*at night-time*)
avant-hier	**the day before yesterday**
Michael est venu me voir **hier**.	Michael came to see me **yesterday**.
Béatrice a appelé **avant-hier**.	Béatrice rang up **the day before yesterday**.

today

aujourd'hui	**today**
On est mardi **aujourd'hui**.	**Today**'s Tuesday.

tomorrow

demain	**tomorrow**
demain matin	**tomorrow morning**
demain soir	**tomorrow evening**, **tomorrow night**
après-demain	**the day after tomorrow**
On est mercredi **demain**.	**Tomorrow** will be Wednesday.
Il faut que je me lève tôt **demain matin**.	I've got to be up early **tomorrow morning**.
On va à une fête **demain soir**.	We're going to a party **tomorrow night**.

BON À SAVOIR!

Remember that the English word *night* may be translated by **la soirée** or **le soir** (*evening*) and **la nuit** (*night-time*) in French.

To say that something happened a certain length of time ago, use **il y a** followed by the period of time in question.

...ago

Elle m'a appelé **il y a une semaine**.	She called me **a week ago**.
Ils ont emménagé dans leur maison **il y a une dizaine de jours**.	They moved into their house **some ten days ago**.
Il est né **il y a trois ans**.	He was born **three years ago**.

One way to talk about how long you've been doing something is to use **cela fait** (or, more informally, **ça fait**) followed by the length of time, the word **que** and the verb in the present tense. For more information on the present tense, see page 272.

for...

Cela fait dix mois **que** nous vivons ici.	We've been living here **for** ten months.
Ça fait dix ans **qu'**ils sont mariés.	They've been married **for** ten years.
Ça fait une semaine **que** je ne l'ai pas vue.	I haven't seen her **for** a week.

You can also use **depuis** (*for*) with a verb in the present tense to say how long something has been happening. For more information on the present tense, see page 272.

for...

Il pleut **depuis** trois jours.	It's been raining **for** three days
Je ne les ai pas vus **depuis** trois semaines.	I haven't seen them **for** three weeks.
Ils ne se sont pas parlé **depuis** des mois.	They haven't spoken to each other **for** months.
J'attends ici **depuis** des heures.	I've been waiting here **for** hours.

L'ALPHABET – THE ALPHABET

When you're in a French-speaking country, you may well need to spell something out in French. French letters are pronounced approximately as shown in the list below. The main difference between the English alphabet and the French one is that French uses accents on vowels (**é**, **à**, **û**, **ë**, etc) and a cedilla on the "c" (**ç**).

A	ah
B	bay
C	say
D	day
E	uh
F	eff
G	jay
H	ash
I	ee
J	jee
K	kah
L	el
M	em
N	en
O	o
P	pay
Q	ku̱
R	err
S	ess
T	tay
U	u̱
V	vay
W	doobluhvay (pronounced like the *v* in *vacancy* in **le wagon** and pronounced as in English in **le web**, **le week-end** and other English loanwords)
X	eeks
Y	ee grayk
Z	zayd

BON À SAVOIR!

All letters are masculine if French. So you would say **ça s'écrit avec un P** (*it's spelt with a P*).

LISTEN OUT FOR

Here are some key phrases you may hear when spelling words out.

Comment ça s'écrit?	How do you spell it?
Est-ce que vous pouvez l'épeler?	Can you spell that for me?
Ça s'écrit G-A-U-T-I-E-R.	That's G-A-U-T-I-E-R.
Je vous l'épelle?	Shall I spell it for you?
Ça s'écrit avec un B.	It's spelt with a B.
B comme Bordeaux.	B for Bordeaux.
Moreau, avec un M majuscule.	That's Moreau with a capital M.
Ça s'écrit avec deux F.	It's spelt with a double F.
Avec un L ou deux?	Is that with one L or two?
Ça devrait être en majuscules.	That should be in capitals.
C'est tout en minuscules.	It's all in small letters.
Comment est-ce qu'on prononce 'ch'?	How do you say 'ch'?
Est-ce que vous pouvez répéter, s'il vous plaît?	Please can you repeat that?

Interesting days and dates

• The French national holiday (**la fête nationale**), known as *Bastille Day* in English, is the 14th of July. French people simply call it **le quatorze juillet**. France has many more bank holidays than the UK, mainly because of all the important dates in the Catholic calendar.

• In Belgium, Switzerland, Quebec and in some parts of France and the former African colonies of Belgium (DRC, Rwanda, Burundi), many people don't use **soixante-dix** (70), **quatre-vingts** (80) and **quatre-vingt-dix** (90) but **septante**, **octante** or **huitante**, and **nonante** instead.

• New Year's Eve, **le 31 décembre**, is also called **la Saint-Sylvestre** in France. New Year's Day is **le premier de l'An**.

• In French-speaking countries the dates of famous events are sometimes commemorated in street names. For example you could find in many towns **l'avenue du 11 novembre** (the date of the WWI armistice).

• You might encounter the word **tantôt**, which is sometimes very confusing even for French speakers! It may mean *soon*, *a little earlier* or *a little later*, and *afternoon*, depending on whether you are in Canada, Belgium or a certain part of France. The most common usage is *sometimes... at other times...* (**tantôt triste... tantôt joyeux...** *sometimes sad, at other times happy*).

• Most Christian names are associated with a Saint's day in French. If it's your Saint's day, people will wish you **Bonne fête!** (*Happy Saint's Day!*). As part of the weather forecast on most TV channels, the presenter reminds the viewers which Saint you are celebrating the following day by saying **Bonne fête à tous les Matthieu** (*Happy Saint's Day to all Matthews*) or whatever name it may be.

In summary...

Bon, résumons... – So, to sum up...

This unit gives you quick access to all the important French structures that you'll have learned in the individual units. They are grouped by function to help you find what you're looking for.

CONTENTS

In summary...

APOLOGIZING

There are several ways you can say *sorry* in French. You can say
excuse-moi to someone you call **tu** and **excusez-moi** to someone
you call **vous**. Alternatively, you can just say **pardon**, especially if
you want to get past someone or if you've bumped into them.

Excuse-moi...

Excuse-moi, je ne savais pas.	**Sorry**, I didn't know.
Excusez-moi, je me suis trompé de numéro.	**Sorry**, I've dialled the wrong number.
Excusez-moi de ne pas vous avoir prévenus avant.	**Sorry** for not letting you know sooner.

Pardon

Pardon! Je peux passer?	**Sorry**! Can I get past?
Pardon! Je t'ai fait mal?	**Sorry**! Did I hurt you?

Another way to say *I'm sorry* is to use **je suis désolé** (or for a
woman **je suis désolée**). You can use **je suis désolé** not only
when you're apologizing but also when you're sympathizing with
someone.

Je suis désolé

Je suis vraiment **désolé**.	**I'm** truly **sorry**.
Je suis désolée de ne pas t'avoir rappelé plus tôt.	**I'm sorry** I didn't call you back earlier.
Je suis désolé pour ce qu'il s'est passé.	**I'm sorry** about what happened.

ASKING FOR AND GIVING EXPLANATIONS

Use **Pourquoi (est-ce que)...?** (*Why...?*) when asking for an explanation. Use **parce que** (*because*) when giving an explanation.

Pourquoi...?

Pourquoi est-ce que vous riez?	**Why** are you laughing?
Pourquoi tu ne veux pas venir avec nous?	**Why** don't you want to come with us?
Pourquoi pas?	**Why** not?

parce que...

Je ne t'en ai pas parlé **parce que** je ne voulais pas t'inquiéter.	I didn't tell you **because** I didn't want to worry you.
J'ai dû partir tôt **parce que** j'avais une réunion.	I had to leave early **because** I had a meeting.

ASKING FOR INFORMATION

When you're asking for information you will need to use question words, for example, **Qu'est-ce que...?** (*What...?*), **Quel...?** (*Which...?*), **Quand...?** (*When...?*), **Où...?** (*Where...?*) and so on.

Qu'est-ce que...?

Qu'est-ce que c'est?	**What** is it?
Qu'est-ce que tu fais dans la vie?	**What** do you do for a living?
Qu'est-ce qu'il a dit?	**What** did he say?
Qu'est-ce qui passe au cinéma en ce moment?	**What's** on at the cinema at the moment?

Quel est...?

Quel est le numéro de l'agence immobilière?	**What's** the number of the letting agency?
Quels sont vos tarifs?	**What are** your rates?
Quelle heure **est**-il?	**What** time **is** it?

> **BON À SAVOIR!**
> Remember to use **quel** for masculine nouns and **quelle** for feminine nouns.

Quand est-ce que...?

Quand est-ce que tu viens dîner à la maison?	**When** are you coming around for dinner?
Quand est-ce que vous vous mariez?	**When** are you getting married?
Quand est le prochain vol pour Londres?	**When** is the next flight to London?

Où...?

Où est le commissariat de police?	**Where**'s the police station?
Où sont les toilettes?	**Where** are the toilets?
Où est-ce que je dois signer?	**Where** do I need to sign?
Où se trouve la mairie?	**Where**'s the town hall?

To ask what time something is due to happen, use **À quelle heure...?** (*What time...?*).

À quelle heure...?

À quelle heure ferme le musée?	**What time** does the museum close?
À quelle heure commence le film?	**What time** does the film start?
À quelle heure est-ce que tu penses partir?	**What time** are you thinking of going?

You use either **Est-ce qu'il y a...?** or **Il y a...?** for both *Is there...?* and *Are there...?*

Est-ce qu'il y a...?

Est-ce qu'il y a une boulangerie dans le quartier?	**Is there** a baker's in the area?
Est-ce qu'il y a des noix dans ce gâteau?	**Are there** any nuts in this cake?
Il y a un menu pour enfants?	**Is there** a children's menu?

To ask how you do something or what something is like, use **Comment...?**.

Comment...?

Comment ça va?	**How** are you?
Comment on fait pour avoir des billets?	**How** do you get tickets?
C'est **comment** l'Ardèche?	**What**'s the Ardèche **like**?
Comment vous appelez-vous?	**What**'s your name?

To ask *how much* or *how many*, use a phrase containing **combien**.

Combien...?

Combien coûte un billet pour Lyon?	**How much is** a ticket to Lyon?
Il reste combien d'oignons?	**How many** onions **are left**?
On met **combien de temps** pour aller à Nice?	**How long** does it take to get to Nice?

212

The simplest way to ask for permission to do something is by using **Est-ce que je peux...?** (*Can I...?*) or **Est-ce que je pourrais...?** (*Could I...?*), followed by a verb in the infinitive. **peux** and **pourrais** come from the verb **pouvoir** (*to be able*). For more information on **pouvoir**, see page 284.

Est-ce que je peux...?

Est-ce que je peux utiliser le téléphone?	**Can I** use the phone?
Je peux vous payer en deux fois?	**Can I** pay you in two instalments?

Est-ce que je pourrais...?

Est-ce que je pourrais rester une semaine de plus?	**Could I** stay for another week?
Je pourrais garer ma voiture ici?	**Could I** park my car here?

Alternatively you can use **Est-ce que ça vous dérange si...?** (*Do you mind if...?*) followed by a verb in the present tense. For more information on the present, see page 272.

Est-ce que ça vous dérange si...?

Est-ce que ça vous dérange si je fume?	**Do you mind if** I smoke?
Est-ce que ça vous dérange si j'invite quelques amis ce soir?	**Do you mind if** I have a few friends over tonight?
Ça vous dérange si j'ouvre la fenêtre?	**Do you mind if** I open the window?

To ask for things in French you can simply name what you want and say **s'il vous plaît** (*please*).

Un..., s'il vous plaît

Un aller simple pour Lille, **s'il vous plaît**.	**A** single to Lille, **please**.
Une limonade, **s'il vous plaît**.	**A** lemonade, **please**.
Deux baguettes **et quatre** croissants, **s'il vous plaît**.	**Two** baguettes **and four** croissants, **please**.

To say what you'd like or what you want, you can use **je voudrais** (*I'd like*), which comes from the verb **vouloir**. For more information on **vouloir**, see page 285.

Je voudrais...

Je voudrais un carnet de timbres, s'il vous plaît.	**I'd like** a book of stamps, please.
Je voudrais deux entrées pour l'exposition, s'il vous plaît.	**I'd like** two tickets for the exhibition, please.
On voudrait un appartement avec vue sur la mer.	**We'd like** a flat with a sea view.

Another way of asking whether something is available is to use **Est-ce que vous avez...?** (*Do you have...?*). **avez** comes from the verb **avoir** (*to have*). For more information on **avoir**, see page 280.

Est-ce que vous avez...?

Est-ce que vous avez de la crème solaire?	**Do you have** suncream?
Vous avez une adresse électronique?	**Do you have** an email address?

To say what you're looking for you can use **je cherche** (*I'm looking for*). For more information on **–er** verbs like **chercher**, see page 269.

Je cherche...

Je cherche un endroit pour camper.	**I'm looking for** somewhere to camp.
Je cherche un restaurant végétarien.	**I'm looking for** a vegetarian restaurant.

To ask someone if they can do something for you, use **Est-ce que vous pouvez...?** (*Can you...?*) or **Est-ce que vous pourriez...?** (*Could you...?*) and then the verb in the infinitive. **pouvez** and **pourriez** come from the verb **pouvoir** (*to be able*). For more information on **pouvoir**, see page 284.

Est-ce que vous pouvez...?

Est-ce que vous pouvez me donner un sac, s'il vous plaît?	**Can you** give me a carrier bag, please?
Est-ce que vous pouvez me photocopier le plan?	**Can you** photocopy the map for me?
Vous pouvez nous apporter la carte des vins?	**Can you** bring us the wine list?

Est-ce que vous pourriez...?

Est-ce que vous pourriez déplacer votre voiture, s'il vous plaît?	**Could you** move your car, please?
Vous pourriez nous donner un reçu?	**Could you** give us a receipt?

You can use **donnez-moi** (or the **tu** form **donne-moi**) followed by **s'il vous plaît** to mean *Can I have..., please?* especially when asking for something at a counter or when asking someone to pass you something.

Donnez-moi...

Donnez-moi une baguette, s'il vous plaît.	**Can I have** a baguette, please?
Donne-moi ton stylo, s'il te plaît.	**Can I have** your pen, please?

If you need to complain, you may want to use **il y a** and **il n'y a pas de** to talk about what there is and what there isn't. Both *there is* and *there are* are **il y a** in French.

Il y a...

Il y a des cafards dans l'appartement.	**There are** cockroaches in the flat.
Il n'y a pas d'eau chaude.	**There isn't any** hot water.

You can also use **il n'y a pas assez de** to say that there isn't enough of something.

Il n'y a pas assez de...

Il n'y a pas assez de renseignements.	**There isn't enough** information.
Il n'y a pas assez de chaises.	**There aren't enough** chairs.

When something has run out, you can use **il ne reste plus de**.

Il ne reste plus de...

Il ne reste plus de papier toilette chez les dames.	**There isn't any** toilet paper **left** in the ladies.
Il ne reste plus de dépliants.	**There aren't any** leaflets **left**.

DESCRIBING PEOPLE AND THINGS

When you're describing people or things, use **il est** (*he is*), or **elle est** (*she is*) or **c'est** (*it is*) followed by an adjective.

Il est...

Il est très grand.	**He's** very tall.
Elle est sympa.	**She's** nice.
Elle n'**est** pas très vieille.	**She's** not very old.

C'est...

C'est beau.	**It's** beautiful.
C'est loin.	**It's** a long way away.
C'est vraiment lourd.	**It's** really heavy.

avoir is used to talk about characteristics that people have. Remember that it's also used with **ans** (*years*) to talk about ages.

Il a...

Il a les cheveux gris.	**He's got** grey hair.
Elle a les yeux bleus.	**She's got** blue eyes.
Il a le teint mat.	**He has** a dark complexion.
J'ai vingt-deux **ans**.	**I'm** twenty two.

To say what someone is wearing, use **il porte** or **elle porte**.

Elle porte...

Elle porte une robe verte.	**She's wearing** a green dress.
Il porte un jean.	**He's wearing** jeans.
Il porte des baskets.	**He's wearing** trainers.

To explain what the problem is, use **il y a** to say both *there is* and *there are*.

Il y a...

Il y a un bruit bizarre.	**There's** a strange noise.
Il n'y a pas de serviettes dans ma chambre.	**There aren't** any towels in my room.
Il y a eu un accident.	**There's been** an accident.

BON À SAVOIR!

The last example uses **il y a** with the past tense of the verb **avoir** (*to have*). For more information on **avoir**, see page 280.

To say what you can't do, use **je n'arrive pas à** (*I can't*) followed by the infinitive.

Je n'arrive pas à...

Je n'arrive pas à démarrer la voiture.	**I can't** get the car to start.
Je n'arrive pas à joindre ma famille.	**I can't** get in touch with my family.
On n'arrive pas à faire marcher le chauffage.	**We can't** get the heating to work.

You use **je ne sais pas...** instead to mean *I can't* when you want to say *I don't know how to*.

Je ne sais pas...

Je ne sais pas bien parler français.	**I can't** speak French very well.
Il ne sait pas conduire.	**He can't** drive.

EXPRESSING OPINIONS ■■■■■■■■

Use **je pense que**, **je trouve que** and **je crois que** to mean *I think*. When these phrases are used in the negative, for example, **je ne pense pas que**, the verb that follows must be in the subjunctive. For more information on the subjunctive, see page 274.

Je pense que...

Je pense que tu devrais réserver à l'avance.	**I think** you should book in advance.
Je pense qu'il va pleuvoir.	**I think** it's going to rain.
Je ne pense pas que ce soit une bonne idée.	**I don't think** it's a good idea.
Qu'est-ce que tu en penses?	**What do you think**?

Je trouve que...

Je trouve que c'est un peu cher.	**I think** it's a bit expensive.
Je trouve que tu as raison.	**I think** you're right.
Je ne trouve pas que ce soit un très bon film.	**I don't think** it's a very good film.

Je crois que...

Je crois que tu te fais du souci pour rien.	**I think** you're worrying about nothing.
Vous croyez que ça en vaut la peine?	**Do you think** it's worth it?
Je ne crois pas qu'on puisse venir.	**I don't think** we're going to be able to make it.

Use **je suis d'accord** to say that you agree and **je ne suis pas d'accord** to say that you disagree.

Je suis d'accord...

Je suis d'accord avec toi.	**I agree with** you.
Nous sommes tous les deux **d'accord**.	**We** both **agree**.
Je ne suis absolument **pas d'accord**.	I completely **disagree**.

MAKING SUGGESTIONS

Use **on pourrait** (*we could*) if you want to suggest doing something with someone.

On pourrait...

On pourrait aller au cinéma.	**We could** go to the cinema.
On pourrait s'asseoir en terrasse.	**We could** sit outside.

If you want to suggest to someone that you do something, you can turn a simple sentence into a suggestion by raising the tone of your voice and making it a question.

On...?

On prend un verre?	**Shall we have** a drink?
On regarde le menu?	**Shall we have a look at** the menu?

Pourquoi pas...? (or **Pourquoi ne pas...?** if you want to sound more formal) can be used to mean *Why not...?*.

Pourquoi pas...?

Pourquoi pas demander à un vendeur?	**Why not** ask a shop assistant?
Pourquoi ne pas s'arrêter à Paris au passage?	**Why not** stop in Paris on the way?

You can also use **Et si...?** followed by the verb in the imperfect tense to suggest doing something. For more information on the imperfect, see page 272.

Et si...?

Et si on passait la nuit ici?	**How about** spending the night here?
Et si on y allait en bateau?	**How about** going there by ferry?
Et si je demandais à l'agent de police?	**How about if** I asked the police officer?
Et si on louait une voiture?	**How about** hiring a car?

You can ask someone if they'd like to do something using **Est-ce que tu veux…?** or **Est-ce que vous voulez…?** (*Would you like…?*) with the infinitive. **veux** and **voulez** come from the verb **vouloir** (*to want*). For more information on **vouloir**, see page 285.

Est-ce que tu veux…?

Est-ce que tu veux venir prendre un verre?	**Would you like to** come and have a drink?
Est-ce que vous voulez voir la cathédrale?	**Would you like to** see the cathedral?

To ask someone if they fancy something, you can use **Ça te dit de…?** (*Do you fancy…?*) or the **vous** form **Ça vous dit de…?**.

Ça te dit de…?

Ça te dit de manger une glace?	**Do you fancy** an ice cream?
Ça vous dit d'aller prendre un café?	**Do you fancy** going for a coffee?

To offer to do something, you can use **laissez-moi** (or the **tu** form **laisse-moi**) to mean *let me*.

Laissez-moi…

Laissez-moi vous aider.	**Let me** help you.
Laisse-moi porter ta valise.	**Let me** carry your suitcase.

Use **Ça ne vous dérange pas que…?** followed by the subjunctive to ask *Is it OK with you if…?*. For more information on the subjunctive, see page 274.

Ça ne vous dérange pas que…?

Ça ne vous dérange pas que je repasse demain?	**Is it OK with you if** I come back tomorrow?
Ça ne te dérange pas que je t'appelle chez toi?	**Is it OK with you if** I call you at home?

If you want to say what would suit you better, you can use **ça m'arrangerait...** (...would be better for me).

Ça m'arrangerait...

Ça m'arrangerait vendredi.	Friday **would be better for me**.
Ça m'arrangerait de vous retrouver là-bas.	**It would suit** me **better** to meet you there.

SAYING WHAT'S HAPPENED

To talk about what has happened, you use the past tense with **avoir** (to have) or **être** (to be) and the past participle (such as been, given, travelled). You can find out more about the past tense on page 269.

J'ai...

J'ai eu un accident.	**I've had** an accident.
Nous avons vu une agression.	**We've witnessed** a mugging.

Je suis...

Je suis arrivée ce matin.	**I arrived** this morning.
Je me suis cassé la jambe.	**I've broken** my leg.
Il est tombé.	**He's fallen**.

SAYING WHAT YOU HAVE TO DO

To say what you have to do, use **je dois** (*I must*) followed by a verb in the infinitive. **dois** is from the verb **devoir**. For more information on **devoir**, see page 281.

Je dois...

Je dois faire le plein.	**I must** fill up the car.
On doit aller les chercher à l'aéroport.	**We have to** pick them up from the airport.

You can also use **il faut que** followed by a verb in the subjunctive. For more information on the subjunctive, see page 274.

Il faut que...

Il faut que je sois à la gare à 14h00.	**I have to** be at the railway station at 2 pm.
Il faut que tu confirmes la réservation.	**You have to** confirm the reservation.
Il faut qu'on achète du pain.	**We need to** buy some bread.

If you want to say that there is something you need to do, you can use **il faudrait que** followed by a verb in the subjunctive. For more information on the subjunctive, see page 274.

Il faudrait que...

Il faudrait que je trouve une carte.	**I need to** find a map.
Il faudrait que je passe un coup de fil.	**I need to** make a phone call.

To talk about what you should do, use **je devrais** (*I should*) followed by an infinitive. **devrais** is from the verb **devoir**. For more information on **devoir**, see page 281.

Je devrais...

Je devrais y aller.	**I should** go.
Vous devriez venir nous voir.	**You should** come and see us.
On devrait faire un peu de ménage.	**We ought to** do some housework.

SAYING WHAT YOU LIKE, DISLIKE, PREFER ▬▬▬▬

To say what you like, use **j'aime bien** (*I like*), which is not as strong as **j'aime** and **j'adore** (*I love*). To say what you dislike, use **je n'aime pas**. **aime** comes from the verb **aimer** (*to love*). For more information on **aimer**, see page 275.

J'aime bien...

J'aime bien ce tableau.	**I like** this painting.
J'aime beaucoup l'Alsace.	**I like** Alsace **a lot**.
Est-ce que tu l'**aimes**?	**Do you love** him?

J'adore...

J'adore la poésie.	**I love** poetry.
J'adore les films en noir et blanc.	**I love** black and white movies.
Il adore cuisiner.	**He loves** cooking.

Je n'aime pas...

Je n'aime pas l'ail.	**I don't like** garlic.
Je n'aime pas du tout prendre le métro.	**I really dislike** taking the underground.

To say what you prefer, use **je préfère**. To say that you prefer A to B, use **je préfère A à B**. **préfère** comes from the verb **préférer**. For more information on **–er** verbs like **préférer**, see page 270.

Je préfère...

Je préfère la chemise grise.	**I prefer** the grey shirt.
Je préfère le train **au** bus.	**I prefer** the train **to** the bus.
Je préfère la cuisine italienne **à la** cuisine française.	**I prefer** Italian cuisine **to** French cuisine.

SAYING WHAT YOU WANT TO DO

To say what you'd like to do, you can use **je voudrais** and **j'aimerais** (*I'd like*).

Je voudrais...

Je voudrais aller au Musée d'Orsay.	**I'd like to** go to the Musée d'Orsay.
Je voudrais gagner plus d'argent.	**I'd like to** earn more money.
Je voudrais relever mes e-mails.	**I'd like to** check my emails.

J'aimerais...

J'aimerais voir le théâtre romain d'Orange.	**I'd like to** see the Roman theatre in Orange.
On aimerait rester ici un peu plus.	**We'd like to** stay here a little longer.

To talk about what you'd rather do, use **je préfère** and **je préférerais** from the verb **préférer** (*to prefer*). For more information on **–er** verbs like **préférer**, see page 270.

Je préfère...

Je préfère partir tôt le matin.	**I'd rather** leave early in the morning.
Je préférerais louer un petit appartement.	**I'd rather** rent a small flat.
On préfère ne pas laisser les bagages dans la voiture.	**We'd rather not** leave the luggage in the car.

If you want to sound more assertive as to what you want or don't want, you can also use **je veux** (I want) from the verb **vouloir** (to want). For more information on **vouloir**, see page 285.

Je veux...

Je veux envoyer cette lettre en recommandé.	**I want to** send this letter recorded delivery.
Je veux acheter une maison dans la région.	**I want to** buy a house in the area.
Je ne veux pas payer de supplément.	**I don't want to** pay a supplement.

TALKING ABOUT YOUR PLANS

To talk about your plans, you can use either **j'ai l'intention de** or **je compte**. They both mean I'm planning to and are followed by a verb in the infinitive.

J'ai l'intention de...

J'ai l'intention de passer deux semaines en Provence.	**I'm planning to** spend two weeks in Provence.
J'ai l'intention de faire construire une maison.	**I'm planning to** have a house built.
On a l'intention d'apprendre l'espagnol.	**We're planning to** learn Spanish.

Je compte...

Je compte loger chez un ami.	**I' m planning to** stay with a friend.
Je ne compte pas rester ici très longtemps.	**I'm not planning to** stay here very long.
On comptait aller au marché demain matin.	**We were planning to** go to the market tomorrow morning.

If you want to say what you're thinking of doing, you can use **je pense** (*I'm thinking of*) or **je pensais** (*I was thinking of*) followed by a verb in the infinitive.

Je pense...

Je pense m'acheter un iPad®.	**I'm thinking of** buying an iPad®.
Je pense arriver vers cinq heures.	**I think I'll** get there at around five pm.
Je pensais inviter Anne à dîner.	**I was thinking of** inviting Anne for dinner.

One easy way of talking about what you're going to do is to use **je vais** (*I'm going to*) followed by a verb in the infinitive. **vais** comes from the verb **aller** (*to go*). For more information on **aller**, see page 279.

Je vais...

Je vais appeler Sam.	**I'm going to** phone Sam.
Je vais envoyer une carte postale à mes parents.	**I'm going to** send a postcard to my parents.
On va visiter un appartement cette semaine.	**We're going to** view a flat this week.

You can use the present tense to talk about something that you're definitely going to do. For more information on the present tense, see page 272.

Je...

Je pars demain à onze heures.	**I'm leaving** tomorrow at eleven.
Je dîne chez Morgane ce soir.	**I'm having dinner** at Morgane's tonight.
On va au Québec dans deux semaines.	**We're going** to Québec in two weeks.
Elle vient la semaine prochaine.	**She's coming** next week.

To talk about what you hope to do, you can use **j'espère** (*I hope* or *I'm hoping to*) followed by an infinitive, or **j'espère que** followed by a verb in the present or the future tense. For more information on **–er** verbs like **espérer**, see page 270. For more information on the present and future tenses, see page 272.

J'espère...

J'espère y retourner un jour.	**I'm hoping to** go back there one day.
J'espère qu'il est déjà sur place.	**I hope** he's already there.
J'espère qu'on se reverra.	**I hope** we'll see each other again.

To say what you may do, you can use **je vais peut-être...** (*I may*) followed by a verb in the infinitive.

Je vais peut-être...

Je vais peut-être organiser une soirée.	**I may** have a party.
Je vais peut-être prendre un verre avec Thomas ce soir.	**I may** go for a drink with Thomas tonight.
Elle va peut-être s'installer en France.	**She may** move to France permanently.

One-stop phrase shop

Je vous demande pardon? – I beg your pardon?

Every day we use a variety of ready-made phrases that just trip off our tongues in English, such as *take a seat*, *hurry up*, *congratulations*, *happy birthday*, *have a nice day*, *thanks* and *the same to you*. In this unit we'll give you all the phrases of this sort that you'll need in French, so that you can say the appropriate thing with confidence.

CONTENTS

One-stop phrase shop

Creating a good first impression is important, so you'll want to say *hello* to people properly. Just as in English, there are several ways of doing this in French. You can simply use the informal **salut** (*hi*) on its own. You can also use **bonjour** (*good morning* or *good afternoon*) or **bonsoir** (*good evening*) which can be followed by **monsieur/madame/mademoiselle** if you want to sound polite.

Hello

Salut.	Hi.
Bonjour.	Good morning *or* afternoon.
Bonsoir.	Good evening.

BON À SAVOIR!
Salut! can be used to mean both *Hi!* and *Bye!*

Goodbye

Au revoir!	Goodbye!
Au revoir à tous!	Goodbye everyone!
Salut!	Bye!
Bonsoir!	Good night!

BON À SAVOIR!
Bonsoir means both *good evening* and *good night*, so you use it both when arriving and leaving somewhere in the evening. You use **bonne nuit** (*good night*) only at bedtime.

See you...!

À plus tard!	**See you** later!
À demain!	**See you** tomorrow!
À la prochaine!	**See you** again!
À lundi!	**See you** on Monday!

One-stop phrase shop

When you're introduced to someone, you need to know how to reply. **enchanté** or **ravi de faire votre connaissance** are used mostly in formal or business situations these days, and very often people just say **bonjour**.

How do you do?

Bonjour, madame. – Bonjour, monsieur.	How do you do? – How do you do?
Enchanté. – Enchanté.	Pleased to meet you. – Pleased to meet you too.
Ravi de faire votre connaissance. – Moi de même.	Pleased to meet you. – Pleased to meet you too.

You may hear French speakers using **bienvenue à** with the name of a town and **bienvenue en** with the name of most countries or regions.

Welcome to...!

Bienvenue!	Welcome!
Bienvenue en France!	Welcome to France!
Bienvenue à Mâcon!	Welcome to Mâcon!
Soyez les bienvenus à Poitiers!	Welcome to Poitiers!

BON À SAVOIR!
bienvenue au is used with the name of a region or country which is masculine, and **bienvenue aux** with the name of a region or country which is plural.

How lovely to see you!

Ça fait plaisir de te revoir!	How lovely to see you again!
Ça fait une éternité que je ne t'ai pas vu!	I haven't seen you for ages!

As in English, there are several ways you can ask someone how they are in French and a variety of ways to reply.

How are you?

Comment ça va? – Bien, merci et toi?	**How are you**? – Fine thanks, and you?
Comment allez-vous? – Bien, merci et vous?	**How are you**? – Fine thanks, and you?
Ça va?	**How are you**?
Ça va bien?	**How's things**?
Salut! **Quoi de neuf**?	Hi! **How's tricks**?
Comment tu te portes?	**How are you feeling**?

I'm...

Ça va bien, merci et toi?	I'm fine thanks. And you?
Pas trop mal!	Not too bad!
On fait aller!	Getting by!
Ça pourrait être pire.	Can't complain.
Beaucoup mieux, merci.	A lot better, thanks.

BON À SAVOIR!

Remember to use the **vous** form to people you don't know.

A knock at the door

Il y a quelqu'un?	Is anybody in?
Qui est-ce?	Who is it?
Un instant!	One moment!
Je viens!	I'm coming!

One-stop phrase shop

Asking someone in

Entrez!	Come in!
Après toi!	After you!
Asseyez-vous donc!	Do sit down!
Fais comme chez toi.	Make yourself at home.

BON À SAVOIR!

When inviting someone to do something in French, you can add **donc** after the verb for emphasis. This is not unlike English where we put *do* before the verb in *do start, do take a seat, do come in* and so on.

PLEASE AND THANK YOU

When requesting something from someone, you should use **s'il vous plaît** (*please*) for someone you don't know, and **s'il te plaît** (*please*) for someone you know well.

Please

Est-ce que je peux avoir un demi, **s'il vous plaît**?	Can I have half a lager, **please**?
Deux kilos d'oranges, **s'il vous plaît**.	Two kilos of oranges, **please**.
Est-ce que vous pouvez me donner l'heure, **s'il vous plaît**?	**Please** could you tell me the time?
Tu peux me passer la télécommande, **s'il te plaît**?	Can you give me the remote control, **please**?
Oui, **s'il vous plaît**.	Yes, **please**.
Oui, **merci**.	Yes, **please**.

BON À SAVOIR!

To say *yes, please*, you can use either **oui, s'il vous plaît** or **oui, merci**.

Thank you!

Merci!	**Thanks**!
Je vous remercie.	**Thank you**.
Merci beaucoup, madame!	**Thank you** very much!
Merci beaucoup pour ton e-mail.	**Thank you** very much for your email.
Non, **merci**.	No, **thank you**.

> **BON À SAVOIR!**
> When you're offered something, stipulate either **oui, merci** or **non, merci**, as **merci** on its own can mean either *yes, thanks* or *no, thanks* depending on your intonation.
>
> The commonest response to **merci** is **de rien** (*not at all*), or the more formal **je vous en prie**.

Not at all

De rien!	Not at all! *or* You're welcome!
Il n'y a pas de quoi!	Don't mention it!
Je vous en prie.	You're welcome.
Merci. – C'est moi qui vous remercie.	Thank you. – No, thank *you*!

ATTRACTING SOMEONE'S ATTENTION ▬▬▬▬

To attract someone's attention, you can use **excusez-moi** or **pardon**, ending your request with **s'il vous plaît**. You can also simply say **s'il vous plaît**.

Excuse me!

Excusez-moi!	**Excuse me**!
Pardon!	**Excuse me**, please!
Pardon, Mademoiselle!	**Excuse me**!
S'il vous plaît!	**Excuse me**, please!

> **BON À SAVOIR!**
> Remember that French speakers tend to be more formal than English speakers. When trying to get someone's attention, you can add **monsieur** (*Sir*), **madame** (*Madam*) or **mademoiselle** (*Miss*).

MAKING SURE YOU'VE UNDERSTOOD

Sometimes you might have problems understanding what's been said or you do not know the right words to express what you want to say in French. Here are some useful phrases to help you when this happens.

I don't understand

Excusez-moi, **je ne comprends pas**.	Sorry, **I don't understand**.
Est-ce que vous pouvez répéter, s'il vous plaît? **Je n'ai pas compris**.	Please could you repeat that? **I didn't understand**.
Excusez-moi, **je n'ai pas compris** ce que vous avez dit.	Sorry, **I didn't understand** what you said.

How do you say...?

Comment est-ce qu'on dit « driving licence » en français?	**How do you say** 'driving licence' in French?
Comment ça s'appelle en français?	**What's this called** in French?

Would you mind...?

Je peux vous demander de parler plus lentement?	**Would you mind** speaking more slowly?
Je peux te demander de répéter ce que tu as dit?	**Would you mind** repeating what you said?

What...?

Pardon, **qu'est-ce que** vous avez dit?	Sorry, **what** did you say?
Pardon, **qu'est-ce que** « couverture » veut dire?	Sorry, **what** does 'couverture' mean?

One-stop phrase shop

To check your facts, you can use **n'est-ce pas?** – which is quite formal – and **non?**. They are used on the end of statements similar to the way we use *isn't it?*, *haven't you?* and so on in English.

...isn't it?

Vous êtes de Paris, **n'est-ce pas**?	You're from Paris, **aren't you**?
Il y a du monde, **non**?	It's busy, **isn't it**?
Vous êtes arrivés hier, **non**?	You arrived yesterday, **didn't you**?
Tu viens, **oui ou non**?	Are you coming **or aren't you**?

BON À SAVOIR!
Adding **oui ou non?** at the end of a question corresponds to the English *or what?*. Just as in English, it is quite informal.

Another way of checking that something is right in French is to add **bien** to the question.

...isn't it?

On est **bien** lundi aujourd'hui?	Today's Monday, **isn't it**?
Tu lui as **bien** dit que c'était d'accord?	You told him it was OK, **didn't you**?
Tu as **bien** les passeports?	You do have the passports, **don't you**?

You can use **vous ne trouvez pas** when addressing several people or someone you don't know well, and **tu ne trouves pas** to someone you're familiar with to say *Don't you think?*

...don't you think?

Ça lui va bien, **tu ne trouves pas**?	It suits her, **don't you think**?
Il fait froid, **vous ne trouvez pas**?	It's cold, **don't you think**?
Vous ne trouvez pas que le vin a un drôle de goût?	**Don't you think** the wine tastes funny?

One-stop phrase shop

To say that you hope someone has a good time, has a good weekend or gets a good night's sleep, use **bon** before a masculine word, **bonne** before a feminine one, or **bien** after a verb.

Have a good...!

Bon voyage!	Have a good trip!
Bon appétit!	Enjoy your meal!
Passe un bon week-end!	Have a great weekend!
Bonnes vacances!	Enjoy your holiday!
Bon rétablissement!	Get well soon!
Amuse-toi bien!	Have fun! *or* Enjoy yourself!
Dors bien!	Sleep well!
Santé!	Cheers! (*when drinking*)

When wishing someone *Happy…!*, you can use **joyeux** or **bon** with a masculine word, or **joyeuse** or **bonne** with a feminine word.

Happy...!

Joyeux Noël!	**Happy** Christmas!
Joyeux *or* **Bon** anniversaire!	**Happy** birthday!
Bonne année!	**Happy** New Year!
Bon anniversaire de mariage!	**Happy** wedding anniversary!

BON À SAVOIR!

Vous de même! and **À toi aussi!** (*The same to you!*) are particularly useful words socially. Use them in reply to expressions such as **Joyeux Noël!** (*Happy Christmas!*) and **Bon appétit!** (*Enjoy your meal!*) if you want to wish the other person the same thing back.

Good luck!

Bonne chance!	**Good luck**!
Bonne chance pour ton examen!	**Good luck** in your exam!
Bonne chance pour ton nouveau travail!	**Good luck** in your new job!

One-stop phrase shop

APOLOGIZING

To say *I'm sorry*, you can use **pardon** or **je m'excuse**.
Alternatively, especially if you've done something more serious,
you can use **je suis désolé**, or **je suis désolée** if you're a woman.
If you need to get past someone, or if you bump into them, just
say **pardon** or **excusez-moi** (*sorry* or *excuse me*).

I'm sorry

Pardon.	**I'm sorry**.
Je m'excuse d'être en retard.	**I'm sorry** I'm late.
Je suis vraiment **désolé**!	**I'm** really **sorry**!
Je suis sincèrement **désolée**!	**I'm** truly **sorry**!

I'm afraid...

Oui, je regrette.	I'm afraid so.
J'en ai bien peur.	I'm afraid so.
Non, je regrette.	I'm afraid not.
J'ai bien peur que non.	I'm afraid not.

REASSURING SOMEONE

If someone apologizes to you or if they tell you about something
they've accidentally done, you can reassure them by saying **ce
n'est pas grave** (*it doesn't matter*) or **ça ne fait rien** (*forget about
it*). There are also a number of other expressions you can use.

It doesn't matter

Ce n'est pas grave.	It doesn't matter.
Ça ne fait rien.	Forget about it.
Ne t'en fais pas!	Don't worry!
Il n'y a pas de problème.	Don't worry about it.
T'inquiète pas! C'est pas grave.	Don't worry about it! It doesn't matter.

BON À SAVOIR!
Remember that in spoken French, you can often omit the **ne** in a
negative sentence. This will make you sound informal.

OPINIONS

To express your opinion in French, you can use **je crois**, **je pense** and **il me semble**, all of which mean I think.

I think so

Je crois que oui.	I think so.
Il me semble, oui.	I think so.
Je suppose que oui.	I suppose so.
J'espère.	I hope so.

I don't think so

Je ne crois pas.	I don't think so.
Je ne pense pas.	I don't think so.
Je suppose que non.	I suppose not.
J'espère que non.	I hope not.

I'm not sure

Je ne suis pas sûr.	I'm not sure.
Je ne suis pas certain.	I'm not sure.
Je ne sais pas.	I don't know.
Tu es sûr?	Are you sure?

BON À SAVOIR!
Remember that if you're a woman, you would say **sûre** or **certaine** instead.

I doubt it

Ça m'étonnerait.	I doubt it.
Ça, j'en doute.	I doubt it.

I don't mind

Ça m'est égal.	I don't mind.
Ça ne me fait rien.	I don't mind.
Peu importe.	It's all the same to me.

AGREEING, DISAGREEING AND DECLINING ▄▄▄

Remember that there are two words to say yes in French: **oui** and **si**. **oui** is the normal word for *yes* and **si** is used to mean *yes* to contradict a negative statement or question such as **Tu ne veux pas manger? – Si!** (*Don't you want to eat? – Yes, I do!*).

Yes

Oui.	Yes.
Bien sûr que oui.	Yes, of course.
Tu n'as pas encore fini? – Si!	Aren't you finished yet? – Yes, I am!
C'est vrai.	That's true.
Tu as raison.	You're right.
Je suis tout à fait d'accord.	I totally agree.

If someone asks you to do something, particularly useful phrases are **D'accord!** (*OK!*), **Bien sûr!** (*Of course!*) or **Sans problème!** (*No problem!*).

OK!

D'accord!	OK!
Bon, d'accord.	OK, then.
Entendu!	OK! *or* Agreed!

Of course

Bien sûr!	Of course!
Oui, bien sûr.	Yes, of course.
Tu m'aides? – Bien sûr!	Will you help me? – Of course I will!
Sans problème!	No problem.

To disagree with someone or refuse something, you can use **non**, or a number of other very common phrases.

No

Non.	No.
Bien sûr que non.	Of course not.
Ce n'est pas vrai.	That's not true.
Eh bien, tu as tort.	Well, you're wrong.
Je ne suis pas d'accord du tout.	I don't agree at all.

There are several words you can use with **je ne peux pas** (*I can't*) to say that you will have to decline to do something, for example **franchement** (*honestly*), **sincèrement** (*truly*), **malheureusement** (*unfortunately*).

I can't

J'aimerais bien, mais malheureusement **je ne peux pas**.	I'd like to but unfortunately **I can't**.
Non, franchement, **je ne peux pas**.	No, **I** honestly **can't**.
J'ai bien peur de **ne pas pouvoir**.	I'm afraid **I can't**.
Je suis sincèrement désolé, mais **je ne vais pas pouvoir** venir.	I'm truly sorry, but **I won't be able to** make it.

If you don't want to commit yourself, **peut-être** is the easiest way of saying *perhaps* in French.

Perhaps

Peut-être.	Perhaps.
C'est possible.	Possibly.
Tu as peut-être raison.	You may be right.
Ça se pourrait.	It could well be.
Ça dépend.	It depends.
On verra.	We'll see.

CONGRATULATING SOMEONE

To congratulate someone on their success, there are lots of useful phrases you can use such as **Félicitations!** (*Congratulations!*) and **Bravo!** (*Well done!*).

Congratulations!

Félicitations!	**Congratulations**!
Bravo!	**Well done**!
Bravo pour ta promotion!	**Congratulations** on your promotion!
Félicitations pour ton succès aux examens!	**Congratulations** on passing your exams!
Bravo, au fait!	**Well done**, by the way!

REACTING TO GOOD AND BAD NEWS

There are a number of very useful expressions to use when someone tells you that they're well or that something good has happened to them.

Glad to hear it

Je suis content de l'apprendre.	That's good to hear.
Je suis bien contente pour toi!	I'm really pleased for you!
C'est une très bonne nouvelle.	That's very good news.
C'est une excellente nouvelle!	What wonderful news!
C'est formidable!	How wonderful!
C'est génial!	That's great!
Génial!	Fantastic!

BON À SAVOIR!

bien is often put in front of adjectives for emphasis, a bit like *really*, for example, **je suis bien content** (*I'm really pleased*), **je suis bien embêté** (*I really don't know what to do*).

To say you're sorry about something bad that's happened, you can use **je suis désolé** (*I'm sorry*).

I'm sorry

Je suis désolé.	**I'm sorry**.
Je suis vraiment **désolé** pour ta tante.	**I'm** really **sorry** to hear about your aunt.
On est sincèrement **désolés pour** ce qu'il s'est passé.	**We're** very **sorry about** what happened.

There are lots of useful expressions which mean *things could be worse* or *it's not that bad*, for example, **ce n'est pas si grave que ça** (*it's not as bad as all that*).

It's not as bad as all that

Ce n'est pas si grave que ça.	It's not as bad as all that.
Ne te laisse pas abattre! Ça aurait pu être pire.	Cheer up! It could have been worse.
Il y a pire.	Things could be worse.

EXCLAMATIONS

In English we often use *What a…!* when saying how something affects us or how we feel about it. In French, you can use **Quel(le)…!** before a noun and **Qu'est-ce que…!** when there is a verb.

What a…!

Quelle peur!	**What a** fright!
Quel dommage!	**What a** shame!
Quelle malchance!	**What** bad luck!
Quelle surprise, dis donc!	**What a** surprise!
Dites donc! **Quel** beau bâtiment!	**What a** beautiful building!

> **BON À SAVOIR!**
> The English *a* is not translated into French in expressions like these.

What a...!

Qu'est-ce que je suis bête!	**What an** idiot I am!
Qu'est-ce que le paysage est beau!	**What a** beautiful landscape!
Qu'est-ce que c'est cher comme restaurant!	**What an** expensive restaurant!

If you want to use the expression *How...!*, you can say **Comme c'est...!** in French.

How...!

Comme c'est intéressant!	**How** interesting!
Comme c'est idiot!	**How** silly!
Comme c'est décevant!	**How** disappointing!

SURPRISE

There are many ways you can express surprise in everyday French.

C'est incroyable!	That's incredible!
Quelle surprise, dites donc!	What a surprise!
Je n'arrive pas à y croire!	I can't believe it!
Ce n'est pas possible!	That's impossible.
Tiens, tiens!	Well, what do you know!
Ah oui?	Really?
Dis donc! Il est drôlement tard!	Oh dear! It's very late!

BON À SAVOIR!
French speakers very often put **dis donc!** or **dites donc!** (equivalent to, though not old-fashioned like *I say!*) either at the beginning or the end of a sentence when they're surprised.

ENCOURAGING SOMEONE

If you need to hurry someone up or get them to do something, you can say **Allez!** (*Come on!*).

Come on!

Allez! On y va!	**Come on**! Let's go!
Allez! On va être en retard.	**Hurry up**! We're going to be late.
Courage! Tu vas y arriver!	**Come on**! You're going to make it!
Encore un effort! Tu y es presque!	**Keep it up**! You're nearly there!
Vite! Le train va partir!	**Quick**! The train is about to leave!
Dépêche-toi! Le film va commencer!	**Hurry up**! The film's about to begin!

BON À SAVOIR!

You use **Allez!** with people you call **tu** and **vous**, but you would use **Dépêchez-vous!** instead of **Dépêche-toi!** with someone you call **vous**.

HANDING SOMEONE SOMETHING

If you're handing someone something, you can say **tiens** (or the **vous** form, **tenez**) to say *here you are*.

Here you are

Tiens.	Here you are.
Tenez.	Here you are.
Prends ça.	Take this.
Voilà.	Here.

DANGERS AND EMERGENCIES

Certain phrases are useful to know in the event of danger or emergencies. Here are some of them, though let's hope you never have to understand or use them.

Look out!

Attention!	Look out!
Fais attention!	Be careful!
Attention à ton sac!	Watch your bag!
Au secours!	Help!
Aidez-moi!	Help me!
Au voleur!	Stop thief!
Au feu!	Fire!

SPEAKING YOUR MIND

If you get into an argument, here are some very common phrases which may come in handy! Be sure to use plenty of body language too.

For goodness sake!

Non mais, franchement!	For goodness sake!
Non mais, ça va pas?	What do you think you're doing?
Tu te prends pour qui?	Who do you think you are?
Non mais, tu rigoles?	Are you joking?
Et puis quoi, encore?	Whatever next!
Je n'y crois pas.	I don't believe it.
C'est hors de question.	It's out of the question.
N'importe quoi!	Nonsense!

BON À SAVOIR!
The French phrase **non mais** at the start of a sentence is a good way of expressing incredulity – it's similar to the English *Honestly!*

CONVERSATIONAL WORDS

Just as in English, there are lots of French words and expressions for linking different points together or for showing what your attitude towards something is. Here are the most useful of them. If you use them they will make you sound more fluent and natural.

ah bon

Ah bon, je ne savais pas. J'ai décidé de ne pas l'inviter. – **Ah bon**?	**Right**, I didn't know. I decided not to invite her. – **Really**?

alors

Je suis fatigué. – **Alors** vas te coucher.	I'm tired. – Go to bed, **then**.

au fait

Au fait, tu joues toujours du saxo?	Do you still play the sax, **by the way**?

> **BON À SAVOIR!**
> You don't usually pronounce consonants at the end of words in French, but you do say the **–t** in **au fait**.

bon

Bon, on y va? **Bon**, à demain alors.	**Right**, shall we go? **Ok**, see you tomorrow then.

c'est ça

Vous êtes ici en vacances ? – Oui, **c'est ça**.	You're here on holiday? – **That's right**.

d'abord

D'abord, on va faire les courses.	**First**, we'll do the shopping.

de toute façon

De toute façon, c'est couvert par l'assurance.	It's covered by the insurance **anyway**.

en fait

En fait, j'ai arrêté de fumer il y a deux mois.	**Actually**, I stopped smoking two months ago.

> **BON À SAVOIR!**
> You don't usually pronounce consonants at the end of words in French, but you do say the **–t** in **en fait**.

enfin

Enfin bref, je ne vais pas pouvoir venir.	**In a word**, I'm not going to be able to come.
Enfin! Je viens de te le dire!	**But** I've just told you!

en plus

Je suis fatigué et **en plus** je n'ai pas envie d'y aller.	I'm tired and **what's more** I just don't feel like going.

ensuite

Qu'est-ce qu'on fait **ensuite**?	**Then** what shall we do?

finalement

Tu as réussi à l'avoir, **finalement**?	Did you manage to get hold of him **in the end**?
Finalement, je vais prendre ce pull.	I'm going to take this jumper **after all**.

quand même

C'est **quand même** bizarre…	**Still**, it is strange…
Quand même! C'est pourtant pas sorcier!	**Honestly!** It's not rocket science!

NOUNS

The gender of nouns

In French all nouns are either masculine or feminine:

• **le** or **un** before a noun tells you that it is masculine
• **la** or **une** before a noun tells you that it is feminine

Whenever you are using a noun, you need to know whether it is masculine or feminine as this affects the form of other words used with it, such as:

• adjectives that describe it
• articles that go before it
• pronouns that replace it

Adjectives, articles and pronouns are also affected by whether a noun is singular or plural.

Nouns referring to people

Most nouns referring to men and boys are masculine.

| un homme | a man |
| un Français | a Frenchman |

Most nouns referring to women and girls are feminine.

| une fille | a girl |
| une Canadienne | a Canadian woman |

Nouns referring to things

In English we call all things – for example, *table, car, book* – 'it'. In French, however, things are either masculine or feminine.

There are a number of rules to tell you which nouns are masculine and which are feminine:

• words ending in **–e** are generally feminine, for example, **une boulangerie** (*a baker's*), **une banque** (*a bank*)

• words ending in a consonant are generally masculine, for example, **un film** (*a film*), **un chien** (*a dog*)

• words ending in **–age**, **–sme**, **–eau**, **–eu**, and **–ou** are often masculine, for example, **le fromage** (*cheese*), **le tourisme** (*tourism*), **un cadeau** (*a present*)

• words ending in **–ion** are often feminine, for example, **une addition** (*a bill*)

In addition, names of days of the week, and months and seasons of the year are masculine, as are the names of languages, for example, **le printemps** (*spring*), **le portugais** (*Portuguese*).

ARTICLES

Translating *the*

In French, articles – the words for *the* and *a* – vary according to the noun they are used with depending on whether it is masculine, feminine, singular or plural. The definite article *the* can be translated as:

	with masculine nouns	with feminine nouns
singular	**le (l')**	**la (l')**
plural	**les**	**les**

> **BON À SAVOIR!**
> **le** and **la** change to **l'** in front of words beginning with a vowel and most words beginning with **h**.

le train	**the** train
la voiture	**the** car
l'autoroute	**the** motorway
l'hôtel	**the** hotel
les clés	**the** keys
les enfants	**the** children

When using the definite article (**le**, **la**, **les**) with the prepositions **à** or **de**, the preposition and the article can combine to make a new form:

• **à + le → au** and **de + le → du**

au cinéma	**at/to the** cinema
du cinéma	**from/of the** cinema

- **à + les → aux** and **de + les → des**

aux maisons   **to the** houses
des maisons   **from/of the** houses

- **à + la/l'** and **de + la/l'** do not change

à l'hôtel   **at/to the** hotel
de la bibliothèque   **from/of the** library

So you would say **je vais à la gare** (*I'm going to the station*) and **je vais au restaurant** (*I'm going to the restaurant*).

Translating *a, an, some, any*

The indefinite articles *a* and *an* can be translated as **un** or **une** depending on whether the word they are used with is masculine or feminine. In the plural **des** is used where in English you would use *some, any*, or use no word at all.

	with masculine nouns	with feminine nouns
singular	**un**	**une**
plural	**des**	**des**

un rendez-vous	**an** appointment
une réunion	**a** meeting
Vous voulez **des** dépliants?	Would you like **some** leaflets?
Vous avez **des** enfants?	Do you have **any** children?
J'ai **des** amis à Lyon.	I have friends in Lyon.

The definite article (**le**, **la**) and indefinite article (**un**, **une**) are not always used in French when they are in English, and vice versa. They are also not always used in the same way.

La France est très belle.	France is very beautiful.
Il est professeur.	He's **a** teacher.
J'ai mal à **la** gorge.	I've got **a** sore throat.

PRONOUNS

Subject pronouns

Subject pronouns are words such as *I*, *he*, *she* and *they* which perform the action expressed by the verb. Here are the subject pronouns in French:

je (j')	I
tu (*informal, singular*)	you
il	he
elle	she
on	we
nous	we
vous (*formal, singular; plural*)	you
ils (*all masculine or masculine and feminine*)	they
elles (*all feminine*)	they

BON À SAVOIR!
je changes to **j'** in front of words beginning with a vowel, most words beginning with **h** and the French word **y**.

How do you say *you* in French?

In English we have only one way of saying *you*. In French there are two words: **tu** and **vous**. The word you use in French depends on:

• whether you are talking to one person or more than one person
• whether you are talking to a friend or family member or someone else

If you are talking to one person you know well, such as a friend, a young person, or a relative, use **tu**.

Tu me prêtes ce CD?	Will **you** lend me this CD?

If you are talking to one person you do not know so well, such as your teacher, your boss or a stranger, use **vous**.

Vous pouvez entrer.	**You** may come in.

BON À SAVOIR!
If you are in doubt as to which form of *you* to use, it is safest to use **vous** and you will not offend anyone.

Using il/elle and ils/elles

In English we generally refer to things (such as *table, book, car*) as 'it'. In French you use **il** for masculine nouns and **elle** for feminine nouns.

Prends cette chaise. **Elle** est plus confortable.	Take this chair. **It**'s more comfortable.

il is also used to talk about the weather, the time and in certain other set phrases, often in the same way as some phrases with *it* in English.

Il pleut.	**It**'s raining.
Il est deux heures.	**It**'s two o'clock.
Il faut partir.	**We** *or* **you** have to go.

ils and **elles** are used in the plural to talk about things, as well as people or animals. Use **ils** for masculine nouns and **elles** for feminine nouns.

Est-ce qu'il reste des billets? – Non, **ils** sont tous vendus.	Are there any tickets left? – No, **they**'re all sold out.

If you're talking about masculine and feminine nouns together, use **ils**.

Emma et Gordon sont en retard; **ils** arriveront dans une heure.	Emma and Gordon are late; **they**'ll get here in an hour.

Using on

on is frequently used in informal, everyday French to mean *we*.

On y va?	Shall **we** go?

on can also have the sense of *someone* or *they*.

On m'a volé mon porte-monnaie.	**Someone**'s stolen my purse.

You can also use **on** as we use *you* in English when we mean people in general.

On peut visiter le château en été.	**You** can visit the castle in the summer.

Direct object pronouns

Direct object pronouns are words such as *me*, *him*, *us* and *them*, which are used instead of a noun. They stand in for the person or thing most directly affected by the action of the verb. Here are the French direct object pronouns:

me (m')	me
te (t') (*informal, singular*)	you
le (l')	him, it
la (l')	her, it
nous	us
vous (*formal, singular; plural*)	you
les	them

J'ai acheté le journal. Tu veux **le** lire?	I've bought the paper. Do you want to read **it**?
Je peux **vous** aider?	Can I help **you**?

Indirect object pronouns

An indirect object pronoun is used instead of a noun to show the person or thing the action is intended to benefit, for example the word *me* in *He gave me a book*. Here are the French indirect object pronouns:

me (m')	me, to me, for me
te (t') (*informal, singular*)	you, to you, for you
lui	him, to him, for him; it, to it, for it
lui	her, to her, for her; it, to it, for it
nous	us, to us, for us
vous (*formal, singular; plural*)	you, to you, for you
leur	them, to them, for them

| Je **lui** ai parlé. | I spoke **to her**. |
| Tu **leur** as téléphoné? | Did you give **them** a ring? |

Emphatic pronouns

An emphatic pronoun is used instead of a noun when you want to emphasize something, for example the word *me* in *Is this for me?*. Here are the French emphatic pronouns:

moi	I, me
toi (*informal, singular*)	you
lui	he, him
elle	she, her
soi	oneself, yourself, ourselves
nous	we, us
vous (*formal, singular; plural*)	you
eux (*masculine*)	they, them
elles (*feminine*)	they, them

Emphatic pronouns are mostly used after a preposition, for emphasis, on their own without a verb, after **c'est** and **ce sont**, and in comparisons.

Venez avec **moi**.	Come with **me**.
Moi, je n'ai pas compris.	**I** didn't understand.
Qui en veut? – **Moi**!	Who wants some? – **I do**!
C'est **toi**?	Is that **you**?

Using en and y

en is used with verbs and phrases usually followed by **de**, such as **être fier de quelque chose** (*to be proud of something*), to avoid repeating the same word.

| Il a un beau jardin et il **en** est très fier. | He's got a beautiful garden and is very proud **of it**. |

en can also replace **du**, **de la**, **de l'** and **des**.

| Je n'ai pas d'argent. Tu **en** as? | I haven't got any money. Have you got **any**? |

When **en** is used with **avoir**, **il y a** or with numbers, it is often not translated in English, but can never be missed out in French.

| J'**en** veux deux. | I want two. |

y is used with verbs and phrases normally followed by **à**, such as **penser à quelque chose** (*to think about something*), to avoid repeating the same word.

Je pensais à l'examen. – Mais arrête d'**y** penser!	I was thinking about the exam. – Well, stop thinking **about it**!

y can also mean *there*. It can be used to replace phrases that would use prepositions such as **dans** and **sur**.

Elle **y** a passé tout l'été.	She spent the whole summer **there**.

y is used in the phrase **il y a** to mean both *there is* and *there are*.

Il y a quelqu'un à la porte.	**There is** someone at the door.
Il y a cinq livres sur la table.	**There are** five books on the table.

ADJECTIVES

Agreement of adjectives

In dictionaries, French adjectives are usually shown in the masculine singular form. You need to know how to change them to make them agree with the noun or pronoun they are describing. To make an adjective agree, you simply add the following endings to the masculine singular adjective in most cases:

• no additional ending for masculine singular
• add **–e** for feminine singular
• add **–s** for the masculine plural
• add **–es** for the feminine plural

un chat **noir**	a **black** cat
une chemise **noire**	a **black** shirt
des chats **noirs**	**black** cats
des chemises **noires**	**black** shirts

If the adjective already ends in an **–e** in the masculine singular form, you do not add another **–e** for the feminine singular.

un sac **jaune**	a **yellow** bag
une chemise **jaune**	a **yellow** shirt

Some very common adjectives have irregular feminine forms, for example, **blanc/blanche**, **favori/favorite**, **sec/sèche** and so on. These irregular feminine forms are shown in the dictionary along with the masculine singular form.

mon sport **favori**	my **favourite** sport
ma chanson **favorite**	my **favourite** song

A very small group of French adjectives have an extra masculine singular form which is used in front of words that begin with a vowel and most words beginning with **h**. These adjectives also have an irregular feminine form:

masc sing	masc sing before vowel	feminine
beau	**bel**	**belle**
fou	**fol**	**folle**
nouveau	**nouvel**	**nouvelle**
vieux	**vieil**	**vieille**

un **beau** jardin	a **beautiful** garden
un **bel** arbre	a **beautiful** tree
un **nouveau** film	a **new** film
un **nouvel** ami	a **new** friend

If the masculine singular form already ends in an **–s** or an **–x**, you do not add another **–s** in the plural.

un fromage **français**	a **French** cheese
des fromages **français**	**French** cheeses

If the masculine singular form ends in **–eau** or **–al**, the masculine plural is usually **–eaux** or **–aux**.

le **nouveau** professeur	the **new** teacher
les **nouveaux** professeurs	the **new** teachers
un livre **original**	an **unusual** book
des livres **originaux**	**unusual** books

Adjectives which do not change

A small number of adjectives (mostly relating to colours) do not change in the feminine or plural. They are called invariable adjectives. These adjectives are often made up of more than one word, for example, **bleu marine** (*navy blue*), or else come from the names of fruits or nuts, for example, **orange** (*orange*) and **marron** (*brown*).

des chaussures **marron**	**brown** shoes
une veste **bleu marine**	a **navy blue** jacket

Word order with adjectives

French adjectives usually go after the noun, and adjectives describing colours, shapes or nationalities always go after the noun.

l'heure **exacte**	the **right** time
des cravates **rouges**	**red** ties
une table **ronde**	a **round** table
la cuisine **italienne**	**Italian** food

There are some very common adjectives which go before the noun: **beau**, **bon**, **grand**, **gros**, **joli**, **long**, **meilleur**, **nouveau**, **petit**.

une **belle** journée	a **lovely** day
Bonne chance!	**Good** luck!

Some adjectives can either go before or after the noun, but their meaning changes depending on where they go, for example, **ancien**, **cher**, **propre**.

un **ancien** collègue	a **former** colleague
un fauteuil **ancien**	an **antique** chair

Chère Julie	**Dear** Julie
un restaurant **cher**	an **expensive** restaurant

ma **propre** chambre	my **own** room
des draps **propres**	**clean** sheets

If two adjectives are used with a noun and they both come after it, they are joined together by **et** (*and*).

une personne intéressante **et** drôle	an interesting, funny person

Comparisons

To say something is bigger, more beautiful and so on, put **plus** (*more*) before the adjective. To say that something is less important, less expensive and so on, put **moins** (*less*) before the adjective.

Emma est **plus** grande.	Emma is tall**er**.
Cet hôtel est **plus** cher **que** l'autre.	This hotel is **more** expensive **than** the other one.
Son dernier livre est **moins** intéressant.	His last book is **less** interesting.

Possessive adjectives

In English a possessive adjective is one of the words *my*, *your*, *his*, *her*, *its*, *our* or *their* used with a noun to show that one person or thing belongs to another. Here are the French possessive adjectives:

	with masculine singular nouns	with feminine singular nouns	with plural nouns
my	**mon**	**ma (mon)**	**mes**
your	**ton**	**ta (ton)**	**tes**
his; her; its; one's	**son**	**sa (son)**	**ses**
our	**notre**	**notre**	**nos**
your	**votre**	**votre**	**vos**
their	**leur**	**leur**	**leurs**

Possessive adjectives agree with the noun they describe, not with the person who owns that thing. For example, **sa** can mean *his*, *her*, *its* and *one's*, but can only be used with a feminine noun.

Mon frère s'appelle Andrew.	**My** brother is called Andrew.
Ma sœur s'appelle Danielle.	**My** sister is called Danielle.
Mes parents sont retraités.	**My** parents are retired.
Sa voiture a été volée.	**His** *or* **her** car was stolen.
Son amie est galloise.	**His** *or* **her** friend is Welsh.

BON À SAVOIR!
ma changes to **mon**, **ta** to **ton**, and **sa** to **son** in front of feminine singular nouns beginning with a vowel and most words beginning with **h**. This makes them easier to say.

QUESTIONS

How to ask a question in French

There are several ways of asking a question in French:

• by using the phrase **est-ce que**
• by making your voice go up at the end of the sentence
• by changing the word order in the sentence

When the phrase **est-ce que** is used to ask a question the word order stays the same as in an ordinary sentence. **est-ce que** comes before the subject, and the verb comes after the subject.

Est-ce que vous allez en ville?	**Are you going** into town?
Quand est-ce que vous arrivez?	**When do you arrive**?

If you are expecting the answer *yes* or *no*, there is a very straightforward way of asking a question. You keep the word order as it would be in an ordinary sentence, but turn it into a question by making your voice go up at the end of the sentence. This will make you sound less formal.

On part tout de suite?	**Are we leaving** right away?
Tu prends un café?	**Are you getting** a coffee?
Tu ne l'**as pas fait**? – Si.	**Haven't you done** it? – Yes(, I have).

> **BON À SAVOIR!**
> **si** is the word you use to reply to a question or statement that contains a negative expression like **ne...pas**.

You can also ask a question by changing the word order in the sentence. To do this you put the verb before the subject and add a hyphen between the verb and the subject. This is quite a formal way of asking a question.

Aimez-vous la France?	**Do you like** France?
Où **vont-ils?**	Where **are they going**?

When the verb ends in a vowel in the **il/elle** form, **-t-** is inserted before the pronoun to make the words easier to say.

Aime-t-il les chiens?	**Does he like** dogs?

In the perfect tense and in other tenses that consist of two or more words, the part of the verb that comes from **avoir** and **être** goes before the pronoun. For more information on the perfect tense, see page 273.

Est-elle restée longtemps?	**Did she stay** long?

NEGATIVES

Making sentences negative

In French, if you want to make a statement negative, you generally use a pair of words, for example, **ne ... pas** (*not*), **ne ... jamais** (*never*) and so on. The verb goes in between these two words. In English, *do* is often used in negative statements. The French verb **faire** is never used in this way.

Je **ne** fume **pas**.	I **don't** smoke.
Jeremy **ne** prend **jamais** les transports en commun.	Jeremy **never** uses public transport.
Il **n'**habite **plus** ici.	He **doesn't** live here **anymore**.

> **BON À SAVOIR!**
> **ne** changes to **n'** in front of a word that starts with a vowel, most words beginning with **h**, and the French word **y**.

In everyday conversation French speakers often miss out the word **ne**. Be careful not to do this yourself in formal situations.

Je peux pas venir ce soir.	**I can't** come tonight.

The French word **ne** is missed out when negatives are used without a verb to answer a question.

Qui a téléphoné? – **Personne**.	Who phoned? – **Nobody**.

moi non plus is the equivalent of English phrases like *me neither, neither do I, neither was I*, and so on. You can use it in all situations without worrying about the tense of the verb.

Je ne suis jamais allée en Italie. – **Moi non plus**.	I've never been to Italy. – **Neither have I**.
Je n'y vais pas et **lui non plus**.	I'm not going and **neither is he**.

Word order with negatives

Negative expressions in French 'sandwich' the verb. **ne** goes before the verb and the other half of the expression comes after the verb.

Il **ne** boit **jamais**.	He **never** drinks.
Je **n'**entends **rien**.	I ca**n't** hear anything.
Je **n'**ai vu **personne**.	I did**n't** see anybody.

However, in the perfect tense and other tenses that consist of two or more words, **pas**, **rien**, **plus** and **jamais** are sandwiched between **avoir** or **être** and the past participle. For more information on the perfect tense, see page 273.

Je **n'**ai **pas** compris.	I **didn't** understand.
Nous **ne** sommes **jamais** allés chez eux.	We've **never** been to their house.

A negative sentence may also contain a pronoun such as **te**, **le**, **lui** and so on or a reflexive pronoun. If so, **ne** comes before the pronoun.

Je **ne** t'entends **pas**.	I ca**n't** hear **you**.
Il **ne se** lève **jamais** avant midi.	He **never** gets up before midday.

After negative expressions, **un**, **une** and **des** change to **de**, as do **du**, **de la**, **de l'**. For example, **Elle a acheté une glace** becomes **elle n'a pas acheté de glace**.

Je ne veux pas **de** café.	I don't want **any** coffee.
Il n'y a plus **d'**eau.	There's no water left.

> **BON À SAVOIR!**
> **de** changes to **d'** in front of words beginning with a vowel, and most words beginning with **h**.

SOME COMMON TRANSLATION DIFFICULTIES ▮▮▮▮

You can't always translate French into English and English into French word for word. The next section points out some common translation difficulties to watch out for.

Prepositions

English phrasal verbs, for example, *to run away*, *to fall down*, are often translated by one word in French.

continuer	to go on
tomber	to fall down

Sentences which contain a verb and preposition in English might not contain a preposition in French, and vice versa.

écouter quelque chose	to listen **to** something
téléphoner **à** quelqu'un	to call somebody

The same French preposition may be translated into English in different ways.

croire **à** quelque chose	to believe **in** something
prendre quelque chose **à** quelqu'un	to take something **from** somebody
rendre quelque chose **à** quelqu'un	to give something back **to** somebody

Singular and plural nouns

A word which is singular in English may not be in French, and vice versa.

les bagage**s**	luggage
mon pantalon	my trouser**s**

-ing

The *-ing* ending in English is translated in a number of different ways in French:

• *to be …-ing* is translated by a verb consisting of one word.

Il **part** demain.	He**'s leaving** tomorrow.

• *-ing* can also be translated by an infinitive or a noun.

J'aime **aller** au cinéma.	I like **going** to the cinema.
Le ski me maintient en forme.	**Skiing** keeps me fit.

to be

The verb *to be* is generally translated by **être**.

Il **est** tard.	It**'s** late.

When you are talking about the physical position of something, **se trouver** can be used.

Où **se trouve** la gare?	Where **is** the station?

In certain set phrases which describe how you are feeling or a state you are in, the verb **avoir** is used.

avoir chaud	**to be** warm
avoir froid	**to be** cold
avoir faim	**to be** hungry
avoir soif	**to be** thirsty
avoir peur	**to be** afraid
avoir tort	**to be** wrong
avoir raison	**to be** right

When you are talking about someone's age, also use the verb **avoir**.

Quel âge **as**-tu?	How old **are** you?
J'**ai** quinze ans.	I**'m** fifteen.

When talking about your health, use the verb **aller**.

Comment **allez**-vous?	How **are** you?
Je **vais** très bien.	I**'m** very well.

it is, it's

In most constructions and phrases which translate *it is* and *it's*, use **c'est**.

C'est moi!	**It's** me!
C'est assez facile.	**It's** quite easy.

it is and *it's* are usually translated by **il est** or **elle est** when referring to a noun, depending on whether the noun is masculine or feminine.

Descends la valise si **elle** n'**est** pas trop lourde.	Bring the case down if **it's** not too heavy.

When you are talking about the time, use **il est**.

Quelle heure **est-il**? – **Il est** sept heures et demie.	What time **is it**? – **It's** half past seven.

When you are describing what the weather is like, use **faire**.

Quel temps **fait-il**? **Il fait** beau. **Il fait** du vent.	What**'s** the weather like? **It's** lovely. **It's** windy.

can, to be able

If you want to talk about someone's physical ability to do something, use **pouvoir**.

Pouvez-vous faire dix kilometres à pied?	**Can** you walk ten kilometres?

When *can* is used with verbs to do with what you can see or hear, you do not use **pouvoir** in French.

Je ne vois rien.	**I can't see** anything.

If you want to say that you don't know how to do something, use **savoir**.

Elle **ne sait pas** nager.	She **can't** swim.

Showing possession

In English, you can use *'s* and *s'* to show who or what something belongs to. In French, you have to use a different construction.

la voiture **de** mon frère la chambre **des** filles	my brother**'s** car the girls**'** bedroom

Introduction to verbs

Verbs are usually used with a noun, with a pronoun such as *I, you* or *he*, or with somebody's name. They can relate to the present, the past and the future – this is called their tense.

Verbs can be either:

• Regular: their forms follow the normal rules
• Irregular: their forms do not follow the normal rules

Regular English verbs have a base form (the form of the verb without any endings added to it, for example, *walk*). The base form can have *to* in front of it, for example, *to walk* – this is called the infinitive.

French verbs also have an infinitive, which ends in **–er**, **–ir** or **–re**, for example, **aimer** (*to love*), **finir** (*to finish*) and **attendre** (*to wait*). Regular French verbs belong to one of these three verb groups, which are called conjugations.

English verbs have other forms apart from the base form and the infinitive: a form ending in *–s (walks)*, a form ending in *–ing (walking)*, and a form ending in *–ed (walked)*. French verbs have many more forms than this, which are made up of endings added to a stem. The stem of a verb can usually be worked out from the infinitive of the verb.

French verb endings change depending on who you are talking about: **je** (*I*), **il/elle/on** (*he/she/we*) in the singular, or **nous** (*we*), **vous** (*you*) and **ils/elles** (*they*) in the plural. French verbs also have different forms depending on whether you are referring to the present, the past or the future.

Irregular verbs

Some verbs in French do not follow the normal rules and are called irregular verbs. These include some very common and important verbs like **avoir** (*to have*), **être** (*to be*), **faire** (*to do* or *to make*) and **aller** (*to go*). The most common irregular verbs are shown in the verb tables, along with a number of others that you may need to use. For more detailed information on all the most important irregular verbs in French, use *Collins Easy Learning French Verbs*.

Regular verbs

There are three groups of regular verbs:

• **–er** verbs: verbs that end in **–er** like **aimer** (shown in full on page 275)
• **–ir** verbs: verbs that end in **–ir** like **finir** (shown in full on page 276)
• **–re** verbs: verbs that end in **–re** like **attendre** (shown in full on page 277)

These are called regular verbs because they follow set patterns. When you have learned these patterns you will be able to form, or conjugate, any regular verb.

To form the stem of the verb for the present, imperfect and present subjunctive of any regular verb, take the infinitive minus the last two letters, for example, **aimer → aim–**; **finir → fin–**; **attendre → attend–**, and add the appropriate ending.

To form the future and conditional tense of any regular verb, take the infinitive of **–er** and **–ir** verbs, for example, **aimer**; **finir**, or the infinitive minus **–e** of **–re** verbs, for example, **attendre → attendr–**, and add the appropriate ending. Verb endings for regular verbs are highlighted in orange in the verb tables on the following pages.

To form the perfect tense of any regular verb, you need:

• to be able to conjugate **avoir** and **être** in the present tense (see pages 280 and 282)
• to be able to form the past participle

To form the past participle of any regular verb, take the infinitive minus the last two letters, for example, **aimer → aim–**; **finir → fin–**; **attendre → attend–**, and add the appropriate ending **–é**, **–i**, or **–u**. The past participles of **aimer**, **finir** and **attendre** are therefore **aimé**, **fini**, and **attendu**.

Spelling changes in –er verbs

Using the patterns of the regular **–er** verb **aimer** on page 275, you can now work out the forms of most **–er** verbs. A few verbs, though, involve a small spelling change. This is usually to do with the way the word is pronounced.

With verbs ending in **–cer** such as **lancer** (*to throw*), **c** becomes **ç** before an **a** or an **o**. This is so the letter **c** is still pronounced like the *c* in the English word *ice*.

je lance	I throw
nous lan**ç**ons	we throw

With verbs ending in **–ger** such as **manger** (*to eat*), **g** becomes **ge** before an **a** or an **o**. This is so the letter **g** is still pronounced like the *s* in the English word *leisure*.

tu manges	you're eating
nous man**ge**ons	we're eating

With verbs ending in **–eler** such as **appeler** (*to call*), the **l** doubles before **–e**, **–es** and **–ent**. The double consonant (**ll**) affects the pronunciation of the word. In **appeler**, the first **e** sounds like the vowel at the end of *teacher*, but in **appelle** the first **e** sounds like the one in the English word *pet*.

Comment t'app**ell**es tu?	What's your name?
Comment vous appelez vous?	What's your name?

There are two exceptions: **geler** (*to freeze*) and **peler** (*to peel*) change in the same way as **lever** (*to lift*). See below.

With verbs ending in **–eter** such as **jeter** (*to throw*), the **t** doubles before **–e**, **–es** and **–ent**. The double consonant (**tt**) affects the pronunciation of the word. In **jeter**, the first **e** sounds like the vowel at the end of *teacher*, but in **jette** the first **e** sounds like the one in the English word *pet*.

je je**tt**e	I throw
nous jetons	we throw

The exceptions to this rule include **acheter** (*to buy*) which changes in the same way as **lever** (*to lift*). See below.

With verbs ending in **–yer** such as **nettoyer** (*to clean*), the **y** changes to **i** before **–e**, **–es** and **–ent**.

je netto**i**e	I clean
nous nettoyons	we clean

Verbs ending in **–ayer**, such as **payer** (*to pay*) and **essayer** (*to try*), can be spelled with either a **y** or an **i**. So **je paie** and **je paye**, for example, are both correct.

With a small number of verbs such as **lever** (*to lift*), **peser** (*to weigh*), **geler** (*to freeze*), **peler** (*to peel*) and **acheter** (*to buy*), **e** changes to **è** before the consonant and the endings **–e**, **–es** and **–ent**. The accent changes the pronunciation too. In **lever** the first **e** sounds like the vowel at the end of *teacher*, but in **lève** and so on the first **e** sounds like the one in the English word *pet*.

j'ach**è**te	I buy
nous achetons	we buy

With verbs such as **espérer** (*to hope*), **préférer** (*to prefer*) and **régler** (*to adjust, to pay*), **é** changes to **è** before the consonant and the endings **–e**, **–es** and **–ent**.

je préf**è**re	I prefer
nous préférons	we prefer

Reflexive verbs

Reflexive verbs are verbs where the action 'reflects back' on the subject. The verb is used with a reflexive pronoun such as *myself*, *yourself* and *herself* in English, for example *I washed myself*; *he shaved himself*. French reflexive verbs are shown in the dictionary as **se** or **s'** (the reflexive pronoun) plus the infinitive, for example **se coucher** (*to go to bed*), **s'appeler** (*to be called*).

Reflexive verbs are much more common in French than they are in English. They are often used to describe things you do (to yourself) every day or that involve a change of some sort (going to bed, sitting down, getting angry, going to sleep). Here are some examples of the most common French reflexive verbs:

s'amuser	to enjoy oneself, to play
s'appeler	to be called
s'asseoir	to sit down
se coucher	to go to bed
se dépêcher	to hurry up
s'habiller	to get dressed
se passer	to take place, to happen, to go
se réveiller	to wake up
se trouver	to be (situated)

To use a reflexive verb in French, you need to decide which reflexive pronoun to use. Here are the French reflexive pronouns:

subject pronoun	reflexive pronoun	meaning
je	**me (m')**	myself
tu	**te (t')**	yourself
il **elle** **on**	**se (s')**	himself herself itself *or* oneself ourselves
nous	**nous**	ourselves
vous	**vous**	yourself (*singular*) yourselves (*plural*)
ils **elles**	**se (s')**	themselves

Il **s'**habille.	He's getting dressed.
Je **m'**appelle Julie.	My name's Julie.
Nous **nous** couchons de bonne heure.	We go to bed early.

You will find an example of a reflexive verb **s'asseoir** conjugated in full on page 278.

The present tense

The present tense is used to talk about what is true at the moment, what happens regularly and what is happening now, for example, *I'm a student*; *he works as a consultant*; *I'm studying French*.

There is more than one way to express the present tense in English. For example, you can either say *I give*, *I am giving* or occasionally *I do give*. In French, you use the same form **je donne** for all these.

In English you can also use the present tense to talk about something that is going to happen in the near future. You can do the same in French.

J'emménage à la fin du mois.	**I'm moving in** at the end of the month.
On sort avec Aurélie ce soir.	**We're going out** with Aurélie tonight.

The future tense

The future tense is used to talk about something that will happen or will be true. There are several ways to express the future tense in English: you can use the future tense (*I'll ask him on Tuesday*), the present tense (*I'm not working tomorrow*), or *going to* followed by an infinitive (*she's going to study in France for a year*). In French you can also use the future tense, the present tense, or the verb **aller** (*to go*) followed by an infinitive.

Elle ne rentrera pas avant minuit.	**She won't be back** before midnight.
Il arrive dans dix minutes.	**He's coming** in ten minutes.
Je vais me faire couper les cheveux.	**I'm going to** have my hair cut.

The imperfect tense

The imperfect tense is one of the tenses used to talk about the past, especially in descriptions, and to say what used to happen, for example *I used to work in Manchester*; *it was sunny yesterday*.

Je ne faisais rien de spécial.	**I wasn't doing anything** special.
C'était une super fête.	**It was** a great party.
Avant, **il était** professeur.	**He used to be** a teacher.

The perfect tense

The perfect tense is made up of two parts: the present tense of **avoir** or **être**, and the French past participle (like *given*, *finished* and *done* in English). To find out how to form the past participle of any regular verb in French, see page 269.

Most verbs form the perfect tense with **avoir**. There are two main groups of verbs which form their perfect tense with **être** instead of **avoir**: all reflexive verbs (see page 271) and a group of verbs that are mainly used to talk about movement or a change of some kind, including:

aller	to go
venir	to come
arriver	to arrive, to happen
partir	to leave, to go
descendre	to go down, to come down, to get off
monter	to go up, to come up
entrer	to go in, to come in
sortir	to go out, to come out
mourir	to die
naître	to be born
devenir	to become
rester	to stay
tomber	to fall

Richard **est parti** de bonne heure.	Richard **left** early.
Tu es sortie hier soir?	**Did you go out** last night?
On est resté trois jours à Toulouse.	**We stayed** in Toulouse for three days.

The imperative

The imperative is a form of the verb used when giving orders and instructions, for example, *Be quiet!*; *Don't forget your passport!*; *Please fill in this form*.

In French, there are several forms of the imperative that are used to give instructions or orders to someone. These correspond to **tu**, **vous** and **nous**. The **nous** form means the same as *let's* in English. For regular verbs, the imperative is the same as the **tu**, **nous** and **vous** forms of the present tense, except that you do not say the pronouns **tu**, **nous** and **vous**. Also, in the **tu** form of **-er** verbs like **aimer**, the final **-s** is dropped.

Arrête de me faire rire!	**Stop** making me laugh!
Venez déjeuner chez nous.	**Come** round to ours for lunch.
Allons voir ce qu'ils font.	**Let's go** and see what they're up to.

The subjunctive

The subjunctive is a verb form that is used in certain circumstances to express some sort of feeling, or to show there is doubt about whether something will happen or something is true. It is used after certain structures in French, for example, **il faut que** and **il faudrait que**.

Il faut que je rentre.	**I have to** get back.
Il faudrait qu'on loue une voiture.	**We should** hire a car.
Je veux que tu viennes avec moi.	**I want** you to come with me.

The conditional

The conditional is a verb form used to talk about things that would happen or that would be true under certain conditions, for instance, *I would help you if I could*. It is also used to say what you would like or need, for example, *Could you give me the bill?*.

Je voudrais deux billets.	**I'd like** two tickets.
Si j'étais toi, **je téléphonerais**.	**I'd call** if I were you.

to love

present

j'	aim**e**
tu	aim**es**
il	aim**e**
nous	aim**ons**
vous	aim**ez**
ils	aim**ent**

imperfect

j'	aim**ais**
tu	aim**ais**
il	aim**ait**
nous	aim**ions**
vous	aim**iez**
ils	aim**aient**

perfect

j'	**ai** aim**é**
tu	**as** aim**é**
il	**a** aim**é**
nous	**avons** aim**é**
vous	**avez** aim**é**
ils	**ont** aim**é**

future

j'	aimer**ai**
tu	aimer**as**
il	aimer**a**
nous	aimer**ons**
vous	aimer**ez**
ils	aimer**ont**

present subjunctive

j'	aim**e**
tu	aim**es**
il	aim**e**
nous	aim**ions**
vous	aim**iez**
ils	aim**ent**

conditional

j'	aimer**ais**
tu	aimer**ais**
il	aimer**ait**
nous	aimer**ions**
vous	aimer**iez**
ils	aimer**aient**

present participle
aim**ant**

past participle
aim**é**

imperative
aim**e** aim**ons** aim**ez**

example phrases

Est-ce que vous **aimez** voyager?	**Do** you **like** to travel?
J'**aimerais** réserver une table pour deux personnes.	**I'd like to** book a table for two people.
Je **n'ai pas aimé** le film.	I **didn't like** the movie.

to finish

	present			**imperfect**
je	fin**is**		je	fin**issais**
tu	fin**is**		tu	fin**issais**
il	fin**it**		il	fin**issait**
nous	fin**issons**		nous	fin**issions**
vous	fin**issez**		vous	fin**issiez**
ils	fin**issent**		ils	fin**issaient**

	perfect			**future**
j'	**ai** fini		je	finir**ai**
tu	**as** fini		tu	finir**as**
il	**a** fini		il	finir**a**
nous	**avons** fini		nous	finir**ons**
vous	**avez** fini		vous	finir**ez**
ils	**ont** fini		ils	finir**ont**

	present subjunctive			**conditional**
je	fin**isse**		je	finir**ais**
tu	fin**isses**		tu	finir**ais**
il	fin**isse**		il	finir**ait**
nous	fin**issions**		nous	finir**ions**
vous	fin**issiez**		vous	finir**iez**
ils	fin**issent**		ils	finir**aient**

present participle
fin**issant**

past participle
fin**i**

imperative
fin**is** fin**issons** fin**issez**

example phrases

J'**ai fini**.	I'**ve finished**.
Elle **n'a pas** encore **fini** de manger.	She **hasn't finished** eating yet.
Tu **finis** le travail à quelle heure?	What time **do** you **finish** work?

to wait

	present		imperfect
j'	attend**s**	j'	attend**ais**
tu	attend**s**	tu	attend**ais**
il	attend	il	attend**ait**
nous	attend**ons**	nous	attend**ions**
vous	attend**ez**	vous	attend**iez**
ils	attend**ent**	ils	attend**aient**

	perfect		future
j'	**ai** attend**u**	j'	attend**rai**
tu	**as** attend**u**	tu	attend**ras**
il	**a** attend**u**	il	attend**ra**
nous	**avons** attend**u**	nous	attend**rons**
vous	**avez** attend**u**	vous	attend**rez**
ils	**ont** attend**u**	ils	attend**ront**

	present subjunctive		conditional
j'	attend**e**	j'	attend**rais**
tu	attend**es**	tu	attend**rais**
il	attend**e**	il	attend**rait**
nous	attend**ions**	nous	attend**rions**
vous	attend**iez**	vous	attend**riez**
ils	attend**ent**	ils	attend**raient**

present participle
attend**ant**

past participle
attend**u**

imperative
attend**s** attend**ons**
attend**ez**

example phrases

Tu **attends** depuis longtemps?	**Have** you **been waiting** long?
Attendez-moi!	**Wait for** me!
Je l'**ai attendu** à la poste.	I **waited for** him at the post office.

S'ASSEOIR

to sit down

	present			imperfect
je	m'assieds		je	m'asseyais
tu	t'assieds		tu	t'asseyais
il	s'assied		il	s'asseyait
nous	nous asseyons		nous	nous asseyions
vous	vous asseyez		vous	vous asseyiez
ils	s'asseyent		ils	s'asseyaient

	perfect			future
je	me suis assis(e)		je	m'assiérai
tu	t'es assis(e)		tu	t'assiéras
il	s'est assis		il	s'assiéra
nous	nous sommes assis(es)		nous	nous assiérons
vous	vous êtes assis(e(s))		vous	vous assiérez
ils	se sont assis		ils	s'assiéront

	present subjunctive			conditional
je	m'asseye		je	m'assiérais
tu	t'asseyes		tu	t'assiérais
il	s'asseye		il	s'assiérait
nous	nous asseyions		nous	nous assiérions
vous	vous asseyiez		vous	vous assiériez
ils	s'asseyent		ils	s'assiéraient

present participle
s'asseyant

past participle
assis

imperative
assieds-toi asseyons-nous
asseyez-vous

example phrases

Je peux m'**asseoir**?	May I **sit down**?
Assieds-toi, Jean-Claude.	**Sit down**, Jean-Claude.
Asseyez-vous, les enfants.	**Sit down**, children.

to go

present

je	**vais**
tu	**vas**
il	**va**
nous	allons
vous	allez
ils	**vont**

imperfect

j'	allais
tu	allais
il	allait
nous	allions
vous	alliez
ils	allaient

perfect

je	suis allé(e)
tu	es allé (e)
il	est allé
nous	sommes allé(e)s
vous	êtes allé(e(s))
ils	sont allés

future

j'	**irai**
tu	**iras**
il	**ira**
nous	**irons**
vous	**irez**
ils	**iront**

present subjunctive

j'	**aille**
tu	**ailles**
il	**aille**
nous	allions
vous	alliez
ils	**aillent**

conditional

j'	**irais**
tu	**irais**
il	**irait**
nous	**irions**
vous	**iriez**
ils	**iraient**

present participle
allant

past participle
allé

imperative
va allons allez

example phrases

Vous **allez** souvent au cinéma?	**Do** you often **go** to the cinema?
Je **suis allé** à Londres.	I **went** to London.
Va voir s'ils sont arrivés.	**Go** and see whether they have arrived.

to have

	present		imperfect
j'	**ai**	j'	**avais**
tu	**as**	tu	**avais**
il	**a**	il	**avait**
nous	**avons**	nous	**avions**
vous	**avez**	vous	**aviez**
ils	**ont**	ils	**avaient**

	perfect		future
j'	**ai eu**	j'	**aurai**
tu	**as eu**	tu	**auras**
il	**a eu**	il	**aura**
nous	**avons eu**	nous	**aurons**
vous	**avez eu**	vous	**aurez**
ils	**ont eu**	ils	**auront**

	present subjunctive		conditional
j'	**aie**	j'	**aurais**
tu	**aies**	tu	**aurais**
il	**ait**	il	**aurait**
nous	**ayons**	nous	**aurions**
vous	**ayez**	vous	**auriez**
ils	**aient**	ils	**auraient**

present participle
ayant

past participle
eu

imperative
aie ayons ayez

example phrases

Il **a** les yeux bleus.	He**'s got** blue eyes.
Vous **avez** réservé?	**Have** you booked?
Emma **aura** deux ans au mois de juillet.	Emma **will be** two in July.

to have, to owe

	present		imperfect
je	dois	je	devais
tu	dois	tu	devais
il	doit	il	devait
nous	devons	nous	devions
vous	devez	vous	deviez
ils	doivent	ils	devaient

	perfect		future
j'	ai dû	je	devrai
tu	as dû	tu	devras
il	a dû	il	devra
nous	avons dû	nous	devrons
vous	avez dû	vous	devrez
ils	ont dû	ils	devront

	present subjunctive		conditional
je	doive	je	devrais
tu	doives	tu	devrais
il	doive	il	devrait
nous	devions	nous	devrions
vous	deviez	vous	devriez
ils	doivent	ils	devraient

present participle
devant

past participle
dû (NB due, dus, dues)

imperative
dois devons devez

example phrases

Je **dois** téléphoner à ma propriétaire.	I **must** ring my landlady.
Vous **devriez** changer vos livres ici.	You **should** change your pounds here.
On **a dû** dormir à l'hôtel.	We **had to** sleep in a hotel.

ÊTRE

to be

	present			imperfect
je	suis		j'	étais
tu	es		tu	étais
il	est		il	était
nous	sommes		nous	étions
vous	êtes		vous	étiez
ils	sont		ils	étaient

	perfect			future
j'	ai été		je	serai
tu	as été		tu	seras
il	a été		il	sera
nous	avons été		nous	serons
vous	avez été		vous	serez
ils	ont été		ils	seront

	present subjunctive			conditional
je	sois		je	serais
tu	sois		tu	serais
il	soit		il	serait
nous	soyons		nous	serions
vous	soyez		vous	seriez
ils	soient		ils	seraient

present participle
étant

past participle
été

imperative
sois soyons soyez

example phrases

Quelle heure **est**-il? – Il **est** dix heures.	What time **is** it? – It**'s** ten o'clock.
Ils **ne sont pas** encore arrivés.	They **haven't** arrived yet.
Il faut qu'on **soit** à la gare dans dix minutes.	We have to **be** at the station in ten minutes' time.

to do, to make

	present			imperfect
je	fais		je	faisais
tu	fais		tu	faisais
il	fait		il	faisait
nous	faisons		nous	faisions
vous	faites		vous	faisiez
ils	font		ils	faisaient

	perfect			future
j'	ai fait		je	ferai
tu	as fait		tu	feras
il	a fait		il	fera
nous	avons fait		nous	ferons
vous	avez fait		vous	ferez
ils	ont fait		ils	feront

	present subjunctive			conditional
je	fasse		je	ferais
tu	fasses		tu	ferais
il	fasse		il	ferait
nous	fassions		nous	ferions
vous	fassiez		vous	feriez
ils	fassent		ils	feraient

present participle
faisant

past participle
fait

imperative
fais faisons faites

example phrases

Qu'est-ce que vous **faites**?	What **are** you **doing**?
Il va **faire** beau demain.	The weather will **be** nice tomorrow.
Je **n'ai pas** encore **fait** la vaisselle.	I **haven't done** the washing up yet.

POUVOIR

to be able

	present			imperfect
je	**peux**		je	**pouvais**
tu	**peux**		tu	**pouvais**
il	**peut**		il	**pouvait**
nous	**pouvons**		nous	**pouvions**
vous	**pouvez**		vous	**pouviez**
ils	**peuvent**		ils	**pouvaient**

	perfect			future
j'	**ai pu**		je	**pourrai**
tu	**as pu**		tu	**pourras**
il	**a pu**		il	**pourra**
nous	**avons pu**		nous	**pourrons**
vous	**avez pu**		vous	**pourrez**
ils	**ont pu**		ils	**pourront**

	present subjunctive			conditional
je	**puisse**		je	**pourrais**
tu	**puisses**		tua	**pourrais**
il	**puisse**		il	**pourrait**
nous	**puissions**		nous	**pourrions**
vous	**puissiez**		vous	**pourriez**
ils	**puissent**		ils	**pourraient**

present participle
pouvant

past participle
pu

imperative
not used

example phrases

Je **peux** vous aider?	**Can** I help you?
Vous **pourriez** me faire un paquet-cadeau?	**Could** you gift wrap it for me?
Je **ne pourrai pas** venir samedi.	I **won't be able to** come on Saturday.

to want

	present			imperfect
je	veux		je	voulais
tu	veux		tu	voulais
il	veut		il	voulait
nous	voulons		nous	voulions
vous	voulez		vous	vouliez
ils	veulent		ils	voulaient

	perfect			future
j'	ai voulu		je	voudrai
tu	as voulu		tu	voudras
il	a voulu		il	voudra
nous	avons voulu		nous	voudrons
vous	avez voulu		vous	voudrez
ils	ont voulu		ils	voudront

	present subjunctive			conditional
je	veuille		je	voudrais
tu	veuilles		tu	voudrais
il	veuille		il	voudrait
nous	voulions		nous	voudrions
vous	vouliez		vous	voudriez
ils	veuillent		ils	voudraient

present participle
voulant

past participle
voulu

imperative
veuille veuillons veuillez

example phrases

Je **voudrais** aller voir un film.	I**'d like to** go and see a movie.
Est-ce que vous **voulez** du café?	**Do** you **want** some coffee?
Elles **voulaient** venir.	They **wanted** to come.

VOCABULARY BUILDER

A

A, an un, une
able to be able to pouvoir
about (*relating to*) au sujet
de; **What is it about?** C'est
à quel sujet?; **I don't know
anything about it** Je ne suis
pas au courant; **at about 10
o'clock** vers dix heures
above above the bed au-
dessus du lit
abroad à l'étranger
abscess l'abcès *m*
accelerator l'accélérateur *m*
to accept accepter; **Do
you accept this card?** Vous
acceptez cette carte?
access l'accès *m*;
wheelchair access accès
aux handicapés
accident l'accident *m*
**accident & emergency
department** les urgences
fpl
accommodation le
logement
according to selon;
according to him selon lui
account le compte
account number le numéro
de compte
to ache faire mal; **My head
aches** J'ai mal à la tête; **It
aches** Ça fait mal
address l'adresse *f*; **Here's
my address** Voici mon
adresse; **What is the
address?** Quelle est
l'adresse?
admission charge l'entrée *f*
to admit (*to hospital*)
hospitaliser
adult l'adulte *m/f*; **for adults**
pour adultes
advance in advance à
l'avance
to advise conseiller
A&E les urgences *fpl*
aeroplane l'avion *m*
afraid to be afraid of avoir
peur de
after après
afternoon l'après-midi *m*; **in
the afternoon** l'après-midi;
this afternoon cet après-

midi; **tomorrow afternoon**
demain après-midi
afterwards après
again encore
against contre; **I'm against
the idea** Je suis contre
age l'âge *m*
agency l'agence *f*
ago a week ago il y a une
semaine; **a month ago** il y
a un mois
to agree être d'accord
air l'air *m*; **by air** en avion
air bed le matelas
pneumatique
air-conditioning la
climatisation
air-conditioning unit le
climatiseur
air freshener le
désodorisant
airline la ligne aérienne
air mail by airmail par avion
airplane l'avion *m*
airport l'aéroport *m*
aisle le couloir
alarm l'alarme *f*
alarm clock le réveil
alcoholic alcoolisé(e)
all tout; **all day** toute la
journée; **all the books** tous
les livres
allergic allergic to
allergique à; **I'm allergic
to...** Je suis allergique à...
to allow permettre; **It's not
allowed** C'est interdit
all right (*agreed*) d'accord;
(*OK*) bien; **Are you all
right?** Ça va?
almost presque
alone tout(e) seul(e)
along le long de; **along the
beach** le long de la plage
alphabet l'alphabet *m*
Alps les Alpes *fpl*
already déjà
also aussi
altogether 20 euros
altogether 20 euros en tout
always toujours
am du matin; **at 4 am** à
quatre heures du matin
ambulance l'ambulance *f*
America l'Amérique *f*

American américain(e)
amount (*total*) le montant
anchovies les anchois *mpl*
and et
angry fâché(e)
animal l'animal *m*
ankle la cheville
another un(e) autre;
another beer, please une
autre bière, s'il vous plaît;
another two salads deux
autres salades
answer la réponse
to answer répondre à
answering machine le
répondeur
answerphone le répondeur
antibiotic l'antibiotique *m*
antifreeze l'antigel *m*
antihistamine
l'antihistaminique *m*
antique shop le magasin
d'antiquités
antiseptic l'antiseptique *m*
any du, de la, des; **Have
you any apples?** Vous avez
des pommes?; **I don't play
tennis any more** Je ne joue
plus au tennis
anyone (*in questions*)
quelqu'un; (*in negative
sentences*) personne
anything (*in questions*)
quelque chose; (*in negative
sentences*) rien
anyway de toute façon
anywhere (*in questions*)
quelque part; (*in negative
sentences*) nulle part; **You
can buy them almost
anywhere** Ça s'achète
presque partout
apart from à part; **apart
from that...** à part ça...
apartment l'appartement *m*
apple la pomme
application form le
formulaire
appointment le
rendez-vous; **I have an
appointment** J'ai rendez-
vous
approximately environ
apricot l'abricot *m*
April avril

arm le bras
to arrange arranger
to arrive arriver
art l'art *m*
art gallery le musée
arthritis l'arthrite *f*
ashtray le cendrier
to ask demander; **to ask for something** demander quelque chose; **I'd like to ask you a question** J'aimerais vous poser une question
aspirin l'aspirine *f*
asthma l'asthme *m*; **I have asthma** Je suis asthmatique
at à; **at home** à la maison; **at 8 o'clock** à huit heures; **at once** tout de suite; **at night** la nuit
attractive séduisant(e)
aubergine l'aubergine *f*
August août
aunt la tante
Australia l'Australie *f*
Australian australien(ne)
automatic car la voiture à boîte automatique
autumn l'automne *m*
available disponible
avocado l'avocat *m*
awake to be awake être réveillé
away far away loin; **he's away** il est parti
awful affreux(-euse)

B
baby le bébé
baby milk (*formula*) le lait maternisé
baby's bottle le biberon
babysitter le/la babysitter
back (*of body*) le dos
backpack le sac à dos
backpacker le routard, la routarde
backpacking to go backpacking voyager sac à dos
bad (*food, weather, news*) mauvais(e)
bag le sac; (*suitcase*) la valise
baggage les bagages *mpl*
baggage allowance le poids (de bagages) autorisé
baggage reclaim la livraison des bagages

baker's la boulangerie
ball (*large: football, rugby*) le ballon; (*small: golf, tennis*) la balle
banana la banane
band (*music*) le groupe
bandage le pansement
bank (*money*) la banque
bank account le compte en banque
banknote le billet de banque
bar (*pub*) le bar; **a bar of chocolate** une tablette de chocolat
barbecue le barbecue; **to have a barbecue** faire un barbecue
barber's le coiffeur
basil le basilic
bath le bain; **to have a bath** prendre un bain
bathroom la salle de bains; **with bathroom** avec salle de bains
battery (*for car*) la batterie; (*for radio, camera*) la pile
to be être
beach la plage; **on the beach** sur la plage
bean le haricot
beautiful beau (belle)
because parce que
become to become ill tomber malade
bed le lit; **double bed** le grand lit; **single bed** le lit d'une personne; **twin beds** les lits jumeaux
bed and breakfast (*place*) la chambre d'hôte; **How much is it for bed and breakfast?** C'est combien pour la chambre et le petit déjeuner?
bedroom la chambre
beef le bœuf
beer la bière
before avant; **before we go** avant de partir; **I've seen this film before** J'ai déjà vu ce film
to begin commencer; **to begin doing** commencer à faire
behind derrière; **behind the house** derrière la maison
beige beige
Belgian belge
Belgium la Belgique

to believe croire
to belong to (*club*) être membre de; **That belongs to me** C'est à moi
below au-dessous de; **below our appartement** au-dessous de chez nous
belt la ceinture
beside à côté de; **beside the bank** à côté de la banque
best le meilleur, la meilleure
better meilleur(e); **better than** meilleur que
between entre
bib (*baby's*) le bavoir
bicycle le vélo; **by bicycle** à vélo
bicycle pump la pompe à vélo
big grand(e); (*car, animal, book, parcel*) gros(se)
bike (*pushbike*) le vélo; (*motorbike*) la moto
bikini le bikini
bill la facture; (*restaurant*) la note
bin (*dustbin*) la poubelle
Biro® le stylo
birthday l'anniversaire *m*; **Happy birthday!** Bon anniversaire!; **My birthday is on...** Mon anniversaire c'est le...
birthday card la carte d'anniversaire
biscuits les biscuits *mpl*
bit a bit (of) un peu (de)
bitter amer(ère)
black noir(e)
black ice le verglas
blanket la couverture
to bleed saigner; **My nose is bleeding** Je saigne du nez
blind (*for window*) le store
blister l'ampoule *f*
blocked bouché(e); **The sink is blocked** L'évier est bouché; **I have a blocked nose** J'ai le nez bouché
block of flats l'immeuble *m*
blog le blog
to blog bloguer
blond (*person*) blond(e)
blood le sang
blood group le groupe sanguin
blood pressure la tension (artérielle)

blouse le chemisier
blow-dry le brushing
blue bleu(e); **dark blue** bleu foncé; **light blue** bleu clair
to board (*bus, train*) monter dans; **What time are we boarding?** À quelle heure embarquons-nous?
boarding card la carte d'embarquement
boat le bateau; (*rowing*) la barque
boat trip l'excursion *f* en bateau
body le corps
boiler la chaudière
bone l'os *m*; (*fish*) l'arête *f*
bonnet (*of car*) le capot
book le livre
to book réserver
booking la réservation
bookshop la librairie
boot (*of car*) le coffre
boots les bottes *fpl*
bored **I'm bored** Je m'ennuie
boring **It's boring** C'est ennuyeux
born **I was born in ...** Je suis né(e) en ...
to borrow **Can I borrow your map?** Je peux emprunter votre plan?
boss le chef
both les deux; **I'd like both T-shirts** Je voudrais les deux tee-shirts; **We both went** Nous y sommes allés tous les deux
bottle la bouteille; **a bottle of wine** une bouteille de vin; **a half-bottle of ...** une demi-bouteille de ...
bottle opener l'ouvre-bouteilles *m*
box office le bureau de location
boy le garçon
boyfriend le copain
bra le soutien-gorge
bracelet le bracelet
brake le frein
to brake freiner
brake fluid le liquide de freins
brake lights les feux *mpl* de stop
brake pads les plaquettes *fpl* de freins

branch (*of bank, shop*) la succursale
brand (*make*) la marque
bread le pain; **wholemeal bread** le pain complet; **sliced bread** le pain de mie en tranches
to break casser
breakdown (*car*) la panne
breakfast le petit déjeuner
to breathe respirer
bride la mariée
bridegroom le marié
bridge le pont
briefcase la serviette
to bring apporter
Britain la Grande-Bretagne
British britannique
broadband le haut débit
broccoli le brocoli
brochure la brochure
broken cassé(e); **My leg is broken** Je me suis cassé la jambe
broken down (*car*) en panne
brooch la broche
brother le frère
brother-in-law le beau-frère
brown marron
bucket le seau
buffet car (*train*) la voiture-bar
building l'immeuble *m*
bulb (*light*) l'ampoule *f*
bumper (*on car*) le pare-chocs
bunch (*of flowers*) le bouquet; (*of grapes*) la grappe
burger le hamburger
burglar le cambrioleur, la cambrioleuse
burglar alarm le système d'alarme
burnt (*food*) brûlé(e)
bus le bus; (*coach*) le car; **by bus** en car
business l'entreprise *f*; **He's got his own business** Il a sa propre entreprise
business card la carte de visite
business class **in business class** en classe affaires
businessman l'homme d'affaires
business trip le voyage d'affaires

businesswoman la femme d'affaires
bus station la gare routière
bus stop l'arrêt *m* de bus
busy occupé(e); **He's very busy** Il est très occupé
but mais
butcher's la boucherie
butter le beurre
button le bouton
to buy acheter
by (*beside*) à côté de; **by the church** à côté de l'église; **a painting by Picasso** un tableau de Picasso; **They were caught by the police** Ils ont été arrêtés par la police; **I have to be there by 3 o'clock** Je dois y être avant trois heures

C

cablecar le téléphérique
café le café
cake (*large*) le gâteau; (*small*) la pâtisserie, le petit gâteau
cake shop la pâtisserie
call (*telephone*) l'appel *m*; **a long distance call** un appel à longue distance
to call (*speak, phone*) appeler
camera l'appareil *m* photo
camera shop le magasin de photo
to camp camper
camping gas le butane
camping stove le camping-gaz®
campsite le camping
can (*to be able to*) pouvoir; (*to know how to*) savoir; **I can't do that** Je ne peux pas faire ça; **I can swim** Je sais nager
can la boîte
Canada le Canada
Canadian canadien(ne)
to cancel annuler
canoeing **to go canoeing** faire du canoë-kayak
can opener l'ouvre-boîtes *m*
cappuccino le cappuccino
car la voiture; **to go by car** aller en voiture
carafe le pichet
car alarm l'alarme *f* de voiture
caravan la caravane
carburettor le carburateur

card (*greetings, business*) la carte; **playing cards** les cartes à jouer
cardigan le gilet
careful Be careful! Fais attention!
car hire la location de voitures
car insurance l'assurance *f* automobile
car park le parking
carriage (*on train*) la voiture
carrot la carotte
to carry porter
case (*suitcase*) la valise; **in any case** de toute façon
cash l'argent *m* liquide
to cash (*cheque*) encaisser
cash desk la caisse
cash dispenser (*ATM*) le distributeur automatique (de billets)
cashpoint le distributeur automatique (de billets)
cassette player le magnétophone
castle le château
casualty department les urgences *fpl*
cat le chat
to catch (*bus, train, plane*) prendre
cathedral la cathédrale
cauliflower le chou-fleur
CD le CD
CD player le lecteur de CD
CD-ROM le CD-ROM
ceiling le plafond
cent (*of euro*) le centime
centimetre le centimètre
central The hotel is very central L'hôtel est très central
central heating le chauffage central
central locking le verrouillage central
centre le centre
century le siècle
cereal la céréale
certificate le certificat
chair la chaise
chairlift le télésiège
chalet le chalet
chambermaid la femme de chambre
change I haven't got any change Je n'ai pas de monnaie; **Can you give me change for ten euros?** Pourriez-vous me donner la monnaie de dix euros?; **Keep the change** Gardez la monnaie
to change to change 50 euros changer 50 euros; **I'm going to change my shoes** Je vais changer de chaussures; **to change trains in Paris** changer de train à Paris; **to change money** changer de l'argent
changing room la cabine d'essayage
Channel (*English*) la Manche
charge (*fee*) le prix; **to be in charge** être responsable
to charge (*money*) prendre; (*battery, phone*) recharger; **Please charge it to my account** Mettez ça sur mon compte s'il vous plaît; **I need to charge my phone** J'ai besoin de recharger mon téléphone
charter flight le vol charter
chatroom le forum de discussion
cheap bon marché
to check (*oil, level, amount*) vérifier
to check in (*at airport*) se présenter à l'enregistrement; (*at hotel*) se présenter à la réception
check-in (*desk*) l'enregistrement *m* des bagages
Cheers! Santé!
cheese le fromage
chemist's la pharmacie
cheque le chèque
cherry la cerise
chewing gum le chewing-gum
chicken le poulet
child l'enfant *m*
children les enfants; **for children** pour enfants
chilli le piment
chips les frites *fpl*
chiropodist le pédicure
chiropractor le chiropracteur
chocolate le chocolat
to choose choisir

chop (*meat*) la côtelette
Christian name le prénom
Christmas Noël *m*; **Merry Christmas!** Joyeux Noël!
Christmas card la carte de Noël
Christmas Eve la veille de Noël
church l'église *f*
cigar le cigare
cigarette la cigarette
cigarette lighter le briquet
cinema le cinéma
circle (*theatre*) le balcon
city la ville
city centre le centre-ville
class first-class la première classe; **second-class** la seconde classe
clean propre
to clean nettoyer
cleaner (*person*) la femme de ménage
clear (*explanation*) clair(e)
clever intelligent(e)
client le client, la cliente
climate le climat
to climb (*mountain*) escalader
climbing to go climbing faire de l'escalade
clinic la clinique
cloakroom le vestiaire
clock l'horloge *f*
close close by proche
to close fermer
closed (*shop, museum, restaurant*) fermé(e)
clothes les vêtements *mpl*
clothes shop le magasin de vêtements
club le club
clutch (*in car*) l'embrayage *m*
coach (*bus*) le car
coach trip l'excursion *f* en car
coal le charbon
coast la côte
coat le manteau
coat hanger le cintre
cockroach le cafard
cocktail le cocktail
code (*dialling code*) l'indicatif *m*
coffee le café; **white coffee** le café au lait; **black coffee** le café noir; **decaffeinated coffee** le café décaféiné

Coke® le Coca®

cold froid; **I'm cold** J'ai froid; **It's cold** Il fait froid; **cold water** l'eau froide

cold (illness) le rhume; **I have a cold** J'ai un rhume

collar le col

colleague le/la collègue

to collect (someone) aller chercher

colour la couleur

colour film (for camera) la pellicule couleur

comb le peigne

to come venir; (to arrive) arriver

to come back revenir

to come in entrer; **Come in! Entrez!**

comfortable confortable

company (firm) la compagnie, la société

compartment (on train) le compartiment

compass la boussole

to complain se plaindre; **We're going to complain to the manager** Nous allons nous plaindre au directeur

complaint (in shop, hotel) la plainte

complete complet(ète)

compulsory obligatoire

computer l'ordinateur m

concert le concert

concert hall la salle de concert

concession la réduction

conditioner l'après-shampooing m

condom le préservatif

conductor (on bus, train) le contrôleur

conference la conférence

to confirm confirmer; **Please confirm** Confirmez, s'il vous plaît

confirmation (flight, booking) la confirmation

Congratulations! Félicitations!

connection (train, plane) la correspondance

consulate le consulat

to consult consulter; **I need to consult my boss** Il faut que je consulte mon patron

to contact joindre; **Where can we contact you?** Où peut-on vous joindre?

contact lens le verre de contact

contact lens cleaner le produit pour nettoyer les verres de contact

to continue continuer

contraceptive le contraceptif

contract le contrat

convenient **Is it convenient?** Cela vous convient?

to cook cuisiner

cooker la cuisinière

cookies les gâteaux mpl secs

cool frais (fraîche)

copy (duplicate) la copie

to copy (photocopy) photocopier

cork le bouchon

corkscrew le tire-bouchon

corner le coin; **the shop on the corner** le magasin au coin de la rue

cornflakes les corn-flakes mpl

corridor le couloir

cost le coût

to cost coûter; **How much does it cost?** Ça coûte combien?

cot le lit d'enfant

cotton le coton

cotton wool le coton hydrophile

cough la toux

to cough tousser

cough mixture le sirop pour la toux

counter (shop, bar) le comptoir

country (not town) la campagne; (nation) le pays; **I live in the country** J'habite à la campagne

couple (two people) le couple; **a couple of ...** deux ...

courgette la courgette

courier service le service de livraisons

course (of meal) le plat; **first course** l'entrée f; **main course** le plat principal

cousin le cousin, la cousine

cover charge (in restaurant) le couvert

crab le crabe

crash (car) l'accident m

crash helmet le casque

cream (food, lotion) la crème

credit (on mobile phone) le crédit

credit card la carte de crédit

crisps les chips fpl

croissant le croissant

to cross (road) traverser

crowded bondé(e)

cruise la croisière

cucumber le concombre

cufflinks les boutons mpl de manchette

cup la tasse

cupboard le placard

current (air, water) le courant

customs (at border) la douane

cut la coupure

to cut couper

to cycle faire du vélo

cycle track la piste cyclable

cycling le cyclisme

D

daily (each day) tous les jours

dairy products les produits mpl laitiers

damage les dégâts mpl

damp humide

to dance danser

dangerous dangereux(-euse)

dark (colour) foncé(e)

date la date

date of birth la date de naissance

daughter la fille

daughter-in-law la belle-fille

day le jour; **every day** tous les jours; **It costs 50 euros per day** Ça coûte 50 euros par jour

dead mort(e)

deaf sourd(e)

dear (expensive, in letter) cher (chère)

decaffeinated décaféiné(e)

December décembre

deckchair la chaise longue

deep profond(e)

deep freeze le congélateur

delay le retard; **How long is the delay?** Il y a combien de retard?

delayed retardé(e)

delicatessen l'épicerie *f* fine

delicious délicieux(-euse)

dental floss le fil dentaire

dentist le/la dentiste

dentures le dentier

deodorant le déodorant

department le rayon

department store le grand magasin

departure lounge la salle d'embarquement

departures les départs *mpl*

desk (*in hotel*) la réception; (*in airport*) le comptoir

desktop l'ordinateur du bureau *m*

dessert le dessert

details **personal details** les coordonnées *fpl*

detergent le détergent

to develop (*photos*) faire développer

diabetic diabétique; **I'm diabetic** Je suis diabétique

to dial (*a number*) composer

dialling code l'indicatif *m*

dialling tone la tonalité

diarrhoea la diarrhée

dictionary le dictionnaire

diesel le gas-oil

diet **I'm on a diet** Je suis au régime; **special diet** le régime spécial

different différent(e)

difficult difficile

digital camera l'appareil *m* photo numérique

dining room (*in hotel*) la salle de restaurant; (*in house*) la salle à manger

dinner (*evening meal*) le diner; **to have dinner** dîner

direct (*train, flight*) direct(e)

directions **to ask for directions** demander le chemin

directory **phone directory** l'annuaire *m*

directory enquiries les renseignements *mpl*

dirty sale

disabled handicapé(e)

to disagree ne pas être d'accord

discount le rabais

dish le plat

dishwasher le lave-vaisselle

disinfectant le désinfectant

disk **hard disk** le disque dur

to dislocate (*joint*) disloquer

disposable jetable

distilled water l'eau distillée

district (*of town*) le quartier; (*of country*) la région

divorced divorcé(e)

dizzy **I feel dizzy** J'ai la tête qui tourne

to do faire

doctor le médecin

documents les papiers *mpl*

dog le chien

dollar le dollar

domestic **domestic flight** le vol intérieur

door la porte

double double; **double bed** le grand lit; **double room** la chambre pour deux personnes

down **to go down the stairs** descendre les escaliers

to download télécharger

downstairs en bas; **the flat downstairs** l'appartement du dessous

draught **There's a draught** Il y a un courant d'air

draught lager la bière pression

drawing le dessin

dress la robe

to dress s'habiller

dressed **to get dressed** s'habiller

drink la boisson

to drink boire

drinking water l'eau *f* potable

to drive conduire

driver le conducteur, la conductrice

driving licence le permis de conduire

dry sec (sèche)

to dry sécher

dry-cleaner's le pressing

due **When is the rent due?** Quand faut-il payer le loyer?; **When is the train due to arrive?** À quelle heure le train doit-il arriver?

during pendant

dust la poussière

duster le chiffon à poussière

duty-free hors taxe

duvet la couette

DVD le DVD

DVD player le lecteur de DVD

E

each chacun, chacune

ear l'oreille *f*

earache **I have earache** J'ai mal à l'oreille/aux oreilles

earlier plus tôt; **I saw him earlier** Je l'ai vu tout à l'heure; **Is there an earlier flight?** Y a-t-il un vol plus tôt?

early tôt

earphones le casque

earrings les boucles *fpl* d'oreille

east l'est *m*

Easter Pâques

easy facile

to eat manger

e-book le livre numérique

ecological écologique

e-commerce le commerce électronique

egg l'œuf *m*; **fried eggs** les œufs sur le plat; **hard-boiled egg** l'œuf dur; **scrambled eggs** les œufs brouillés; **soft-boiled egg** l'œuf à la coque

eggplant l'aubergine *f*

either **I've never been to Corsica – I haven't either** Je ne suis jamais allé en Corse – Moi non plus

Elastoplast® le sparadrap

electric électrique

electrician l'électricien *m*

electric razor le rasoir électrique

electronic électronique

elevator l'ascenseur *m*

email le e-mail; **to email sb** envoyer un e-mail à qn

email address l'adresse e-mail

embassy l'ambassade *f*

emergency l'urgence *f*

empty vide

end la fin

engaged (*to be married*) fiancé(e); (*phone, toilet*) occupé(e)
engine le moteur
England l'Angleterre *f*
English anglais(e); (*language*) l'anglais *m*
Englishman l'Anglais
Englishwoman l'Anglaise
to enjoy aimer; **I enjoy swimming** J'aime nager; **I enjoy dancing** J'aime danser; **Enjoy your meal!** Bon appétit!
enough assez; **I haven't got enough money** Je n'ai pas assez d'argent; **That's enough** Ça suffit
enquiry desk les renseignements *mpl*
to enter entrer
entrance l'entrée *f*
entrance fee le prix d'entrée
envelope l'enveloppe *f*
equipment l'équipement *m*
escalator l'escalator *m*
essential indispensable
estate agent's l'agence *f* immobilière
euro l'euro *m*
Europe l'Europe *f*
European européen(ne)
even even on Sundays même le dimanche; **even though, even if** même si; **even if it rains** même s'il pleut
evening le soir; **this evening** ce soir; **tomorrow evening** demain soir; **in the evening** le soir; **at 7 o'clock in the evening** à sept heures du soir
evening meal le dîner
every chaque; **every time** chaque fois
everyone tout le monde
everything tout
everywhere partout
examination (*school, medical*) l'examen *m*
example for example par exemple
excellent excellent(e)
except for sauf; **except for me** sauf moi
exchange in exchange for en échange de

to exchange échanger
exchange rate le taux de change
excursion l'excursion *f*
excuse Excuse me! Excusez-moi!; (*to get by*) Pardon!
exhaust pipe le pot d'échappement
exhibition l'exposition *f*
exit la sortie
expensive cher (chère)
to expire (*ticket, passport*) expirer
to explain expliquer
express (*train*) le rapide
express to send a letter express envoyer une lettre en exprès
extra (*in addition*) supplémentaire; **Can you give me an extra blanket?** Pouvez-vous me donner une couverture supplémentaire?; **There's an extra charge** Il y a un supplément
eye l'œil *m*
eyeliner l'eye-liner *m*
eye shadow le fard à paupières

F
fabric le tissu
face le visage
fair (*hair*) blond(e); **That's not fair** Ce n'est pas juste
fair (*funfair*) la fête foraine; **a trade fair** une foire commerciale
fake faux (fausse)
fall (*autumn*) l'automne *m*
to fall over tomber; **He fell over** Il est tombé
family la famille
famous célèbre
fan (*handheld*) l'éventail *m*; (*electric*) le ventilateur; **I'm a jazz fan** Je suis un fan de jazz; **She's a U2 fan** C'est une fan de U2; **He's a Liverpool fan** C'est un supporter de Liverpool
far loin; **Is it far?** C'est loin?; **How far is it?** C'est loin?
farm la ferme
farmhouse la ferme
fashionable à la mode
fast rapide; **too fast** trop vite

fat (*plump*) gros (grosse); (*in food, on person*) la graisse
father le père
father-in-law le beau-père
fault (*defect*) un défaut; **It's not my fault** Ce n'est pas de ma faute
favourite préféré(e)
fax le fax; **by fax** par fax
to fax (*document*) faxer; **to fax someone** envoyer un fax à quelqu'un
February février
to feed nourrir
to feel sentir; **I feel sick** J'ai la nausée; **I don't feel well** Je ne me sens pas bien
ferry le ferry
festival le festival
to fetch aller chercher
few with a few friends avec quelques amis; **few tourists** peu de touristes
fiancé le fiancé
fiancée la fiancée
fig la figue
file (*computer*) le fichier
to fill remplir
to fill in (*form*) remplir
to fill up (*with petrol*) faire le plein; **Fill it up please!** (*car*) Le plein s'il vous plaît!
fillet le filet
filling (*in tooth*) le plombage
film (*at cinema*) le film; (*for camera*) la pellicule
to find trouver
fine (*to be paid*) la contravention
finger le doigt
to finish finir
finished fini(e)
fire (*electric, gas*) le radiateur; (*open, accidental*) le feu
fire alarm l'alarme *f* d'incendie
firm la compagnie
first premier(ière)
first aid les premiers secours *mpl*
first class de première classe; **to travel first class** voyager en première classe
first name le prénom
fish (*food*) le poisson
to fish pêcher
fishing la pêche

fishmonger's le marchand de poisson, la marchande de poisson

to fit (*clothes*) **It doesn't fit me** Ça ne me va pas

fitting room le salon d'essayage

to fix (*repair*) réparer

fizzy gazeux(euse); **fizzy water** l'eau gazeuse

flash (*for camera*) le flash

flask (*thermos*) le Thermos®

flat (*appartment*) l'appartement *m*

flat (*battery*) à plat; **It's flat** (*beer*) C'est éventé

flat tyre le pneu crevé

flavour (*taste*) le goût; **Which flavour?** (*of ice cream*) Quel parfum?

flaw le défaut

fleas les puces *fpl*

flesh la chair

flex (*electrical*) le fil

flight le vol

flippers les palmes *fpl*

floor (*of room*) le sol; (*of building*) l'étage *m*; **Which floor?** Quel étage?; **on the ground floor** au rez-de-chaussée; **on the first floor** au premier étage; **on the second floor** au deuxième étage

floppy disk la disquette

flour la farine

flower la fleur

flu la grippe

fly la mouche

to fly (*person*) aller en avion; (*bird*) voler

fly sheet le double toit

fog le brouillard

foggy It's foggy Il y a du brouillard

food la nourriture

foot le pied; **to go on foot** aller à pied

football le football

football match le match de football

for pour; **for me** pour moi; **for you** pour toi, pour vous; **for five euros** pour cinq euros; **I've been here for two weeks** Ça fait deux semaines que je suis ici; **She'll be away for a month**

Elle sera absente pendant un mois

foreign étranger(ère)

foreigner l'étranger, l'étrangère

forever pour toujours

to forget oublier; **I've forgotten his name** J'ai oublié son nom; **to forget to do** oublier de faire

fork (*for eating*) la fourchette

form (*document*) le formulaire

fortnight quinze jours

forward en avant

four-wheel drive vehicle le quatre-quatre

France la France; **in/to France** en France

free (*not occupied*) libre; (*costing nothing*) gratuit(e); **Is this seat free?** Ce siège est libre?

freezer le congélateur

French français(e); (*language*) le français

French fries les frites *fpl*

French people les Français *mpl*

frequent fréquent(e)

fresh frais (fraîche)

Friday vendredi

fridge le frigo

fried frit(e)

friend l'ami *m*, l'amie *f*

friendly gentil(le)

frog la grenouille

frogs' legs les cuisses *fpl* de grenouille

from de; **Where are you from?** Vous êtes d'où?; **from nine o'clock** à partir de neuf heures

front le devant; **in front of** devant

frozen (*food*) surgelé(e)

fruit le fruit

fruit juice le jus de fruit

fruit salad la salade de fruits

frying-pan la poêle

fuel (*petrol*) l'essence *f*

fuel tank le réservoir d'essence

full (*tank, glass*) plein(e); (*restaurant, hotel*) complet(ète)

full board la pension complète

funfair la fête foraine

funny amusant(e)

furnished meublé(e)

furniture les meubles *mpl*

G

gallery la galerie

game le jeu

garage (*for petrol*) la station-service; (*for parking, repair*) le garage

garden le jardin

garlic l'ail *m*

gas le gaz

gas cooker la gazinière

gas cylinder la bouteille de gaz

gate la porte

gay (*person*) homo

gear la vitesse; **first gear** la première; **second gear** la seconde; **third gear** la troisième; **fourth gear** la quatrième; **reverse gear** la marche arrière

gearbox la boîte de vitesses

gents (*toilet*) les toilettes *fpl* (pour hommes)

genuine authentique

to get (*to have, to receive*) avoir; (*to fetch*) aller chercher

to get in (*vehicle*) monter

to get out (*vehicle*) sortir

gift le cadeau

gift shop la boutique de souvenirs

girl la fille

girlfriend la copine

to give donner

to give back rendre

glass (*for drinking, material*) le verre; **a glass of water** un verre d'eau; **a glass of wine** un verre de vin

glasses (*spectacles*) les lunettes *fpl*

gloves les gants *mpl*

to go aller; **to go home** rentrer à la maison

to go back retourner

to go in entrer

to go out sortir

God Dieu *m*

goggles (*for swimming*) les lunettes *fpl* de natation; (*for skiing*) les lunettes *fpl* de ski

golf le golf

golf ball la balle de golf
golf clubs les clubs mpl de golf
golf course le terrain de golf
good bon (bonne); **very good** très bien; **good afternoon** bonjour; **good evening** bonsoir; **good morning** bonjour; **good night** bonne nuit
goodbye au revoir
good-looking beau, bel (belle)
gram(me) le gramme
grandchildren les petits-enfants mpl
granddaughter la petite-fille
grandfather le grand-père
grandmother la grand-mère
grandparents les grands-parents mpl
grandson le petit-fils
grapefruit le pamplemousse
grapes le raisin
grated (cheese) râpé(e)
greasy gras(se)
great (wonderful) formidable
Great Britain la Grande-Bretagne
green vert(e)
grey gris(e)
grill (part of cooker) le gril
grilled grillé(e)
grocer's l'épicerie f
ground floor le rez-de-chaussée; **on the ground floor** au rez-de-chaussée
groundsheet le tapis de sol
group le groupe
guarantee la garantie
guesthouse la pension
guide (person) le/la guide
guidebook le guide
guided tour la visite guidée
guitar la guitare
gums (in mouth) les gencives fpl
gym (gymnasium) le gymnase
gynecologist le/la gynécologue

H

hair les cheveux mpl
haircut la coupe (de cheveux)
hairdresser le coiffeur, la coiffeuse
hairdryer le sèche-cheveux
half la moitié; **half of the cake** la moitié du gâteau; **half an hour** une demi-heure
half board la demi-pension
ham (cooked) le jambon; (cured) le jambon cru
hamburger le hamburger
hand la main
handbag le sac à main
handicapped handicapé(e)
handlebars le guidon
hand luggage les bagages mpl à main
handsome beau, bel (belle)
hangover la gueule de bois
to hang up (telephone) raccrocher
to happen What happened? Qu'est-ce qui s'est passé?
happy heureux(-euse)
happy birthday! bon anniversaire!
harbour le port
hard (not soft) dur(e); (not easy) difficile
hardly I've hardly got any money Je n'ai presque pas d'argent
hardware shop la quincaillerie
hat le chapeau
to have avoir; **I have ...** J'ai ...; **I don't have ...** Je n'ai pas ...; **to have to** devoir; **I've done it** Je l'ai fait; **I'll have a coffee** Je vais prendre un café
hay fever le rhume des foins
he il
head la tête
headache le mal de tête; **I have a headache** J'ai mal à la tête
headlights les phares
headphones les écouteurs
to hear entendre
heart le cœur
heart attack la crise cardiaque
heartburn les brûlures fpl d'estomac
heater l'appareil m de chauffage
heating le chauffage
heavy lourd(e)

heel le talon
hello bonjour!; (on telephone) allô?
helmet le casque
to help aider; **Can you help me?** Vous pouvez m'aider?; **Help!** Au secours!
her la, l'; lui; elle (belonging to her) son, sa, ses (agrees with the noun that follows); **I saw her last night** Je l'ai vue hier soir; **I don't know her** Je ne la connais pas; **I gave her the book** Je lui ai donné le livre; **with her** avec elle; **I'm older than her** Je suis plus âgé qu'elle; **her passport** son passeport; **her room** sa chambre; **her suitcases** ses valises
here ici; **Here is ...** Voici ...; **Here's my passport** Voici mon passeport
Hi! Salut!
high haut(e)
hill la colline
hill-walking la randonnée en montagne
him le, l'; lui **I saw him last night** Je l'ai vu hier soir; **I don't know him** Je ne le connais pas; **I gave him the letter** Je lui ai donné la lettre; **with him** avec lui
hip la hanche
hire car hire la location de voitures; **bike hire** la location de vélos; **boat hire** la location de bateaux; **ski hire** la location de skis
to hire louer
hire car la voiture de location
his son, sa, ses (agrees with the noun that follows); **his passport** son passeport; **his room** sa chambre; **his suitcases** ses valises
historic historique
hobby le passe-temps; **What hobbies do you have?** Quels sont tes passe-temps?
to hold tenir; (contain) contenir
hole le trou
holiday les vacances fpl; (public) le jour férié; **on holiday** en vacances
home la maison; **at home**

à la maison
homeopathic homéopathique
honey le miel
honeymoon la lune de miel
to hope espérer; **I hope so** J'espère que oui; **I hope not** J'espère que non
hors d'œuvre le hors-d'œuvre
horse racing les courses *fpl* de chevaux
horse-riding l'équitation *f*
hospital l'hôpital *m*
hostel (*youth hostel*) l'auberge *f* de jeunesse
hot chaud(e); **hot water** l'eau chaude; **I'm hot** J'ai chaud; **It's hot** (*weather*) Il fait chaud
hotel l'hôtel *m*
hour l'heure *f*; **half an hour** une demi-heure
house la maison
house wine le vin en pichet
how (*in what way*) comment; **How much/ many?** Combien?; **How are you?** Comment allez-vous?
hungry to be hungry avoir faim
hurry I'm in a hurry Je suis pressé
to hurt Have you hurt yourself? Tu t'es fait mal?; **My back hurts** J'ai mal au dos; **That hurts** Ça fait mal
husband le mari

I
I je
ice la glace; **ice cube** le glaçon; **with/without ice** avec/sans glaçons
ice box (*for picnics*) la glacière; (*in fridge*) le compartiment à glace
ice cream la glace
ice lolly l'esquimau *m*
idea l'idée *f*
if si
ignition l'allumage *m*
ignition key la clé de contact
ill malade
illness la maladie
immediately immédiatement
immersion heater le

chauffe-eau électrique
immobilizer (*on car*) le dispositif antidémarrage
to import importer
important important(e)
impossible impossible
to improve améliorer
in dans; en; au, à; **in ten minutes** dans dix minutes; **in France** en France; **in Canada** au Canada; **in London** à Londres; **in the hotel** à l'hôtel; **in front of** devant
included compris(e)
indicator (*in car*) le clignotant
indigestion l'indigestion *f*
infection l'infection *f*
information les renseignements *mpl*
information desk les renseignements *mpl*
inhaler (*for medication*) l'inhalateur *m*
injection la piqûre
injured blessé(e)
injury la blessure
inn l'auberge *f*
inquiry desk le bureau de renseignements
insect l'insecte *m*
insect repellent le produit antimoustiques
inside à l'intérieur
instant instant coffee le café instantané
instead instead of au lieu de
insulin l'insuline *f*
insurance l'assurance *f*
insurance certificate l'attestation *f* d'assurance
to insure assurer
insured assuré(e)
intend to intend to avoir l'intention de
interesting intéressant(e)
international international(e)
internet l'Internet *m*; **on the internet** sur Internet; **Do you have internet access?** Vous avez accès à l'Internet?
interpreter l'interprète *m/f*
interval (*theatre*) l'entracte *m*
into dans; en; **to get into a car** monter dans une

voiture; **to go into the cinema** entrer dans le cinéma; **to go into town** aller en ville
to introduce présenter
invitation l'invitation *f*
to invite inviter
invoice la facture
Ireland l'Irlande *f*
Irish irlandais(e); (*language*) l'irlandais *m*
iron (*for clothes*) le fer à repasser
to iron repasser
ironing board la planche à repasser
ironmonger's la quincaillerie
island l'île *f*
it il, elle
itchy It's itchy Ça me démange

J
jack (*for car*) le cric
jacket la veste; **waterproof jacket** l'anorak *m*
jam (*food*) la confiture
jammed coincé(e)
January janvier
jar (*of honey, jam*) le pot
jeans le jean
jelly (*dessert*) la gelée
jeweller's la bijouterie
jewellery les bijoux *mpl*
Jewish juif (juive)
job le travail
to jog faire du jogging
to join (*club*) s'inscrire à
journey le voyage
juice le jus; **a carton of juice** un carton de jus
July juillet
jumper le pull
jump leads les câbles *mpl* de raccordement pour batterie
June juin
just just two deux seulement; **I've just arrived** Je viens d'arriver
to keep (*retain*) garder

K
kettle la bouilloire
key la clé
kid (*child*) le gosse
kidneys les reins *mpl*
kilo(gram) le kilo
kilometre le kilomètre

kind (*person*) gentil(le)
kind (*sort*) la sorte; **What kind?** Quelle sorte?
to kiss embrasser
kitchen la cuisine
knee le genou
knickers la culotte
knife le couteau
to know (*facts*) savoir; (*person, place*) connaître; **I don't know** Je ne sais pas; **I don't know Paris** Je ne connais pas Paris; **to know how to do sth** savoir faire quelque chose; **to know how to swim** savoir nager

L
label l'étiquette *f*
lace (*fabric*) la dentelle
ladies (*toilet*) les toilettes *fpl* (pour dames)
lady la dame
lager la bière; **bottled lager** la bière en bouteille; **draught lager** la bière pression
lake le lac
lamb l'agneau *m*
lamp la lampe
to land atterrir
landlady la propriétaire
landline la ligne fixe
landlord le propriétaire
landslide le glissement de terrain
lane la ruelle; (*of motorway*) la voie
language la langue
language school l'école *f* de langues
laptop le portable
large grand(e)
last dernier(ière); **the last bus** le dernier bus; **the last train** le dernier train; **last time** la dernière fois; **last week** la semaine dernière; **last year** l'année dernière; **last night** (*evening*) hier soir; (*night-time*) la nuit dernière
late tard; **The train is late** Le train a du retard; **Sorry we are late** Excusez-nous d'arriver en retard
later plus tard
to laugh rire
launderette la laverie

automatique
laundry service le service de blanchisserie
lavatory les toilettes *fpl*
lavender la lavande
lawyer l'avocat *m*, l'avocate *f*
lead (*electric*) le fil
leak la fuite
to leak **It's leaking** Il y a une fuite
to learn apprendre
lease (*rental*) le bail
least **at least** au moins
leather le cuir
to leave (*a place*) partir; (*to leave behind*) laisser; **I left it at home** Je l'ai laissé à la maison; **What time does the train leave?** À quelle heure le train part-il?
leek le poireau
left on/to the left à gauche
left-luggage locker la consigne automatique
left-luggage office la consigne
leg la jambe
legal légal(e)
leisure centre le centre de loisirs
lemon le citron
lemonade la limonade
to lend prêter; **Can you lend me your pen?** Tu peux me prêter ton stylo?
lens (*of camera*) l'objectif *m* (*contact lens*) la lentille
less moins; **less than me** moins que moi; **A bit less, please** Un peu moins, s'il vous plaît
lesson la leçon
to let (*to allow*) permettre; (*to hire out*) louer
letter la lettre
letterbox la boîte aux lettres
lettuce la laitue
licence le permis
to lie down s'allonger
lift (*elevator*) l'ascenseur *m*; **Can you give me a lift to the swimming pool?** Vous pouvez me déposer à la piscine?
lift pass (*skiing*) le forfait
light (*not heavy*) léger(ère)
light la lumière; **Have you got a light?** Avez-vous du feu?

light bulb l'ampoule *f*
lighter le briquet
lighthouse le phare
lightning les éclairs *mpl*
like (*similar to*) comme; **a city like Paris** une ville comme Paris
to like aimer; **I like coffee** J'aime le café; **I don't like ...** Je n'aime pas ...; **I'd like to ...** Je voudrais ...
lime (*fruit*) le citron vert
line (*queue*) la file; (*row, telephone*) la ligne
linen le lin
lingerie la lingerie
lips les lèvres *fpl*
lipstick le rouge à lèvres
to listen to écouter
litre le litre
little petit(e); **a little** un peu
to live (*in a place*) habiter; **I live in London** J'habite à Londres
liver le foie
living room le salon
loaf le pain
lobster le homard
local local(e)
lock (*on door, box*) la serrure
to lock fermer à clé
locker (*for luggage*) le casier
locksmith le serrurier
log (*for fire*) la bûche
lollipop la sucette
London Londres; **to/in London** à Londres
long long(ue); **for a long time** longtemps
long-sighted hypermétrope
to look after garder
to look at regarder
to look for chercher
loose (*not fastened*) desserré(e); **It's come loose** (*unscrewed*) Ça s'est desserré; (*detached*) Ça s'est détaché
lorry le camion
to lose perdre
lost (*object*) perdu(e); **I've lost ...** J'ai perdu ...; **I'm lost** Je suis perdu(e)
lost property office le bureau des objets trouvés
lot **a lot of, lots of** beaucoup de; **a lot of people** beaucoup de monde; **a lot**

of fruit beaucoup de fruits
lotion la lotion
loud fort(e)
loudspeaker le haut-parleur
lounge (*in hotel, airport*) le salon
love l'amour
to love (*person*) aimer; (*food, activity*) adorer; **I love you** Je t'aime; **I love swimming** J'adore nager
lovely beau, bel (belle)
low bas(se)
lucky chanceux(-euse); **to be lucky** avoir de la chance
luggage les bagages *mpl*
luggage allowance le poids maximum autorisé
luggage rack le porte-bagages
luggage tag l'étiquette *f* à bagages
luggage trolley le chariot (à bagages)
lump (*swelling*) la bosse
lunch le déjeuner
lung le poumon
luxury le luxe

M
mad fou (folle)
magazine la revue
maid (*in hotel*) la domestique
maiden name le nom de jeune fille
mail le courrier; **by mail** par la poste
main principal(e)
main course (*of meal*) le plat principal
main road la route principale
make (*brand*) la marque
to make faire; **made of wood** en bois
make-up le maquillage
man l'homme *m*
to manage (*to be in charge of*) gérer
manager le directeur, la directrice
manageress la directrice
manicure les soins *mpl* de manucure
manual (*gear change*) manuel(le)
many beaucoup de
map (*of region, country*) la

carte; (*of town*) le plan;
road map la carte routière;
street map le plan de la ville
March mars
margarine la margarine
marina la marina
mark (*stain*) la tache
market le marché; **Where is the market?** Où est le marché?; **When is the market?** Le marché, c'est quel jour?
marmalade la marmelade d'oranges
married marié(e); **I'm married** Je suis marié(e); **Are you married?** Vous êtes marié(e)?
mass (*in church*) la messe
massage le massage
match (*game*) le match
matches les allumettes *fpl*
material (*cloth*) le tissu
to matter **It doesn't matter** Ça ne fait rien; **What's the matter?** Qu'est-ce qu'il y a?
mattress le matelas
May mai
mayonnaise la mayonnaise
mayor le maire
maximum le maximum
me me, m'; moi; **Can you hear me?** Vous m'entendez?; **He scares me** Il me fait peur; **It's me** C'est moi; **without me** sans moi; **with me** avec moi
meal le repas
to mean vouloir dire; **What does this mean?** Qu'est-ce que ça veut dire?
meat la viande
medicine le médicament
Mediterranean Sea la Méditerranée
medium (*size*) moyen(ne)
medium rare (*meat*) à point
to meet (*by chance*) rencontrer; (*by arrangement*) voir; **I'm meeting her tomorrow** Je la vois demain
meeting la réunion
melon le melon
member (*of club*) le membre
to mend réparer
menu la carte; **set menu** le menu

message le message
to message envoyer un message
metal le métal
meter le compteur
metre le mètre
microwave oven le four à micro-ondes
midday midi; **at midday** à midi
middle le milieu; **in the middle of the street** au milieu de la rue; **in the middle of May** en plein mois de mai
middle-aged d'une cinquantaine d'années
midge le moucheron
midnight minuit; **at midnight** à minuit
migraine la migraine; **I have a migraine** J'ai la migraine
mild (*weather, cheese*) doux (douce); (*curry*) peu épicé(e)
milk le lait; **with/without milk** avec/sans lait; **fresh milk** le lait frais; **hot milk** le lait chaud; **long-life milk** le lait longue conservation; **powdered milk** le lait en poudre; **soya milk** le lait de soja
milkshake le milk-shake
millimetre le millimètre
mince (*meat*) la viande hachée
to mind **Do you mind if I...?** Ça vous gêne si je...?; **I don't mind** Ça m'est égal
mineral water l'eau minérale
minidisc le minidisque
minimum le minimum
minute la minute
mirror le miroir; (*in car*) le rétroviseur
Miss Mademoiselle
to miss (*train, flight*) rater
missing (*disappeared*) disparu(e); **My son is missing** Mon fils a disparu
mistake l'erreur *f*
to mix mélanger
mobile number le numéro de portable
mobile phone le portable
modem le modem

modern moderne
moisturizer la crème hydratante
moment at the moment en ce moment; **just a moment** un instant
monastery le monastère
Monday lundi
money l'argent *m*
month le mois; **this month** ce mois-ci; **last month** le mois dernier; **next month** le mois prochain
moped le vélomoteur
more plus; **more expensive** plus cher; **more than before** plus qu'avant; **more wine** plus de vin; **more than 10** plus de dix; **Do you want some more tea?** Voulez-vous encore du thé?; **There isn't any more** Il n'en reste plus
morning le matin; **in the morning** le matin; **this morning** ce matin; **tomorrow morning** demain matin
mosque la mosquée
mosquito le moustique
mosquito repellent le produit antimoustiques
most the most interesting le plus intéressant; **most of the time** la plupart du temps; **most people** la plupart des gens
mother la mère
mother-in-law la belle-mère
motor le moteur
motorbike la moto
motorboat le bateau à moteur
motorway l'autoroute *f*
mountain la montagne
mountain bike le VTT, le vélo tout-terrain
mountaineering l'alpinisme *m*
mouse la souris
mouth la bouche
to move bouger
movie le film
Mr Monsieur; **Mr Dupond** M. Dupond
Mrs Madame; **Mrs Leclerc** Mme Leclerc
Ms Madame
much beaucoup; **too much**

trop; **too much money** trop d'argent; **I feel much better** Je me sens beaucoup mieux
mugging l'agression *f*
museum le musée
mushrooms les champignons *mpl*
music la musique
Muslim musulman(e)
mussels les moules *fpl*
must I must buy some presents Il faut que j'achète des cadeaux
mustard la moutarde
my mon, ma, mes (*agrees with the noun that follows*); **my passport** mon passeport; **my room** ma chambre; **my suitcases** mes valises

N

nail (*metal*) le clou; (*finger*) l'ongle *m*
nail file la lime à ongles
name le nom; **My name is...** Je m'appelle...; **What is your name?** Comment vous appelez-vous?
nanny la garde d'enfants; **We have a nanny** Nous avons une dame qui vient garder les enfants à la maison
napkin la serviette de table
nappy la couche
narrow étroit(e)
nationality la nationalité
natural naturel(le)
nature reserve la réserve naturelle
navy blue bleu marine
near près de; **near the bank** près de la banque; **Is it near?** C'est près d'ici?
necessary nécessaire
neck le cou
necklace le collier
nectarine le brugnon
to need (to) avoir besoin de; **I need** j'ai besoin de; **we need** nous avons besoin de; **I need to phone** J'ai besoin de téléphoner
needle l'aiguille *f*; **a needle and thread** du fil et une aiguille
negative (*photo*) le négatif

neighbours les voisins *mpl*
nephew le neveu
net le Net
neutral (*gear*) le point mort
never jamais; **I never drink wine** Je ne bois jamais de vin
new nouveau (nouvelle)
news (*TV, radio*) les informations *fpl*
newsagent's le marchand de journaux
newspaper le journal
news stand le kiosque
New Year le Nouvel An; **Happy New Year!** Bonne année!
New Year's Eve la Saint-Sylvestre
New Zealand la Nouvelle-Zélande
next prochain(e); (*after*) ensuite; **the next train** le prochain train; **the next stop** le prochain arrêt; **next week** la semaine prochaine; **next Monday** lundi prochain; **next to** à côté de; **What did you do next?** Qu'est-ce que vous avez fait ensuite?
nice (*kind*) gentil(le); (*pretty*) joli(e); (*good*) bon(ne)
niece la nièce
night (*night-time*) la nuit; (*evening*) le soir; **at night** la nuit; **per night** par nuit; **last night** (*evening*) hier soir; (*night-time*) la nuit dernière; **tomorrow night** (*evening*) demain soir; (*night-time*) la nuit prochaine; **tonight** (*evening*) ce soir; (*night-time*) cette nuit
nightclub la boîte de nuit
no non; (*without*) sans; **no thanks** non merci; **no smoking** défense de fumer; **no problem** pas de problème; **no ice** sans glaçons; **no sugar** sans sucre; **There's no hot water** Il n'y a pas d'eau chaude
nobody personne; **Nobody came** Personne n'est venu
noise le bruit
noisy It's very noisy Il y a beaucoup de bruit

non-alcoholic sans alcool
none aucun(e)
non-smoking (*seat, compartment*) non-fumeurs
normally (*usually*) généralement; (*as normal*) normalement
north le nord
Northern Ireland l'Irlande *f* du Nord
nose le nez
nosebleed to have a nosebleed saigner du nez
not ne pas; **I am not going** Je n'y vais pas
note (*banknote*) le billet; (*written*) le mot
note pad le bloc-notes
nothing rien; **nothing else** rien d'autre
notice There's a notice on the door C'est affiché sur la porte
November novembre
now maintenant; **now and then** de temps en temps
number (*quantity*) le nombre; (*of room, house*) le numéro; **phone number** le numéro de téléphone
numberplate (*of car*) la plaque d'immatriculation
nurse l'infirmier *m*, l'infirmière *f*
nursery slope la piste pour débutants
nuts (*to eat*) les noix et les arachides *fpl*
to obtain obtenir

O

occasionally de temps en temps
occupation (*work*) la profession
October octobre
of de; **a glass of wine** un verre de vin; **made of cotton** en coton
off (*light, heater*) éteint(e); (*tap, gas*) fermé(e); (*milk*) tourné(e); **I'm off** Je m'en vais
office le bureau
often souvent; **How often do you go to the gym?** Tu vas à la gym tous les combien?

oil l'huile *f*
oil gauge la jauge de niveau d'huile
OK! d'accord!
old vieux, vieil (vieille); **How old are you?** Quel âge avez-vous?; **I'm... years old** J'ai... ans
olive l'olive *f*
olive oil l'huile *f* d'olive
on (*TV, light*) allumé(e); (*tap, gas*) ouvert(e); (*engine*) en marche
on sur; **on the table** sur la table; **on the TV** à la télé; **on the second floor** au deuxième étage; **on Friday** vendredi; **on Fridays** le vendredi; **on time** à l'heure
once une fois; **once a week** une fois par semaine; **at once** tout de suite
onion l'oignon *m*
only seulement; **How much was it? – Only 10 euros** C'était combien? – Seulement dix euros; **We only want to stay for one night** Nous ne voulons rester qu'une nuit; **the only day I'm free** le seul jour où je suis libre
open ouvert(e)
to open ouvrir
opening hours les heures *fpl* d'ouverture
opera l'opéra *m*
operation (*surgical*) l'opération *f*
operator (*phone*) le/la standardiste
opposite en face de; **opposite the bank** en face de la banque; **quite the opposite** bien au contraire
optician l'opticien, l'opticienne
or ou; **Tea or coffee?** Du thé ou du café?; **I don't eat meat or fish** Je ne mange ni viande ni poisson
orange (*fruit*) l'orange *f* (*colour*) orange
orange juice le jus d'orange
order out of order en panne
to order (*in restaurant*) commander; **I'd like to order** Je voudrais commander

organic biologique
to organize organiser
other autre; **the other car** l'autre voiture; **the other one** l'autre; **Have you any others?** Vous en avez d'autres?
ought I ought to call my parents Je devrais appeler mes parents
our (*sing*) notre; (*plural*) nos; **our room** notre chambre; **our passports** nos passeports; **our baggage** nos bagages
out (*light*) éteint(e); **She's out** Elle est sortie; **He lives out of town** Il habite en dehors de la ville
outdoor (*pool*) en plein air
outside dehors; **It's outside** C'est dehors; **outside the house** en dehors de la maison
oven le four
over (*on top of*) au-dessus de; (*finished*) terminé(e); **over the window** au-dessus de la fenêtre; **over here** ici; **It's over there** C'est là-bas; **over the holidays** pendant les vacances
to overcharge faire payer trop cher
overdone (*food*) trop cuit(e)
to owe devoir; **I owe you...** Je vous dois...
own propre; **It's his own company** C'est sa propre société; **on my own** tout seul
to own (*land, house, company*) être propriétaire de
owner le/la propriétaire
oxygen l'oxygène *m*
oyster l'huître *f*

P

pacemaker le stimulateur (cardiaque)
to pack (*luggage*) faire les bagages
package tour le voyage organisé
packet le paquet
paid payé(e)
pain la douleur

painful douloureux(-euse)
painkiller l'analgésique *m*
to paint peindre
painting (*picture*) le tableau
pair la paire
palace le palais
pale pale blue bleu pâle
pan (*saucepan*) la casserole; (*frying pan*) la poêle
panniers (*for bike*) les sacoches *fpl*
panties la culotte
pants (*men's underwear*) le slip
panty liner le protège-slip
paper le papier
paragliding le parapente
parcel le colis
pardon Pardon? Comment?; I beg your pardon? Pardon?
parents les parents *mpl*
park le parc
to park garer (la voiture)
parking meter le parcmètre
partner (*business*) l'associé *m*, l'associée *m* (*boyfriend/girlfriend*) le compagnon, la compagne
party (*group*) le groupe; (*celebration*) la fête; (*in the evening*) la soirée
pass (*bus, train*) la carte; (*mountain*) le col
to pass Can you pass me the salt, please? Vous pouvez me passer le sel, s'il vous plaît?
passenger le passager, la passagère
passport le passeport
password le mot de passe
pasta les pâtes *fpl*
pastry (*cake*) la pâtisserie
path le chemin
patient (*in hospital*) le patient, la patiente
to pay payer; I'd like to pay Je voudrais payer; Where do I pay? Où est-ce qu'il faut payer?
payment le paiement
peach la pêche
peanut la cacahuète *f*
pear la poire
peas les petits pois
pedestrian le piéton, la piétonne
to peel éplucher

peg (*for clothes*) la pince à linge; (*for tent*) le piquet
pen le stylo
pencil le crayon
pensioner le retraité, la retraitée
people les gens *mpl*
pepper (*spice*) le poivre; (*vegetable*) le poivron
per par; per day par jour; per person par personne
performance (*in theatre*) le spectacle; (*in cinema*) la séance
perfume le parfum
perhaps peut-être
perm la permanente
permit le permis
person la personne
petrol l'essence *f*; unleaded petrol l'essence sans plomb
petrol pump la pompe à essence
petrol station la station-service
petrol tank le réservoir
pharmacy la pharmacie
phone le téléphone; by phone par téléphone
to phone téléphoner
phonebook l'annuaire *m*
phone call l'appel *m*
phonecard la télécarte
photo la photo; to take a photo prendre une photo
photocopy la photocopie
to photocopy photocopier
photograph la photographie
to pick (*choose*) choisir
pickpocket le pickpocket
picnic le pique-nique; to have a picnic pique-niquer
picture (*painting*) le tableau; (*photo*) la photo
pie (*fruit, meat*) la tourte
piece le morceau
pig le cochon
pill la pilule
pillow l'oreiller *m*
pilot le pilote
pin l'épingle *f*
pineapple le pamplemousse
pink rose
pipe (*drains*) le tuyau
pity What a pity! Quel dommage!
pizza la pizza
place l'endroit *m*

place of birth le lieu de naissance
plain (*yoghurt*) nature
plan (*of town*) le plan
plane (*aircraft*) l'avion *m*
plaster (*sticking plaster*) le sparadrap; (*for broken limb, on wall*) le plâtre
plastic en plastique
plastic bag le sac en plastique
plate l'assiette *f*
platform (*railway*) le quai; Which platform? Quel quai?
play (*theatre*) la pièce
to play (*games*) jouer à; (*instrument*) jouer de; I play the guitar Je joue de la guitare
please s'il vous plaît
pleased content(e); Pleased to meet you! Enchanté(e)!
plug (*electrical*) la prise; (*for sink*) le bouchon
to plug in brancher
plum la prune
plumber le plombier
pm de l'après-midi
poached (*egg, fish*) poché(e)
pocket la poche
police la police
policeman l'agent *m* de police
police station le commissariat; (*in small town*) la gendarmerie
policewoman la femme agent
polish (*for shoes*) le cirage
polite poli(e)
pool la piscine
poor pauvre
popular populaire
pork le porc
porter (*in hotel*) le portier; (*at station*) le porteur
portion la portion
Portugal le Portugal
Portuguese portugais(e); (*language*) le portugais
possible possible
post by post par courrier
to post poster
postbox la boîte aux lettres
postcard la carte postale
postcode le code postal
poster l'affiche *f*
postman le facteur

post office la poste
postwoman la factrice
pot (*for cooking*) la casserole
potato la pomme de terre;
  baked potato la pomme de
  terre cuite au four; **boiled
  potatoes** les pommes
  vapeur; **fried potatoes** les
  pommes frites; **mashed
  potatoes** la purée; **roast
  potatoes** les pommes
  de terre rôties; **sauteed
  potatoes** les pommes de
  terre sautées
potato salad la salade de
  pommes de terre
pottery la poterie
pound (*money*) la livre
powder la poudre
powdered en poudre
power (*electricity*) le
  courant
pram le landau
prawn la crevette rose
to prefer préférer
pregnant enceinte; **I'm
  pregnant** Je suis enceinte
to prepare préparer
prescription l'ordonnance *f*
present (*gift*) le cadeau
president le président
pressure la pression
pretty joli(e)
price le prix
price list le tarif
priest le prêtre
print (*photo*) la photo
to print imprimer
printer l'imprimante *f*
printout la sortie papier
private privé(e)
probably probablement;
  **He'll probably come
  tomorrow** Il viendra
  probablement demain
problem le problème
programme (*TV, radio*)
  l'émission *f*
to promise promettre
to pronounce prononcer;
  How's it pronounced?
  Comment ça se prononce?
public public(ique)
public holiday le jour férié
pudding le dessert
to pull tirer
pullover le pull
pulse le pouls

pump (*for bike*) la pompe;
  petrol pump la pompe à
  essence
puncture la crevaison
purple violet(te)
purpose le but; **on purpose**
  exprès
purse le porte-monnaie
to push pousser
pushchair la poussette
to put (*place*) mettre
Pyrenees les Pyrénées *mpl*

Q
quality la qualité
quantity la quantité
quarter le quart; **a quarter
  of an hour** un quart d'heure
question la question; **to
  ask a question** poser une
  question
queue la queue
to queue faire la queue
quick rapide
quickly vite
quiet (*place*) tranquille
quilt la couette
quite (*rather*) assez; **quite
  good** pas mal; **quite
  expensive** assez cher; **I'm
  not quite sure** Je n'en suis
  pas tout à fait sûr; **quite a
  lot** pas mal

R
racket la raquette
radiator le radiateur
radio la radio; **car radio**
  l'autoradio *m*
railway le chemin de fer
railway station la gare
rain la pluie
to rain **It's raining** Il pleut
raincoat l'imperméable *m*
rare (*uncommon*) rare; (*steak*)
  saignant(e)
raspberry la framboise
rat le rat
rate (*price*) le tarif
rate of exchange le taux de
  change
rather plutôt; **rather
  expensive** plutôt cher;
  I'd rather stay in tonight
  J'aimerais mieux rester à la
  maison ce soir
raw cru(e)
razor le rasoir

razor blades les lames de
  rasoir
to read lire
ready prêt(e)
real vrai(e)
really vraiment
receipt le reçu
reception desk la réception
receptionist le/la
  réceptionniste
to recharge (*battery*)
  recharger
recipe la recette
to recognize reconnaître
to recommend recommander
red rouge
refill la recharge
refund le remboursement
region la région
to register (*at hotel*)
  s'inscrire sur le registre
registered (*letter*)
  recommandé(e)
registration form la fiche
relation (*family*) le parent,
  la parente
relationship les rapports *mpl*
to remain rester
remember se rappeler; **I
  don't remember** Je ne
  m'en rappelle pas; **I can't
  remember his name** Je ne
  me souviens pas de son nom
remote control la
  télécommande
rent le loyer
to rent louer
rental la location
to repair réparer
to repeat répéter
to reply répondre
to require exiger; **What
  qualifications are required?**
  Quels sont les diplômes
  requis?
to rescue sauver
reservation la réservation
to reserve réserver
reserved réservé(e)
resident (*in country*) le
  résident, la résidente;
  (*in street*) le riverain, la
  riveraine; (*in hotel*) le/la
  pensionnaire
rest (*relaxation*) le repos;
  (*remainder*) le reste; **the rest
  of the money** le reste de
  l'argent

to rest se reposer
restaurant le restaurant
restaurant car le wagon-restaurant
retired retraité(e)
to return (*to go back*) retourner
return ticket le billet aller-retour
retweet le retweet
to retweet retweeter
to reverse faire marche arrière; **to reverse the charges** appeler en PCV
reverse gear la marche arrière
rice le riz
rich (*person, food*) riche
to ride (*on horseback*) monter à cheval; (*on bike*) faire du vélo
right (*correct*) exact(e); **to be right** avoir raison; **You're right** Tu as raison; **That's right** C'est vrai; **on/to the right** à droite
right of way la priorité
ring (*on finger*) la bague
ripe mûr(e)
river la rivière
Riviera (*French*) la Côte d'Azur
road la route
roast rôti(e)
roll (*bread*) le petit pain
roof le toit
room (*in house*) la pièce; (*in hotel*) la chambre; (*space*) la place; **double room** la chambre pour deux personnes; **single room** la chambre pour une personne; **family room** la chambre pour une famille
room number le numéro de chambre
room service le service dans les chambres
rosé wine le rosé
row (*line, theatre*) la rangée
rubber (*material*) le caoutchouc; (*eraser*) la gomme
rubbish les ordures *fpl*
rucksack le sac à dos
to run courir
rush hour l'heure *f* de pointe

S
sad triste
saddle la selle
safe (*for valuables*) le coffre-fort
safe sans danger; **Is it safe?** Ce n'est pas dangereux?
safety belt la ceinture de sécurité
safety pin l'épingle *f* de sûreté
to sail (*sport, leisure*) faire de la voile
sailboard la planche à voile
sailing (*sport*) la voile
sailing boat le voilier
salad la salade; **green salad** la salade verte; **mixed salad** la salade composée; **salad dressing** la vinaigrette
sales (*in shops*) les soldes *fpl*
sales assistant le vendeur, la vendeuse
salesman le vendeur
sales rep le représentant, la représentante
saleswoman la vendeuse
salmon le saumon
salt le sel
salt water l'eau salée
salty salé(e)
same même; **Have a good weekend! – The same to you!** Bon week-end! – Vous de même!
sand le sable
sandals les sandales *fpl*
sandwich le sandwich; **toasted sandwich** le croque-monsieur
sanitary towels les serviettes *fpl* hygiéniques
sardines les sardines *fpl*
satellite dish l'antenne *f* parabolique
satellite TV la télévision par satellite
Saturday samedi
sauce la sauce
saucepan la casserole
saucer la soucoupe
sausage la saucisse
savoury salé(e)
to say dire
scarf (*headscarf*) le foulard; (*woollen*) l'écharpe *f*
scenery le paysage
schedule l'horaire *m*

school l'école *f*; **at school** à l'école; **to go to school** aller à l'école; **after school** après l'école; **primary school** l'école primaire
scissors les ciseaux *mpl*
score (*of match*) le score; **What's the score?** Quel est le score?; **to score a goal** marquer un but
Scotland l'Écosse *f*
Scottish écossais(e)
screen (*on computer, TV*) l'écran *m*
screw la vis
screwdriver le tournevis
scuba diving la plongée sous-marine
sea la mer
seafood les fruits *mpl* de mer
seaside le bord de la mer; **at the seaside** au bord de la mer
season (*of year*) la saison; **high season** la haute saison; **in season** de saison
season ticket la carte d'abonnement
seat (*chair*) le siège; (*in bus, train*) la place
seatbelt la ceinture de sécurité
second second(e); **a second** une seconde
second class de seconde classe; **to travel second class** voyager en seconde classe
secretary le/la secrétaire
to see voir
self-service le libre-service
to sell vendre; **Do you sell...?** Vous vendez...?
Sellotape® le Scotch®
to send envoyer
senior citizen la personne du troisième âge
sensible raisonnable
separated séparé(e)
separately **to pay separately** payer séparément
September septembre
septic tank la fosse septique
serious (*accident, problem*) grave
to serve servir

service (*in restaurant, shop*) le service; (*church*) l'office *m*; **Is service included?** Le service est compris?; **service charge** le service; **service station** la station-service

to service (*car, washing machine*) réviser

serviette la serviette

set menu le menu à prix fixe

several plusieurs; **several times** plusieurs fois

shade l'ombre *f*; **in the shade** à l'ombre

shallow peu profond(e)

shampoo le shampooing

to share partager

to shave se raser

shaver le rasoir

shaving cream la crème à raser

she elle

sheet (*for bed*) le drap

sherry le xérès

ship le navire

shirt la chemise

shock absorber l'amortisseur *m*

shoe la chaussure

shoelaces les lacets *mpl*

shoe polish le cirage

shoe shop le magasin de chaussures

shop le magasin

shop assistant le vendeur, la vendeuse

shopping les courses *fpl*; **to go shopping** (*for pleasure*) faire du shopping; (*for food*) faire les courses

shopping centre le centre commercial

shop window la vitrine

short court(e)

shorts le short

short-sighted myope

shoulder l'épaule *f*

show le spectacle

to show montrer

shower (*bath*) la douche; (*rain*) l'averse *f*; **to take a shower** prendre une douche

shower gel le gel douche

shrimp la crevette

shut (*closed*) fermé(e)

to shut fermer

shutters (*outside*) les volets *mpl*

shuttle service la navette

sick (*ill*) malade; **I feel sick** J'ai envie de vomir

side le côté

side dish la garniture

sightseeing to go sightseeing faire du tourisme

to sign signer

signature la signature

silk la soie

silver l'argent *m*

SIM card la carte SIM

similar similar to semblable à; **They're similar** Ils se ressemblent

since (*time*) depuis; (*given that*) puisque; **since 1974** depuis 1974; **since you're not French** puisque vous n'êtes pas français

to sing chanter

single (*unmarried*) célibataire; (*bed, room*) pour une personne

single ticket l'aller *m* simple

sister la sœur

sister-in-law la belle-sœur

to sit s'asseoir; **Sit down, please!** Asseyez-vous, s'il vous plaît!

site (*website*) le site

size (*clothes*) la taille; (*shoes*) la pointure

skateboard le skate-board

ski le ski

to ski faire du ski

ski boots les chaussures *fpl* de ski

to skid déraper

skiing le ski

ski instructor le moniteur, la monitrice de ski

ski lift le remonte-pente

skimmed skimmed milk le lait écrémé

skin la peau

ski pass le forfait

ski pole, ski stick le bâton de ski

ski run, ski piste la piste de ski

skirt la jupe

to sleep dormir; **to go to sleep** s'endormir

sleeper (*on train*) la couchette

sleeping bag le sac de couchage

sleeping car la voiture-lit

sleeping pill le somnifère

slice (*bread, cake, ham*) la tranche

sliced bread le pain de mie en tranches

slide (*photograph*) la diapositive

slightly légèrement

slow lent(e)

slowly lentement

small petit(e); **smaller than** plus petit(e) que

smell l'odeur *f*; **a bad smell** une mauvaise odeur; **a nice smell** une bonne odeur

to smile sourire

to smoke fumer; **I don't smoke** Je ne fume pas; **Can I smoke?** Je peux fumer?

SMS le SMS

snack to have a snack manger un petit quelque chose

snail l'escargot *m*

snow la neige

to snow neiger; **It's snowing** Il neige

snowboarding to go snowboarding faire du snowboard

snow chains les chaînes *fpl*

so (*therefore*) alors; (*in comparisons*) aussi; **The shop was closed so I didn't buy it** Le magasin était fermé, alors je ne l'ai pas acheté; **It's not so expensive as the other one** Ce n'est pas aussi cher que l'autre; **so do I** moi aussi; **so much/so many...** tellement de...; **I think so** Je crois

soap le savon

socket (*for plug*) la prise de courant

socks les chaussettes *fpl*

sofa bed le canapé-lit

soft drink la boisson non alcoolisée

software le logiciel

sole (*shoe*) la semelle

some du, de la, des; **Would you like some bread?** Voulez-vous du pain?; **some books** des livres; **some of them** quelques uns

someone quelqu'un

something quelque chose

sometimes quelquefois

son le fils

son-in-law le gendre

song la chanson

soon bientôt; **as soon as possible** dès que possible

sore to have a sore throat avoir mal à la gorge

sorry Sorry! Pardon!; **I'm sorry!** Je suis désolé(e)!

sort la sorte

soup la soupe

sour aigre

south le sud

souvenir le souvenir

space la place

spade la pelle

Spain l'Espagne *f*

Spaniard l'Espagnol *m*, l'Espagnole *f*

Spanish espagnol(e)

spare parts les pièces *fpl* de rechange

spare tyre le pneu de rechange

spare wheel la roue de secours

sparkling sparkling water l'eau gazeuse; **sparkling wine** le mousseux

to speak parler; **Do you speak English?** Vous parlez anglais?

speaker (*loudspeaker*) le haut-parleur

special spécial(e)

speciality la spécialité

speedboat le hors-bord

speed limit la limitation de vitesse

speedometer le compteur

to spell How is it spelt? Comment ça s'écrit?

to spend (*money*) dépenser

spicy épicé(e)

spinach les épinards *mpl*

spirits (*alcohol*) les spiritueux *mpl*

spite in spite of malgré

spoon la cuiller

sport le sport

sports centre le centre sportif

sports shop le magasin de sports

spring (*season*) le printemps

square (*in town*) la place

squash le squash

squid le calmar

stadium le stade

stain la tache

stairs l'escalier *m*

stalls (*in theatre*) l'orchestre *m*

stamp le timbre

to stand être debout

start le début; **at the start of the film** au début du film; **from the start** dès le début

to start commencer; (*car*) démarrer; **What time does it start?** À quelle heure est-ce que ça commence?; **The car won't start** La voiture ne veut pas démarrer

starter (*in meal*) le hors d'œuvre

station la gare

stationer's la papeterie

stay le séjour; **Enjoy your stay!** Bon séjour!

to stay (*remain*) rester; **I'm staying at the... hotel** Je suis à l'hôtel...; **Where are you staying? – In a hotel** Où logez-vous? – À l'hôtel; **to stay the night** passer la nuit; **We stayed in Paris for a few days** Nous avons passé quelques jours à Paris

steak le bifteck

to steal voler

steamed cuit(e) à la vapeur

steering wheel le volant

stepbrother le demi-frère

stepdaughter la belle-fille

stepfather le beau-père

stepmother la belle-mère

stepsister la demi-sœur

stepson le beau-fils

stereo la chaîne (stéréo)

sterling la livre sterling

steward (*on plane*) le steward

stewardess (*on plane*) l'hôtesse *f*

sticking-plaster le sparadrap

still still water l'eau *f* plate

sting la piqûre

to sting piquer

stockings les bas *mpl*

stomach l'estomac *m*; **He's got stomachache** Il a mal au ventre

stone la pierre

stop bus stop l'arrêt *m* de bus

to stop arrêter; **Do you stop at the station?** Vous vous arrêtez à la gare?; **to stop doing** arrêter de faire; **to stop smoking** arrêter de fumer

store (*shop*) le magasin

storey l'étage *m*

straightaway tout de suite

straight straight on tout droit

strange bizarre

straw (*for drinking*) la paille

strawberry la fraise

street la rue

street map le plan de la ville

strike la grève; **to be on strike** être en grève

striped rayé(e)

stroke (*medical*) l'attaque *f* (d'apoplexie)

strong fort(e)

stuck It's stuck C'est coincé

student l'étudiant *m*, l'étudiante *f*

student discount le tarif étudiant

stuffed farci(e)

stupid stupide

subway (*train*) le métro; (*passage*) le passage souterrain

suddenly soudain

suede le daim

sugar le sucre

to suggest suggérer

suit (*man's*) le costume; (*woman's*) le tailleur

suitcase la valise

summer l'été *m*

summer holidays les vacances *fpl* d'été

sun le soleil

to sunbathe prendre un bain de soleil

sunblock l'écran *m* total

sunburn le coup de soleil

suncream la crème solaire

Sunday le dimanche

sunglasses les lunettes *fpl* de soleil

sunny It's sunny Il fait beau

sunroof le toit ouvrant

sunscreen (*lotion*) l'écran *m* solaire

sunshade le parasol
sunstroke l'insolation *f*
suntan le bronzage
suntan lotion le lait solaire
supermarket le supermarché
supplement le supplément
to surf faire du surf; **to surf the Net** surfer sur Internet
surfboard la planche de surf
surname le nom de famille
surprise la surprise; **What a surprise!** Quelle surprise!
sweater le pull
sweatshirt le sweat
sweet (*not savoury*) sucré(e)
sweet (*dessert*) le dessert; **sweets** les bonbons *mpl*
to swim nager
swimming pool la piscine
swimsuit le maillot de bain
swing (*for children*) la balançoire
Swiss suisse
switch le bouton
to switch off éteindre
to switch on allumer
Switzerland la Suisse
swollen enflé(e)

T
table la table
tablecloth la nappe
tablesppon la grande cuiller
table tennis le tennis de table
tablet (*medicine*) le comprimé; (*computer*) la tablette
tailor's le tailleur
to take (*medicine, sugar*) prendre; (*take with you*) emporter; (*exam*) passer; (*subject at school*) faire; **Do you take sugar?** Vous prenez du sucre?; **I'll take you to the airport** Je vais vous emmener à l'aéroport; **How long does it take?** Ça prend combien de temps?; **It takes about one hour** Ça prend environ une heure; **We take credit cards** Nous acceptons les cartes de crédit
take away (*food*) à emporter
to take off (*plane*) décoller; (*clothes*) enlever

to take out sortir
to talk to parler à
tall grand(e)
tampons les tampons *mpl* hygiéniques
tangerine la mandarine
tank petrol tank le réservoir
tap le robinet
tap water l'eau *f* du robinet
tart la tarte
taste le goût
to taste goûter; **Can I taste some?** Je peux goûter?
taxi le taxi
taxi driver le chauffeur de taxi
taxi rank la station de taxis
tea le thé; **herbal tea** la tisane; **lemon tea** le thé au citron; **tea with milk** le thé au lait
teabag le sachet de thé
to teach enseigner
teacher le professeur
team l'équipe *f*
teapot la théière
teaspoon la petite cuiller
teenager l'adolescent *m*, l'adolescente *f*
teeth les dents *fpl*
telephone le téléphone
to telephone téléphoner
telephone call le coup de téléphone
telephone number le numéro de téléphone
television la télévision; **on television tonight** à la télévision ce soir
to tell dire
temperature la température; **to have a temperature** avoir de la fièvre
tenant le/la locataire
tennis le tennis
tennis ball la balle de tennis
tennis court le court de tennis
tennis racket la raquette de tennis
tent la tente
tent peg le piquet de tente
terminal (*airport*) l'aérogare *f*
terrace la terrasse
to test (*to try out*) tester

to text envoyer un SMS (à); **I'll text you** Je t'enverrai un SMS
text message le SMS, le texto
than que; **Diana sings better than me** Diana chante mieux que moi; **more than you** plus que toi; **more than five** plus de cinq
thank you merci; **thank you very much** merci beaucoup
that ce, cet, cette; **that cat** ce chat; **that man** cet homme; **that dress** cette robe; **that one** celui-là, celle-là; **to think that...** penser que...
the le, la, l', les
theatre le théâtre
their (*sing*) leur; (*plural*) leurs; **their car** leur voiture; **their children** leurs enfants
them les; leur; eux; elles; **I didn't know them** Je ne les connaissais pas; **I gave them some brochures** Je leur ai donné des brochures; **It's for them** C'est pour eux
there (*over there*) là; **there is, there are** il y a; **there was** il y avait; **there'll be** il y aura
therefore donc
thermometer le thermomètre
these ces; **these ones** ceux-ci, celles-ci
they ils, elles
thick (*not thin*) épais(se)
thief le voleur, la voleuse
thin (*person*) mince
thing la chose; **my things** mes affaires
to think penser
thirsty I'm thirsty J'ai soif
this ce, cet, cette; **this cat** ce chat; **this man** cet homme; **this dress** cette robe; **this one** celui-ci, celle-ci
those ces; **those ones** ceux-là, celles-là
throat la gorge
through par; **to go through Rouen** passer par Rouen; **a through train** un train

direct; **from May through to September** de mai jusqu'à septembre

Thursday jeudi

ticket (for plane, train, theatre, concert) le billet; (for bus, tube, cinema, museum) le ticket; **a single ticket** un aller simple; **a return ticket** un aller-retour; **a book of tickets** un carnet de tickets

ticket collector le contrôleur, la contrôleuse

ticket office le guichet

tide (sea) la marée; **low tide** la marée basse; **high tide** la marée haute

tidy bien rangé(e)

tie la cravate

tight (fitting) serré(e)

tights le collant

till (cash desk) la caisse

till (until) jusqu'à; **till 2 o'clock** jusqu'à deux heures

time le temps; **this time** cette fois; **What time is it?** Quelle heure est-il?; **on time** à l'heure

timetable l'horaire m

tin (can) la boîte

tin-opener l'ouvre-boîtes m

tip (to waiter) le pourboire

tipped (cigarette) à bout filtre

tired fatigué(e)

tissues les kleenex® mpl

to à; (with name of country) en, au; **to London** à Londres; **to France** en France; **to Canada** au Canada; **to the airport** à l'aéroport; **from nine o'clock to half past three** de neuf heures à trois heures et demie; **something to drink** quelque chose à boire

toast le pain grillé

tobacconist's le bureau de tabac

today aujourd'hui

toe le doigt de pied

together ensemble

toilet les toilettes fpl

toilet paper le papier hygiénique

toiletries les articles fpl de toilette

toll (motorway) le péage

tomato la tomate; **tinned tomatoes** les tomates en boîte

tomato soup la soupe à la tomate

tomorrow demain; **tomorrow morning** demain matin; **tomorrow afternoon** demain après-midi; **tomorrow evening** demain soir

tongue la langue

tonic water le tonic

tonight (this evening) ce soir; (during the night) cette nuit

too (also) aussi; (excessively) trop; **My sister came too** Ma sœur est venue aussi; **The water's too hot** L'eau est trop chaude; **too late** trop tard; **too much** trop; **too much noise** trop de bruit; **too many** trop; **too many people** trop de gens

tooth la dent

toothache le mal de dents

toothbrush la brosse à dents

toothpaste le dentifrice

toothpick le cure-dent

top the top floor le dernier étage

top (of bottle) le bouchon; (of pen) le capuchon; (of pyjamas, bikini) le haut; (of hill, mountain) le sommet; **on top of** sur

total (amount) le total

to touch toucher

tough (meat) dur(e)

tour (trip) l'excursion f; (of museum) la visite; **guided tour** la visite guidée

tour guide le/la guide

tour operator le tour-opérateur

tourist le/la touriste

tourist information office l'office du tourisme

towel la serviette

tower la tour

town la ville; **town centre** le centre-ville; **town plan** le plan de la ville

toy le jouet

toyshop le magasin de jouets

traffic la circulation

traffic jam l'embouteillage m

traffic lights les feux mpl

traffic warden le contractuel, la contractuelle

train le train; **by train** par le train; **the next train** le prochain train; **the first train** le premier train; **the last train** le dernier train

trainers les baskets fpl

tranquillizer le tranquillisant

to translate traduire

to travel voyager

travel agent's l'agence f de voyages

travel guide le guide

travel insurance l'assurance f voyage

travel sickness le mal des transports

traveller's cheque le chèque de voyage

tray le plateau

treatment le traitement

tree l'arbre m

trip l'excursion f

trolley (for luggage, shopping) le chariot

trousers le pantalon

truck le camion

true vrai(e)

trunk (luggage) la malle

trunks swimming trunks le maillot (de bain)

to try essayer

to try on (clothes, shoes) essayer

t-shirt le tee-shirt

Tuesday mardi

tuna le thon

to turn tourner

to turn off (light, cooker, TV) éteindre; (tap) fermer

to turn on (light, cooker, TV) allumer; (tap) ouvrir

turquoise (colour) turquoise

tweet le tweet

to tweet tweeter

twice deux fois; **twice a week** deux fois par semaine

twin twin room la chambre à deux lits

twins (male) les jumeaux; (female) les jumelles

twisted tordu(e)

tyre le pneu

tyre pressure la pression des pneus

U

ugly laid(e)
ulcer l'ulcère m; **mouth ulcer** l'aphte m
umbrella le parapluie; (*sunshade*) le parasol
uncle l'oncle m
uncomfortable inconfortable
under sous; **children under 10** les enfants de moins de 10 ans
undercooked pas assez cuit(e)
underground le métro
underpants (*men's underwear*) le slip
to understand comprendre; **I don't understand** Je ne comprends pas; **Do you understand?** Vous comprenez?
underwear les sous-vêtements mpl
unfortunately malheureusement
United Kingdom le Royaume-Uni
United States les États-Unis mpl
university l'université f
unleaded petrol l'essence f sans plomb
unlikely peu probable
to unlock ouvrir
to unpack déballer ses affaires
unpleasant désagréable
up up here ici; **up there** là-haut; **What's up?** Qu'est-ce qu'il y a?; **up to 50** jusqu'à 50; **up to now** jusqu'à présent
upstairs en haut; **the people upstairs** les gens du dessus
urgent urgent(e)
us nous; **Can you help us?** Pouvez-vous nous aider?
USA les USA mpl
to use utiliser
useful utile
usual habituel(le)
usually d'habitude

V

vacancy (*in hotel*) la chambre libre
vacant libre
vacation les vacances fpl
vacuum cleaner l'aspirateur m
valid valable
valuable d'une grande valeur
value la valeur
VAT la TVA
veal le veau
vegan végétalien(ne); **I'm vegan** Je suis végétalien(ne)
vegetables les légumes mpl
vegetarian végétarien(ne); **I'm vegetarian** Je suis végétarien(ne)
very très; **very much** beaucoup; **I like it very much** Je l'aime beaucoup
vest le maillot de corps
via par
video camera la caméra vidéo
view la vue
village le village
vinegar le vinaigre
vineyard le vignoble
virus le virus
visa le visa
visit le séjour
to visit visiter
visiting hours les heures fpl de visite
visitor le visiteur, la visiteuse
voicemail la messagerie vocale
voucher le bon

W

waist la taille
to wait for attendre
waiter le serveur
waiting room la salle d'attente
waitress la serveuse
to wake up se réveiller
Wales le pays de Galles
walk la promenade; **to go for a walk** faire une promenade
to walk marcher; (*go on foot*) aller à pied
walking boots les chaussures fpl de marche
walking stick la canne
wall le mur
wallet le portefeuille
to want vouloir
ward (*hospital*) la salle

wardrobe l'armoire f
warehouse l'entrepôt m
warm chaud(e); **It's warm outside** Il fait bon dehors
to warm up (*milk, food*) faire chauffer
to wash laver
washing machine la machine à laver
washing powder la lessive
washing-up liquid le produit à vaisselle
wasp la guêpe
waste bin la poubelle
watch la montre
to watch (*look at*) regarder
water l'eau f; **bottled water** l'eau en bouteille; **cold water** l'eau froide; **drinking water** l'eau potable; **hot water** l'eau chaude; **sparkling water** l'eau gazeuse; **still water** l'eau plate
water heater le chauffe-eau
watermelon la pastèque
to waterski faire du ski nautique
watersports les sports mpl nautiques
waves (*on sea*) les vagues fpl
way in l'entrée f
way out la sortie
we nous
weak (*coffee, tea*) léger(ère); (*person*) faible
to wear porter
weather le temps
weather forecast la météo
web (*internet*) le Web
website le site web
wedding le mariage
wedding present le cadeau de mariage
Wednesday mercredi
week la semaine; **last week** la semaine dernière; **next week** la semaine prochaine; **per week** par semaine; **this week** cette semaine; **during the week** pendant la semaine
weekday le jour de semaine
weekend le week-end; **next weekend** le week-end prochain; **this weekend** ce week-end
to weigh peser

weight le poids
welcome! bienvenu(e)!
well bien; **I'm very well** Je vais très bien; **He's not well** Il est souffrant
well done (*steak*) bien cuit(e)
Welsh gallois(e); (*language*) le gallois
west l'ouest *m*
wet mouillé(e); **wet weather** le temps pluvieux
wetsuit la combinaison de plongée
what? quoi?; **What colour is it?** C'est de quelle couleur?; **What is it?** Qu'est-ce que c'est?; **I saw what happened** J'ai vu ce qui arrivé; **Tell me what you did** Dites-moi ce que vous avez fait
wheel la roue
wheelchair le fauteuil roulant
when? quand?
where? où?
whether si; **I don't know whether to go or not** Je ne sais pas si je dois y aller ou non
which? quel(le)?; **Which one?** Lequel, laquelle?; **Which ones?** Lesquels, lesquelles?
while **in a while** bientôt; (*very soon*) tout à l'heure
whisky le whisky
white blanc (blanche)
who? qui?
whole entier(ière)
wholemeal bread le pain complet
whose **Whose is it?** C'est à qui?
why? pourquoi?
wide large
widow la veuve

widower le veuf
wife la femme
wild (*animal*) sauvage
to win gagner
window la fenêtre; (*in car, train*) la vitre; **shop window** la vitrine
windscreen le pare-brise
windscreen wipers les essuie-glaces *mpl*
to windsurf faire de la planche à voile
windy **It's windy** Il y a du vent
wine le vin; **dry wine** le vin sec; **house wine** le vin en pichet; **red wine** le vin rouge; **rosé wine** le vin rosé; **sparkling wine** le vin mousseux; **white wine** le vin blanc; **wine list** la carte des vins
wing mirror le rétroviseur latéral
winter l'hiver *m*
with avec; **with ice** avec des glaçons; **with milk** avec du lait
without sans; **without ice** sans glaçons; **without milk** sans lait
woman la femme
wonderful merveilleux (-euse)
wood le bois
wooden en bois
wool la laine
woollen en laine
word le mot
work le travail; **at work** au travail
to work (*person*) travailler; (*machine, car*) marcher; **It doesn't work** ça ne marche pas
world le monde
worried inquiet(-iète)
worse pire

worth **It's worth...** Ça vaut...
to wrap (*parcel*) emballer
wrapping paper le papier cadeau
wrist le poignet
to write écrire; **Please write it down** Vous pouvez l'écrire, s'il vous plaît?
wrong faux (fausse); **What's wrong?** Qu'est-ce qu'il y a?

X
X-ray la radiographie

Y
yacht le yacht
year l'an *m*; l'année *f*; **a year ago** il y a un an; **this year** cette année; **next year** l'année prochaine; **last year** l'année dernière
yearly annuel(le)
yellow jaune
yes oui; **yes, please** oui, merci
yesterday hier; **yesterday morning** hier matin; **yesterday evening** hier soir
yet **not yet** pas encore
yoghurt le yaourt; **plain yoghurt** le yaourt nature
yolk le jaune d'œuf
you (*familiar*) tu; (*polite, plural*) vous
young jeune
your (*familiar sing*) ton, ta; (*familiar plural*) tes; (*collective or polite singular*) votre; (*collective or polite plural*) vos
youth hostel l'auberge *f* de jeunesse

Z
zip la fermeture éclair
zoo le zoo
zoom lens le zoom
zucchini la courgette